T0316709

THE GLOBAL MANAGEMENT SERIES

Marketing Perspectives

Andrew MacLaren, Tom Farrington and
Kevin O'Gorman

Goodfellow Publishers Ltd

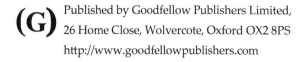

Published by Goodfellow Publishers Limited,
26 Home Close, Wolvercote, Oxford OX2 8PS
http://www.goodfellowpublishers.com

First published 2017

British Library Cataloguing in Publication Data: a catalogue record for this title is
available from the British Library.
Library of Congress Catalog Card Number: on file.

ISBN: 978-1-911396-18-5

This book is part of the Global Management series

ISSN: 2514-7862

Copyright © Andrew MacLaren, Tom Farrington and Kevin O'Gorman, 2017

All rights reserved. The text of this publication, or any part thereof, may not be
reproduced or transmitted in any form or by any means, electronic or mechanical,
including photocopying, recording, storage in an information retrieval system,
or otherwise, without prior permission of the publisher or under licence from
the Copyright Licensing Agency Limited. Further details of such licences (for
reprographic reproduction) may be obtained from the Copyright Licensing
Agency Limited, of Saffron House, 6–10 Kirby Street, London EC1N 8TS.

All trademarks used herein are the property of their repective owners, The use
of trademarks or brand names in this text does not imply any affiliation with or
endorsement of this book by such owners.

  Design and typesetting by P.K. McBride, www.macbride.org.uk

Cover design by Cylinder

Printed by Baker & Taylor, www.baker-taylor.com

Contents

Acknowledgments

We would like to sincerely thank all of the contributors to this book, beginning with the authors. Your hard work and flexibility has helped to produce a book of which we can all be proud. Thanks must also go to those at Goodfellow Publishers. Sally, Tim, and Mac have been as helpful, attentive, and encouraging as ever. Our students have also played vital roles in shaping the chapters, by providing active test audiences for much of the material that follows. Let's face it, without students there would be no book: so thanks to you for believing in us, and for believing in yourselves.

AM, TF & KDO

Dedication

To all the students I have taught, I have learned as much from you as you have from me; that learning helped produce this book...thank you.
AM

To Becca, AM, M & FD: thanks for everything.
TF

Biographies

Matthew Alexander is a senior lecturer in the Department of Marketing at the University of Strathclyde in Glasgow. His research interests are focused within the services domain around the complementary concepts of Service Dominant Logic, value co-creation and customer engagement. Within this he has a particular focus on the behavioural manifestations of engagement and their impact within society. His research has been published in a wide range of quality academic journals including the *Journal of Service Research* and *Annals of Tourism*.

Ross Curran is a lecturer in marketing at Dundee Business School, University of Abertay, Dundee. His primary research interests focus on nonprofit marketing and volunteer management practices, as well as areas of authenticity and heritage in tourist consumption. His recent work is published in *Tourism Management*, the *Journal of Nonprofit and Voluntary Sector Quarterly*, and the *International Journal of Contemporary Hospitality Management*.

Elaine Collinson is Associate Professor in the Department of Management in the School of Social Sciences at Heriot-Watt University. She is Director of Postgraduate Studies within the school, Deputy Director of the Corporate Executive Development. With over 25 years' experience in the Higher Education sector, she has held roles, primarily in an academic and research capacity but also in developing transnational education and industry links across the globe. As Director of Postgraduate Programmes at Heriot-Watt University, she teaches on the International Marketing Management suite of programmes, specialising in Branding & Communications, Strategic Marketing Management, Entrepreneurial Marketing. She works closely with industry involving her wide network of contacts on the programmes in order to ensure business relevance for students. Throughout her academic career she has published in the areas of Small Business Marketing, Entrepreneurship and Academic & Industry Collaboration.

Tom Farrington is a Post-Doctoral Research Associate in Management and Organisation at Heriot-Watt University's School of Social Sciences. Tom has taught at South East European University in Tetovo and at the University of

Edinburgh, where he received his doctorate, and where he was Co-Director of the Scottish Universities' International Summer School. Tom's research is mainly focused on management practice, business ethics, and constructions of identity. He has a particular interest in cultural heritage and tourism, focussing on issues such as authenticity and social responsibility, with expertise in critical, cultural, and literary theory. His work has most recently appeared in the *Journal of Marketing Management*, the *International Journal of Contemporary Hospitality Management*, and the *Journal of Sustainable Tourism*.

Keith Gori is a PhD student in the School of Social Sciences at Heriot-Watt University. His doctoral research centres on understanding the social and cultural significance of consumption in historical context, with a specific interest in the British home front during the Second World War. He is involved in a range of marketing and consumer research projects utilising multiple theoretical and methodological approaches. He has published a number of journal articles and chapters in edited texts and has presented at conferences both in the UK and overseas. He teaches on management, marketing and methods courses in the Department of Business Management. He holds BA and MA degrees in history from the University of Sheffield.

Kevin O'Gorman is Professor of Management and Business History and Director of Internationalisation in the School of Social Sciences at Heriot-Watt University. He trained in Glasgow, Salamanca and Rome as a philosopher, theologian and historian. His research interests have a dual focus: Origins, history and cultural practices of hospitality, and philosophical, ethical and cultural underpinnings of contemporary management practices. Using a wide range of methodological approaches he has published over 140 journal articles, books, chapters, and conference papers in business and management.

Darren Jubb is a PhD student at Heriot-Watt University, Edinburgh. His primary research interest is considering the role that accounting plays in shaping popular culture, with a current emphasis on how accounting influences the cultural practice of record production. Darren received an MA Hons in Accountancy from Heriot-Watt University in 2010 before working in professional accountancy practice for a number of years. During this period he qualified as a Chartered Accountant with the Institute of Chartered Accountants Scotland.

Andrew MacLaren is Assistant Professor of Marketing, Heriot-Watt University. His main research interests focus on the service industry. His outlook is international and he works throughout Europe, the USA, the Middle

East and India. He has published widely in the field on multiple topics, contributing in the domains of theory, method and industry practice.

Rodrigo Perez Vega is a Lecturer in Marketing at Henley Business School. His research interest are on social media, digital marketing and social influence marketing. Prior to finishing his PhD, Rodrigo had marketing experience in several digital marketing and brand management roles within FMCG and service industries.

Lindsay Stringfellow is a Senior Lecturer in Marketing at the University of Exeter. Her PhD thesis examined the interplay between social capital and the development of small professional firms. Her research interests are broadly in the sociology of the professions, with a particular interest in small practitioners. Her work often takes a Bourdieusian perspective, and focuses critically on issues of status, legitimacy and power in the professions, particularly accounting. Her interest in Pierre Bourdieu also spans into cultural reproduction, where she has examined taste and the impact of celebritisation on the culinary field, as well as across new forms of media.

Preface

"Living in age of advertisement, we are perpetually disillusioned. The perfect life is spread before us every day, but it changes and withers at a touch."

J.B. Priestley, 'The Disillusioned', 1929

Given the ever-quickening pace of technological innovation, and the increasing urgency with which this newness mediates social interactions, it is difficult for us to fully envision the types of marketing jobs our graduates will go on to do. With this in mind, we offer this book as a series of perspectives on both the fundamentals of marketing, and the state-of-the-art in each topic. It is vital that students and scholars read these chapters critically, with a view to adapting the principles and ideas within to the particular nuances and challenges of their pursuits in marketing. Readers should always be aware that marketing is not a simple case of *this plus that equals success*; marketers are required to continually encounter and re-encounter that most unpredictable of variables: the human being.

Marketing is a strange beast in some ways. It is often seen from the outside as rather a glamorous activity, an idea that is fashioned from images of glitzy product launches and Hollywood's portrayal of 'ad execs' flying around the world, sowing the seeds of their creative ideas. Marketing goes a lot deeper than that and, as such, represents a heck of a lot more graft than is betrayed by the champagne and jet travel. Working in marketing is a stimulating blend of numbers, statistics, algorithms, creativity, emotional intelligence, cultural sensitivity, charm, wit and maybe even a bit of good old fashioned luck. Not many jobs encompass such a varied range of functions, which makes it stimulating yet elusive, since it's not always completely possible to fathom why one thing works the first time you do it and then fails the next time. The challenge of marketing is both a cause and a consequence of the ever-fluctuating, unpredictable and uncertain world we live in today. The developed world is a consumer's world; it is built for and by consumerism, and is measured by it too. This is not necessarily a good thing, but it also puts a function like marketing at the axis of deciding whether consumerism can build a better world or send it into terminal decline.

From international DJs, to chocolate companies, to charities and hotels, this book takes a tour through both the theory and the application of some useful, widespread and interesting perspectives on marketing. Unfortunately, it's not exhaustive and readers are encouraged to use the suggested reading and the works cited within the chapters to deepen their knowledge and understanding even further.

Our publisher suggested we might like to include some humour in the preface, so we're going to leave you with a marketing joke:

Q: Why did the marketer fail at honey harvesting?

A: Instead of tapping the hive, she insisted on going B2B.

Hahaha…sorry! We hope you enjoy the book.

1 Introduction

Tom Farrington and Andrew MacLaren

"Anybody here work in Marketing?...kill yourself, seriously!"

Bill Hicks, 1994

Since this book is about different perspectives on the marketing concept, this first chapter lays down the broad foundations of marketing as a subject. It is not exhaustive, but the foundational concepts of marketing such as brand, consumer behaviour and the marketing mix are presented in order to give a reference point for the discussions that will take place in the rest of the book.

The quotation used to introduce this chapter, and indeed this book, is a provocative one. It certainly is not resoundingly positive and it betrays a cynical and suspicious perspective on the enigmatic concept of marketing. We should, make it clear at this point, that the quotation comes from a live comedy show and it was said entirely in a sarcastic and symbolic way – it is not intended to represent support or empathy with self-harm. Marketing is simultaneously both vague and precise; it is abundantly evident around us, yet it is also mysterious and hidden. As we write this sentence, a quick glance around reveals the evidence of over 20 examples of marketing endeavour, from the branding on the computer to the carcass of an Amazon parcel torn-up this morning ... think of all the different stages that had to be brilliantly understood and resolved in order for someone to go from finding a book on Amazon.com to having it delivered to their door on a Saturday morning! Marketing activities infiltrate every facet of our lives, and ironically enough Bill Hicks himself relied on marketing activities to build his career and bring the audience into the theatre, where he delivered the above quote at his comedy gig in the 1990s.

'Marketing' is an umbrella term for a vast range of organisational activities, linked by one simple idea: understanding and providing appropriate value for the end users (or stakeholders). Marketing is therefore not just the

TV advert for a cosmetics brand broadcast deliberately during a programme known to be watched by a predominantly middle-aged female audience, it is also the reason behind that parcel being delivered on a Saturday and it is the reason why there are no words on the instruction manuals for IKEA furniture. It is a significant reason behind constant innovation in the things that make our lives better, healthier, easier, more productive, longer…

What is marketing?

A study on brand recognition by Valkenburg and Buijzen (2005) found that children as young as two could identify popular brands such as Mercedes-Benz, McDonald's and Nike. This simple study demonstrates the power of marketing activities – the essence of a business proposition can be distilled so effectively into a brand that children who can barely talk can recognise it.

This book is called *Marketing Perspectives* for a reason; it gives you a tour through some different perspectives on the marketing challenge that many of you reading this may face later in your careers. Some of the chapters give you a perspective on marketing from concrete, specific points of view, such as the chapter on money or the one on customers. Others are more niche, such as the chapter on celebrities or the one that looks specifically at services. This book will help you understand how marketing fits into most aspects of our lives and helps everything from hospitals to chip shops to international DJs connect to their customers/users and maximise the value that everyone gains. In every chapter you will find a case study that gives you a focussed, real life example of the concepts discussed in that chapter.

Marketing as a business philosophy (Value)

In recent times we have evolved away from thinking of marketing as a purely cultural production. This was the mindset that created the 4 Ps framework and encouraged us to understand marketing as a basic formula for considering these ideas (McCarthy, 1960). These are important but we have to appreciate that our understanding has moved beyond this to include attention towards the organic and fluxing world of consumer use and meaning. It includes the production that takes place amongst the consumer population and indeed the consumption that takes place within the producer population, as Peñaloza and Venkatesh (2006) discuss.

This relates to Lusch and Vargo's (2006) notions of co-creation and network theory, which place marketing as a more loosely defined concept, which Peñaloza and Venkatesh (2006) state is a 'socially-constructed' phenomenon. They support the idea of moving towards a hybrid interpretation of marketing that accommodates the interpretation of value in exchange and value in use.

What do we mean by this? Let's look at mobile smartphones, one of the most fundamentally disruptive developments of the last 10 years. We can conceptualise smartphones from many different perspectives. We can look at them from a value in exchange perspective, the tradeable commodity that is the phone itself and the measurable values of phone bills, data costs, app purchases. But we can also look at the use of smartphones; the way markets are being shaped by the social evolution that smartphones create. Some of you will be using a smartphone right now. They change the way we communicate, expect to interact and value items.

In 1941, Turner Morris stated that "The emphasis…is upon the services of goods, not upon the goods themselves…Goods are wanted because they are capable of performing services." (Holbrook, 1995: 116), and Abbott (1955) asserted that "People want products because they want the experience-bringing services which they hope the products will render." (ibid., 116)

The contemporary economy has evolved through the development of services and experiences, and this has been significantly supported by the Internet and digital technology. One of the things for which marketing is often criticised is 'disease-mongering'. This phrase comes from the pharmaceutical industry, where companies are accused of researching diseases in order to create treatments that they can sell to consumers, sometimes inflating the threat or severity of a disease in order to achieve greater sales of the treatment they've developed. Disease-mongering extends to all areas of the economy, and if we take a critical look at some contemporary business propositions, then we can see how marketing can act to package and promote certain needs in order to achieve profitability.

A powerful example of marketing packaging a product in a way that amplifies and changes our perceptions of how much we need it is the health and fitness industry. It is likely that many of the people reading this book will pay a subscription to a gym. Without realising it, over the last twenty years, membership of a gym has become synonymous with maintaining a healthy lifestyle: it feels like the only way to stay fit is to make sure you have a gym membership. But gyms for the masses are a recent development. In the recent past, gyms were reserved only for elite athletes and members of subcultures like bodybuilding. However, the concept of health and fitness has been appropriated by marketers, and we are now all too accustomed to seeing images of finely-tuned torsos being used to promote a lifestyle in which health and fitness is an important element.

Gyms are full of potential for marketers. The number of memberships you sell is not proportionate to the size of gym you need to build. Statistics tell us that the average gym user will use the gym twice a week, and most gyms have a greater number of inactive members than active members. This is useful to marketers because they can use the dream of healthy lifestyle and rippling muscles to sell a membership of a gym, safe in the knowledge that the realisation of that dream is dependent solely on the customer, and the monthly membership fee can act as a surrogate for the sense that somebody is doing something about improving their health and fitness. Most gym memberships burn a bigger hole in your wallet than they do calories.

This can be thought of as disease-mongering because it translates directly: marketers tell us that there is this new scary disease called health and fitness, and the way that you treat it is by exercising. But fear not! They've developed state-of-the-art treatment centres, to which you can gain access for a monthly membership, and there are special medicines and supplements that you can buy to help with your treatment, such as protein powders. The fact of the matter is that for many people it is difficult to see beyond gyms and the health and fitness industry in the pursuit of a healthy lifestyle, yet people weren't falling over dead through lack of fitness before gyms appeared on the scene.

This is a cynical view of the function of marketing, but it demonstrates neatly the role that marketing plays in a business environment; how marketing conceptualises an idea, packages it, and then positions it in front of consumers in a way that makes them wonder how they could have ever lived without it.

The Chartered Institute of Marketing defines marketing as "the management process responsible for identifying, anticipating and satisfying customer requirements, profitably." One of the core things that marketing does is find a way of presenting a product or service to us in a way that differentiates it from other things available to us in our environment. That includes articulating its features and benefits relative to what we already know, so you will often see things identified as bigger, faster, smaller, thinner, lighter (and so on), in an attempt to accentuate specific features and benefits. Marketing also walks a tightrope of understanding what is currently familiar to us and conventional, and what is novel and different. Seth Godin's famous example of the purple cow demonstrates this. He mentioned how if we were to drive past a field of purple cows they would stand out to us because we were familiar with the concept of a cow, yet these cows were presented in a distinctive way, enough for us to take notice of them. Marketing makes use of balancing the novel and the conventional in a way that moves us to take notice.

Silk soya milk revolutionised the soya milk industry by presenting soya milk in a novel way for soya products, but an entirely conventional way for milk products. Soya milk had been a permanent feature of the dried and canned foods aisle in the supermarket for many years, consigning it to a life of obscure recipes and alternative diets. But Silk decided that, through some shrewd marketing, they could get more conventional consumers to take notice of it. They decided that, rather than packaging Silk in a tin, and placing it in a tin in the dried goods aisle, they would put it in a milk carton, and store it in the refrigerated aisle along with all the other milk. Suddenly, people took notice of the product, because it aligned with their conventional understanding of what milk products look like and where they should be found, but it was now understood to be a distinctive healthy alternative to dairy milk. The result was sales of Silk soya milk skyrocketed; competitor brands took notice, and started to do the same thing. Ever since, the refrigerated aisle has been where we expect to find soya milk in the supermarket, even though it does not need to be refrigerated any more than a tin of baked beans.

Buyer behaviour

Marketing as a subject takes all the good bits from several other disciplines: it borrows heavily from psychology, anthropology, and sociology. You can see the links when you consider that marketing activities are largely about understanding consumers and aligning products and services to their needs, wants, aspirations and desires. Buyer behaviour forms a cornerstone of marketing fundamentals because understanding and analysing the way in which consumers behave allows the marketing function to do its job more effectively. Understanding buyer behaviour is based on five key questions:

- Where do customers buy what they buy?
- What criteria do they apply to their choices?
- When do they make purchases?
- How do they make purchases?
- Who in the wider consumer community are the most important customers?

If we can answer these questions accurately, it makes our marketing activities more effective and efficient.

People are also capable of forming attachments to brands and products in the same way that they form attachments to people. By understanding how the psychology of these attachments works, marketers can build even greater loyalty and attachment among their customers.

The psychological elements of marketing are particularly important when considering consumer behaviour. It is necessary to identify what motivates people to buy certain things. Equally, people's attitudes, beliefs, and personal characteristics will affect the choices they make. It is also necessary to understand the perceptions that different consumer groups have of your business. These perceptions often inform other elements such as motives and attitudes. For example, your brand may have the reputation of being expensive, but knowing that it is perceived as expensive can be valuable to you if you know that consumers are aware that by purchasing your products, their friends will recognise that they can afford an expensive brand, which in turn may be something that is valued by their personality type. The concept of cognitive dissonance is when someone's beliefs are strengthened by the very thing that discredits those beliefs. Often in a marketing scenario, due to that fact that people have paid money to have the things they have, when the value of those possessions is somehow challenged, consumers will try their hardest to twist that information in a way that affirms their decision to purchase it rather than undermining that decision.

Segmentation

Marketers follow a process of segmentation, targeting, and positioning, when conceptualising a marketing strategy.

- **Segmentation** involves dividing a market into distinct groups. These distinct groups can be defined based on a broad range of characteristics. These may be do with financial value, or number of people, or more refined criteria, such as specific needs or behaviours.

- Once market segments have been identified, the marketer is looking to select those segments that have the potential of yielding the greatest amount of value for the business. Once again, the criteria used to decide on the **target** will depend on the business's overall strategy. You could be targeting a mass consumer group for market penetration, or perhaps a narrow, niche consumer group for increased profitability.

- Once that target market has been decided upon, the marketer must **position** the product in such a way to make it clear, distinctive, and desirable, relative to competitors.

Segmentation is a particularly critical process in getting a marketing strategy off the ground. Identifying a market that will have an appetite for your product, and which you understand well enough in order to grow successfully, can mean the difference between success and failure.

Take, as an example, the camera industry. We can understand the market to be differentiated based on basic needs. Many consumers will simply want a functional product that allows them to capture photographs at an affordable price. This would be considered the mass consumer. A smaller proportion of the overall market will have specific needs, which they expect the product to cater to, such as portability. So we understand as marketers that there is demand among a certain group for a product to be made more portable and for a premium price to be charged due to the value placed on portability. There will also be a portion of the market which requires high quality photographs to be taken with the product. This means that more sophisticated equipment will need to be used, and once more a premium price will be charged for those who wish to gain access to that quality of product. But we may also know that within that particular segment (looking for high quality equipment), there is an even narrower group, who want the very highest quality of equipment. There are far fewer of these people, but their willingness to pay an absolute premium price for the very best quality of equipment means there is value to be found and money to be made by successfully targeting them.

As a marketer, there are multiple threats to how we can get our products into the hands of the consumers who we know will want them. One significant threat is that competitors produce a product that is more popular than ours. Another threat is innovation in a parallel industry challenging the legitimacy of our product. It is very likely that while you are reading this, you are thinking "I don't need to buy a camera because I have one on my smartphone." This is an example of those who market smartphones finding a way to capture the imaginations of people who enjoy taking photographs in a more effective way. In fact, the issue for the manufacturers of cameras has nothing to do with photography at all; it has everything to do with connectivity. The innovation of smartphones has revolutionised the way we are able to interact as humans, and the basic ability to take a photograph with your phone has led to the basic expectation that once a photograph has been taken it can be shared instantly. In turn, this innovation has led to the marketers and product developers in the camera industry to innovate in their own way, with new market segments being invented in order to sustain business despite the shrinking of the mass-market camera segment. So cameras have become waterproof, shockproof, and the basic quality of picture for a regular retailing camera has increased significantly, as a means of differentiating it from smartphone cameras. This is segmentation, targeting, and positioning in action.

Marketing communications

Marketing communications are the form of marketing activities of which we are generally most aware. These are the activities that come to our attention in our day to day lives, whether it's a pop-up on your laptop, an email in your inbox, or an advert on the television. Marketing communications are designed to get some of your attention and effect some form of action from you as a consumer. Marketing communications typically have the objective of doing one of four things: differentiate, reinforce, inform, or persuade. Sometimes they might do mixture of those things, or do them in sequence, but for most marketing communications, if you were to ask the question "what is this advert doing?", you could most often answer the question with one of these four actions. The only exception to this in the contemporary Internet age is that some marketing communications are aimed purely to entertain, and this strategy serves to amplify our goodwill towards the brand in question.

■ Brands

Brands are a daily feature in our lives. In the contemporary world you have probably seen close to twenty brands before you even got out of bed in the morning. From your branded pyjamas to the symbol on your smartphone, to the app that you use to check your social media first thing when you wake up. We mentioned earlier than children as young as two years-old can recognise brands, and while that fact may horrify you, it also communicates the pivotal reason why brands are so important in marketing. A good brand, supported by a good marketing apparatus, is simple and well-conceived enough that our brains can relate it easily and quickly to what it represents. Brands act as a sort of memory aid for a larger set of characteristics and features that we understand to relate to that particular business or organisation.

The anatomy of a brand breaks down into four different things: attributes, identity, positioning, and value.

- **Brand attributes** are intangible characteristics of the brand. Brand attributes are often things that people would describe as being, such as: relevant, credible, consistent, sustainable. These terms translate into attributes that a brand will try to develop for itself, for example, in the 1990s, United Colours of Benetton put significant effort into making its brand relevant and credible in relation to matters of equality.

- **Brand identity** is defined by the tangible characteristics of a brand, for example, its appearance, from colour schemes to taglines, to symbols associated with it. All of these elements are designed to reflect the attributes of the brand.

- The **positioning** of the brand will be considered relative to the positioning of other brands in the same competitive territory. Each brand will naturally represent a position in the market, and it is essential that the attributes and the identity of the brand coherently reflect the position chosen. In supermarkets there are clear brand strategies associated with positions in the market whereby Waitrose (which has a sophisticated appearance and presents the coat of arms of the British Royal Family beside its brand without any tagline) communicates a distinctive set of attributes and the distinctive identity compared to other supermarkets such as Asda (which has a less sophisticated brand identity reinforcing its low price strategy in its tagline – 'Save Money, Live Better').

- **Value** represents a form of capital that is associated directly with the brand itself, which represents trust from the customers and also literally increases the perceived value of any product bearing that brand. For example, in the car industry, a car bearing the brand of Aston Martin commands a higher price than a car bearing a Ford badge, simply because there is significantly more prestige attached to the Aston Martin badge. Brands therefore accrue value in their own right, which is important for marketers in developing product ranges whereby products that are low cost to produce may be sold at proportionately higher prices, simply because they bear a brand with high brand value.

Exercise

Stop reading, put down the book, grab a pen and note down every brand you can see around you where you are right now…How many did you see?

The 4Ps

The concept of marketing can be distilled into the '4Ps'. These are product, place, price, and promotion, and they form the foundation for understanding marketing as a subject. They represent marketing in its broadest functional sense, which is a concept that incorporates product development and design all the way through to completing transactions with customers, and aftersales care.

■ Product

As marketing is fundamentally concerned with the needs of consumers, it must contribute to the development of a product, therefore the cost of production, and the features and benefits of any product, need to be conceived with a strong understanding of marketing. For example, Apple has released a new iPhone almost every year since it was first launched in 2007. This is not because unexpected innovation took place in the twelve months between each new release, but because the release of every product has been planned based on a clever marketing strategy. This means that every time a new product is released it has new features that are valued by the customer base.

■ Price

Price is arguably the most important element of marketing. This is because it is the only activity that directly relates to revenue generation. All other marketing activities are a cost, but setting the price leads to earning revenues. Pricing is also the most versatile function in the marketing mix. If you want to alter your product design, then it will take weeks or even months to reorient your production to accommodate that change, whereas you can change the price of any product simply by putting a new label on the tag, or by typing in a new price on your website. This can be in response to a range of developments in your competitive environment. It might be that a new competitor has appeared and you need to reduce your price to meet their competitive pricing strategy, or you might be trying to get rid of stock of a certain product. Or, it may be a reflection of the perishability of the product, whether that be a fresh fruit salad that is about to go out of date (in which case you would lower the price), or a seat on an aeroplane that takes off in four hours' time (in which case you could increase the price).

■ Place

Place broadly refers to where your product can be found, and how you get it into your customers' hands. The marketing concept of place has become even more complex and sophisticated since the dawn of the Internet. Place includes consideration for how you get your product from manufacture and production through distribution channels to retailers and into the hands of your customers. So place involves the calculations of how to reach your customers in the most cost-efficient way, without using channels that diminish the value of the product for your target customers.

Promotion

Promotion is the part of marketing that we all see every day. Promotion activities animate and incentivise, trying to get our attention and convert our activity into some form of value creation for the business, whether that be to visit their shop, or buy their product, or encourage a friend to do the same. Promotional activities are designed to convert action into value for the business. Promotional activities can be anything from television adverts to competitions in a magazine, or even discount vouchers after you've made your first purchase. Most promotional activities operate on the conventional wisdom within marketing that once you have become a customer, you are far more likely to increase the level of custom you offer to the business. So it is in a business's interest to offer discounts to customers for their continued custom into the future.

Criticism of the 4Ps

The 4Ps marketing mix has been used consistently by marketing practitioners and educators since it was originally conceived by E. Jerome McCarthy (1960). As we embark on a book that brings in multiple perspectives though, it is only right to point out that the 4Ps model has received its fair share of criticism over the years, with many researchers claiming it has less value as a theoretical base for research. This diminishes marketing's ability to contribute to the wider academic community, since the 4Ps has been widely adopted as a fundamental element to marketing as a subject. Van Waterschoot and Van den Bulte (1992: 85) note that:

> *"The properties or characteristics that are the basis for classification have not been identified.*
>
> *The categories are not mutually exclusive.*
>
> *There is a catch-all subcategory that is continually growing in importance."*

Van Waterschoot and Van den Bulte (1992) are saying that the 4Ps are practical tools but are not representative of marketing functions at their core level. They suggest that there are four generic marketing functions that underpin the 4Ps: configuration, valuation, facilitation, and symbolisation. They are also suggesting that in order for the marketing mix to be truly effective as a theoretical framework, the categories have to be distinct and autonomous, whereas in their current form they have direct influence on one another and often overlap. They also consider the catch-all subcategory to be 'Sales Promotion', which is related to all the other categories. This is an important distinction because typically the fourth P, 'Promotion' includes 'Sales Promotion' as a concept, yet sales promotion might be something that is required in the functions relating to any other of the 4Ps. This makes the category of 'Promotion' less easy to justify as a distinct category in its own right when the concept of 'Sales Promotion' is often used as a term for any promotion that does not fit into the traditional main forms of promotion, which are: personal selling, advertising and publicity.

Despite the critical debate that exists around the concept of the 4Ps and the efficacy of the categories for theoretical work, it remains a useful framework within which to structure our understanding of marketing, and practition-ers continue to apply the 4Ps. Further suggestions and criticisms have been made in recent times and the debate continues (see: Goi, 2009; Goldsmith, 1999; Zineldin & Philipson, 2007), but for the purposes of this textbook, we will continue basing our structuring of marketing as a concept around the 4Ps model.

How this book works

This book has a traditional structure; each chapter is devoted to a specific marketing topic. The theoretical basis for each topic will be presented and practical examples from the real world will be given to show you how these theories are used by practitioners. All the chapters feature case studies, which give you in-depth understanding of how these concepts are put into practice.

You will also find exercises within the chapters designed to make you think in a different way about the concepts being discussed. Then at the end of each chapter there are a few short questions which help highlight the key points throughout the chapter. These will help with your revision of the material.

Case study: Calvin Harris

Ever wondered who was the biggest selling song-writer in the UK in 2011 and 2012?

It wasn't Beyoncé, it wasn't Rihanna or Lady Gaga, it was a young man from Dumfries in southern Scotland. His name is Adam Wiles but he is better known as Calvin Harris. The rise of Calvin Harris as a globally recognisable name and brand within music is remarkable on several fronts. First, his sheer popularity and appeal make him a compelling case, second for his conscious chameleon-like changes during his career, and third for his continuous reference to himself and his approach as a strategic product that is considered from a marketing perspective.

Strategic marketing decisions

His first single, *Acceptable in the 80s*, had a soul quality to it so he decided to give himself a racially ambiguous name, rather than using his real name, Adam Wiles, in order to make the single seem more credible as a soul song. And so the artist known as Calvin Harris was born: "My first single was more of a soul track, and I thought Calvin Harris sounded a bit more racially ambiguous. I thought people might not know if I was black or not. After that, I was stuck with it." (Harris, 2016)

And so Calvin Harris broke onto the music scene in the UK in 2006 with debut single *Acceptable in the 80s*, which peaked in the UK charts at number 10. It launched Harris's ascent into public consciousness in the UK as an electro-singer-songwriter-performer, playing at festivals and releasing a best-selling debut album, *I Created Disco*, which peaked at number 8 in the UK album charts as well as achieving broad international success.

This was the birth of Calvin Harris the music product. The importance of this decision to change names lies in the structuring of meaning around the name. The intention here was at the very least for people to perhaps subconsciously assume that the name Calvin Harris belonged to a black soul singer and thus make a soul record seem more musically credible. This founded the direction he took from then on in his career, which was to manage Calvin Harris as though it was a musical commodity, rather than just his stage name.

At this time Harris was asked to produce music for internationally renowned artists such as Kylie Minogue; he topped the singles charts in the UK for the first time ;and he began work on his second album, *Ready For The Weekend*. Harris at this point was a performing act, meaning he appeared with a band and performed his songs live at gigs and promoted them on TV and radio by offering live performances. He continued to collaborate with a large number of acclaimed international artists and received production and writing credits on a host of highly successful songs. In interviews he was particularly candid about his deliberate commercial approach:

> "Well I'm making songs for the radio. I'm not making songs for people who look at Drowned In Sound or whatever. I'm a commercial act! That's what we're trying to present me as, so, you know, you've got to respect that."

However, when he was asked about how well he was doing at playing the part of a commercial popstar, he responded:

> "Not that well (Laughs). I love being accommodating in the musical sense, but I'm not very good at going out or trying to get my picture taken or getting off with celebrities or that kind of thing. I'm terrible at that so I've given up on it, and I don't think I'm going to be a celebrity any time soon. But as far as music goes, I'd like to think of it as being an accessible thing I do! (Harris, 2011)

After supporting Rihanna on her world tour in 2011, Harris took the decision that he wanted to become known for his work behind the scenes rather than as a performing act, specifically he wanted to rebrand from being a popstar to a DJ/producer. His next album, *18 Months*, became the first album ever to have eight top ten singles on it and it signified Harris's arrival on the scene as a bona fide international DJ. Fortunately for Harris, around this time, dance music was taking the world by storm, heralded as the saviour of Las Vegas, its raging popularity in the USA turned it into a five billion dollar industry in a matter of years, and Harris was the perfect package for this new wave of DJ dominance: he had the popstar pedigree, the understanding of the relationship between dance and pop, the networks and relationships with the royalty of the pop world and he understood the potential earnings of DJing compared to conventional pop star touring. A DJ could earn twice as much as a popstar without the need for dancers, an elaborate stage or even the necessity to play only their own songs. Harris could jet around the world from one nightclub to another and promote his music and earn money with relative ease.

Perhaps you could say the rest is history. At the time of writing this case study, Harris has emerged as one of the most recognisable names in music across the globe. A relationship with Taylor Swift (another one of the most popular, successful and dominant acts in pop music) cemented his profile in the popular consciousness and they were also identified as the highest earning couple in global music. Harris's musical profile continues to evolve as he has begun releasing lower tempo, more pop-orientated music with artists such as Migos, Pharrell Wiliams and Frank Ocean…developing his reputation as a respected producer and broadening the appeal of Calvin Harris the brand.

Revision questions

1 What are the four categories of the marketing mix and what are the four functions that underpin them?

2 Marketing borrows from several other academic disciplines, name three of them.

3 What were the three areas of criticism directed towards the 4Ps concept?

4 Complete the sentence: Marketing has evolved from being concerned with value in exchange to also being concerned with value in _____.

5 What are the four parts of the anatomy of a brand?

Directed further reading

Peñaloza, L., & Venkatesh, A. (2006). Further evolving the new dominant logic of marketing: from services to the social construction of markets. *Marketing Theory*, **6**(3), 299-316.

Valkenburg, P. M., & Buijzen, M. (2005). Identifying determinants of young children's brand awareness: Television, parents, and peers. *Journal of Applied Developmental Psychology*, **26**(4), 456-468

Van Waterschoot, W., & Van den Bulte, C. (1992). The 4P classification of the marketing mix revisited. *The Journal of Marketing*, 83-93.

References

Abbott, L. (1955), *Quality and Competition: An Essay in Economic Theory*, New York, NY: Columbia University Press.

Goi, C. L. (2009). A review of marketing mix: 4Ps or more? *International journal of marketing studies,* **1**(1), 2.

Goldsmith, R. E. (1999). The personalised marketplace: beyond the 4Ps. *Marketing Intelligence & Planning,* **17**(4), 178-185.

Harris, C. (2011) *Calvin Harris Interview/Interviewer: P. Justice.*

Harris, C. (2016) *This is why Calvin Harris named himself Calvin Harris/Interviewer: M. Nissim & L. Corner*. Digital Spy.

Holbrook, M. B. (1995). *Consumer Research: Introspective Essays on the Study of Consumption*, London: SAGE Publications.

Lusch, R.F. and Vargo, S.L. (2006). Service-dominant logic: Reactions, reflections and refinements. *Marketing Theory*, **6**(3), 281-288.

McCarthy, E. J. (1960). *Basic Marketing: A Managerial Approach*. Homewood, IL: Richard D. Irwin. Inc.,

Peñaloza, L., & Venkatesh, A. (2006). Further evolving the new dominant logic of marketing: from services to the social construction of markets. *Marketing Theory*, **6**(3), 299-316.

Valkenburg, P. M., & Buijzen, M. (2005). Identifying determinants of young children's brand awareness: Television, parents, and peers. *Journal of Applied Developmental Psychology*, **26**(4), 456-468.

Van Waterschoot, W., & Van den Bulte, C. (1992). The 4P classification of the marketing mix revisited. *The Journal of Marketing*, 83-93.

Zineldin, M., & Philipson, S. (2007). Kotler and Borden are not dead: myth of relationship marketing and truth of the 4Ps. *Journal of Consumer Marketing*, **24**(4), 229-241.

2 History

Keith Gori

"History is not just events and chronology; it is carried forward in the human consciousness. The past is alive in the present and may shape the emerging future."

Andrew Pettigrew, Business Historian

Historical research is a growing field within the academic discipline of marketing. This chapter looks at why it is important to study the history of marketing and provides a brief (albeit incomplete) analysis of some major marketing developments in history. The case study of Cadbury offers an example of a company with a rich marketing history.

Why study (marketing) history?

A generally accepted understanding of history is the study of the past by those in the present; or, as Carr (1990: 55) puts it, the, "process of interaction between the historian and his facts, an unending dialogue between the present and the past...both the inquiry conducted by the historian and the facts of the past into which he enquires."

We can understand, then, what history is in this way, but the question remains as to why we should be interested in or by it. Historians and philosophers of history have engaged in lengthy debates over both the purpose of studying history and on what that history might include. As Stearns (1998: 1) writes, "People live in the present. They plan for and worry about the future. History, however, is the study of the past." Stearns (1998) sets out a number of propositions on which the study of history can be justified:

1 **It helps us understand people and societies.** History offers a mass of information about how people and societies behave, the understanding of which is difficult (though many disciplines try). Stearns (1998) argues

that history offers the only extensive evidence base on which to analyse how societies function.

2   **It helps us to understand change and how things came to be.** Stearns (1998) claims that the past causes the present. Although history is about much more than chronological patterns, it is clear that we cannot understand the significance of certain contemporary issues without trying to understand their root causes.

3   **Its has importance in our own lives and for providing identity.** Stearns (1998) celebrates the beauty of history well told and of the 'pastness of the past', arguing that history is enjoyable and interesting. Moreover it provides identity, be it a family identity, a national identity, or a political identity.

4   **It provides moral understanding and is essential for good citizenship.** He suggests that history provides a terrain for moral contemplation, and allows us to question the characters and events of the past in relation to our own moral views. By doing so, it is hoped that advancement can be made in the present.

Taking these four examples we can argue that marketing needs history in the same way. Marketing needs to understand the processes by which the people, organisations and systems in which it operates have come to be as they are. History can be interesting for students of marketing, marketers and others to engage with the discipline's past. It provides the discipline with identity, assists in moral understanding and helps to ensure that marketing can act for progress for business, consumers, and wider society.

Marketing in the Ancient World

Marketing is a relatively young academic discipline, having received sustained scholarly attention for just over a century, and although there has been some historical attention given to both theory and practice in this period (Jones, 2010), historical research in marketing is not as well developed as it is in, for example, business, management or accounting. Jones (2009a) claims that the development of these fields is in a more advanced position due to their having a longer standing critical and pluralist culture, or having considerable contribution from scholars working in history departments rather than business or management schools. Given the wide-ranging debate, and the growing prominence of interpretive and qualitatively driven research in marketing and consumer research, it is perhaps unsurprising that there has been a considerable growth in the volume of historical research during recent decades. As the qualitative, interpretive methods generally utilised in historical research have increasingly thrived, so a space has been created for historical research in marketing. This growth in historical research in marketing has included the development of a biennial conference devoted to the subject (running since 1983), increased publication of historically orientated articles in marketing journals, and more recently the development of a dedicated journal, the *Journal of Historical Research in Marketing* (Jones, 2010).

Historical research in marketing has developed in two broad areas: marketing history, and the history of marketing thought. Marketing history tends to analyse companies, industries or economies in order to explore the histories of advertising, retailing, product design, distribution, and other elements of the marketing mix; whereas the history of marketing thought scrutinises the philosophical development of marketing ideas, concepts and theory (Jones, 2009b; 2010). Both approaches offer the historical depth of analysis that any successful field ought to pursue, and have gone a long way towards correcting the "poverty of ahistorical analysis" from which the discipline suffered (Fullerton, 1987: 97). Beyond the 'specialist' marketing historians that engage in these kinds of research, many marketing publications begin with a 'potted history' of the theoretical concepts and approaches under investigation and the contextual means through which this is being studied. Though not particularly common, students on both undergraduate and postgraduate degree programmes can take a historical marketing issue or development as the basis for their dissertations or theses, particularly given the increasing use and accessibility of online archives and materials (Gori & Perez-Vega, 2015).

Having questioned why we might be interested in the history of marketing, the chapter continues with some historical analysis of the concept of marketing and its development in society. Organising a history of a vast period of time and a broad concept such as marketing could be approached in a number of ways, including chronologically by geography, or arranged by topics within the broader subject (e.g. distribution, promotion etc). Here a chronological approach is taken, although this can prove difficult in itself. Ideally, such a periodization should hinge on key events rather than being organised by a more binary dating system such as discussion of each decade or century (Hollander et al., 2005). For example, historians have often talked about the long-eighteenth (Baines, 2004), the long-nineteenth (Hobsbawm, 1962; 1975; 1987) or the short-twentieth century (Hobsbawm, 1994) to acknowledge and embrace this. The pitfalls can be seen in Egan's (2008) history of twentieth century marketing which often falls into the trap of discussing decade-by-decade developments, without acknowledging some of the important continuities and disparities evolving through longer periods. Here a brief history of marketing is presented, which attempts to track only some changes through key events and turning points. The pivotal points discussed here are:

■ The pre-modern expansion of trade between groups of people;

■ Progress achieved during the development of ancient civilisations in Greece and Rome;

■ The regression of marketing in the warring middle ages;

■ Its re-emergence amidst the growth of the later middle ages and early modern periods including the impact of colonial expansion;

■ The industrial revolution and its expansion of trade and consumption;

■ The mass consumption of the post-Second World War era.

'Pre-modern' marketing

It has been suggested that trading practices go back 40,000 years to the Upper Paleolithic era, in which archaeological evidence can be found for rudimentary bartering (a form of verbal negotiation, often expected to take place in a trading context):

> *"For some 40,000 years, prior to the retail revolution in marketing practice, during the sixth century BCE, the major form of trade was barter, the exchange of goods for goods, particularly the silent trade. Barter was crucial to the evolution of early modern man and appears to have provided the competitive advantage that led to the rise of Homo Sapiens and the demise of Homo Neanderthalis." (Shaw 2016: 38)*

The bartering described here continued through the Stone, Bronze and Iron Ages, and supported the development of civilisations for many thousands of years. Central to this was silent trade, often featuring no direct contact, which facilitated trade between groups with no shared language or at very different stages of technological advancement. Originally, silent trade developed in Africa between West Africans and North Africans. They didn't share a common language and there was always the threat of territorial conflict during physical encounters. However, each group had surplus of a commodity valued by the other group. For the North Africans, this surplus was salt, while West Africans had surplus gold. The North Africans wanted gold to trade with Europeans, and the West Africans required salt as it enabled them to preserve their food. In order to trade without a common language, and without the risk of conflict, a middleman would arrange a meeting point, where the West Africans would deposit their gold and leave, and the North Africans would retrieve the gold and in return leave salt. The silent trade was enacted in the spirit of continuity, so the North Africans would leave a disproportionately large amount of salt (which they had in abundance), in order to ensure the West Africans were satisfied and would continue to supply them with gold in the future. This evolved to silent bartering, where a common language of hand signals was developed to allow direct interactions between traders; a simplified form of visual communication, which did not necessitate a common spoken language. Such forms of market communication are still seen today on trading floors in the financial services industry.

Exercise

Can you think of physical symbols that would be essential in communicating in a trade scenario? What would they be? Think of things such as 'final offer', 'opening offer', 'counter-offer', 'deposit', 'collateral', 'insurance'.

Although these practices have existed much beyond these periods into modern history, fewer and fewer groups use them. This is because trade by barter is inefficient and reliant on both parties in the exchange having the exact products that the other wants and in appropriate quantities. Barter involves an opportunity cost, since traders must transport and collect goods, in order to meet the other participant or to deposit them for a silent trade. Bartering goods also involves difficulty in negotiating the value of goods, and storing value for future use. Although it had stimulated terrific development over a long period this inefficiency was replaced during Antiquity by the development of a more efficient system and one in which we can see many resemblances to the system we now identify as marketing (Shaw, 2015).

The origins of marketing systems: Antiquity

Beginning in Athens, trading during Antiquity moved from a system dominated by bartering to one bearing significant resemblance to the basic fundamental components of modern exchange. This transition can be seen in analysis of the descriptions of trade that appear in the Bible. Describing the Jerusalem of the Old Testament, Grossman (1983) clearly presents a system in which trade is most often operated through commissioned merchants of King

Solomon rather than independent traders, and in which bartering remains the common system. Describing the picture of trade 1000 years later, as presented in the New Testament, Mulvihill (1983) shows that markets and a marketing system are commonplace, having "spread from Greece into every nook and cranny of the civilized world" (Shaw 2016: 29).

The philosophical underpinnings of a system integrating society and economy, and concerns caused by such a system, can be found in ancient writings such as those of the Socratic philosophers (Shaw, 1995; Shaw & Jones, 2002). Plato's *The Republic* describes how a state comes into being because no one individual is self-sufficient, but rather has a range of basic needs such as food, shelter and clothing which must be satisfied in an efficient manner. Shaw (1983: 147) summarises Plato's description in terms of a market economy:

> *"Comparative advantage leads to a division of labour resulting in efficiency in production. But the division of labour also results in a separation of producers and consumers. To bridge this gap market exchange is required. The exchange process requires work, work takes time, and time has an opportunity cost. Hence, marketing institutions emerge because of increased efficiency of exchange."*

This spread was prompted by the increasing requirement for a more efficient system to satisfy the needs and wants of the populace than that provided by barter trade. This was achieved through three important developments: the proliferation of central marketplaces, the appearance of sedentary retailers, and the adoption of coined money.

Money was crucial to the development of a recognisably modern marketing system, because it served both as a medium of exchange and as a store of value. Shaw (2016, p. 28) states:

> *"Simply, bartering involves product or service X exchanged for product or service Y, which requires a double coincidence of product or service desires. Marketing involves product or service X exchanged for M = money, which serves as a middleman that, in turn, can be exchanged for any product or service a, b, c … z; or held for a future date."*

Whereas goods could perish, decline in value, vary in size or be difficult to quantify and split for exchange, money retained its value much longer (only declining through inflation or debasement) and offered a store of value, which individuals could increase over time, building capital wealth.

As money allowed trade negotiations to be carried out more easily and for individuals to accumulate and store wealth, so developments in the organisation of trading allowed for easier exchange of goods through central marketplaces and sedentary retailing. In cities of the ancient world, labour became increasingly specialised and thus increasingly efficient. However, this necessitated increasing trade for people to satisfy all of their needs, and a separation of producers meant that selling one's own goods and acquiring others remained laborious. Retailers became prevalent, to whom goods were sold in bulk, allowing labour to continue relatively uninterrupted. Marketplaces developed, such as the *agora* in Athens (from the 6th century BC), in which these specialist retailers could predictably be found, and various retailing and advertising practices began to develop: singing about products, shop signage, and increasingly elaborate layouts of 'stores' (Shaw, 2015; 2016; Vennarruci, 2015). Given the time taken to transition from barter to market exchange, the speed with which this system spread is remarkable, with similar practices observed to develop in India between the sixth and third centuries BC, and in China during the Han Dynasty.

What followed was perhaps the most sustained and widespread advance in the development of marketing systems. Many of these developments regressed through the Dark Ages before slowly re-emerging, following a mini-Ice Age around the year 1000 AD. Shaw (2016) notes that warring, destruction to infrastructure such as roads, and the decline of currency systems of the early medieval period caused a return to predominantly agricultural production and barter trade. This slowed the expansion of trading systems and marketing developments dramatically, although the later medieval period did see the introduction of key financial instruments and trade fairs and guilds. This development continued through the Renaissance period, with new trading routes opened in the wake of European colonialism, making an array of new luxury goods available for purchase. Such trading mainly targeted the wealthy, and it was not until the onset of industrialisation and the growth of increasingly urban labour forces that development drove towards what has been termed 'modern marketing'.

'Modern' marketing

The Industrial Revolution brought a shift from predominantly agricultural to industrial production, and a movement of labour that saw cities and mill-towns expand rapidly. Technological developments created the conditions for more efficient and cheaper production of goods. In Britain, per capita income doubled in the second half of the nineteenth century, with disposable income growing even more quickly. It also brought much poverty, squalor and a desperately poor standard of living for many workers (including child labourers), but from a marketing perspective the long-term impact is profound: the Industrial Revolution created a system in which goods were produced much more cheaply and efficiently, and the populace were increasingly able to purchase them.

The role of marketers and marketing developed in response to these changes. Egan (2008) lays out a range of developments in marketing thought and practice that contribute to making the twentieth century a 'century of marketing,' in which an independent discipline and the specialist role of the 'marketer' truly developed. For Egan (2008: 3), "modern marketing began, developed and flourished in the USA... [where] ... it was recognised early on as a subject worthy of academic endeavour". These early American courses covered distribution, advertising and salesmanship, and justifications of the role of marketing, which could be considered at this time as a form of applied economics (Egan, 2008; Ellis et al., 2011). Jones and Monieson (1990) note that there were earlier marketing courses being taught in Germany, describing the influence of the German Historical School of Economics, which many American scholars, who trained in Germany, brought back to the USA. These scholars subscribed to an inductive, positivist epistemology, and sought to develop a science of marketing from which improvements could be made to the market. Jones and Monieson (1990) also highlight the importance these scholars attached to the notion of distributive justice, and ensuring all in the market were treated fairly.

A shift towards the management of a marketing strategy is something that dominated marketing thinking in this period, with the likes of Ralph Butler Starr and Arch W. Shaw highlighting the importance of co-ordination, planning and management operations, production and distribution (Bartels, 1976). Ellis et al. (2011) argue that much of this thinking in the marketing field was derived from the work and influence of Frederick Wilmslow Taylor, who developed the concept of managing according to scientific principles, at the turn of the twentieth century (also known as Taylorism). Ellis et al. (2011) cite a number of scholars and practitioners as influential figures in applying Taylorism to marketing practice; so the 'art' of salesmanship was transformed into the 'science' of selling. The development of marketing was much influenced by the impact of two world wars in the first half of the twentieth century, though in different ways. The need for production on a large scale saw massive capacity increases in the US and, unlike Europe, America was not ravaged by the destruction of war, so this capacity remained once the conflict had ceased. This unprecedented capacity for production presented a much more competitive landscape for business. The need to understand consumer needs, wants and desires became ever more important. The post-war period can be seen as one in which the emphasis of marketing thought increasingly shifted from production to consumption.

The post-war period has often been discussed in terms of the consumer boom and the growth of a consumer society, but various historians, anthropologists and sociologists have developed accounts which show how the consumer society developed over a much longer period. For example, McCracken (1988) argues that the consumer revolution needs to be seen as part of a larger transformation in Western societies going back as far as the sixteenth century. Various explanations for the development of consumer society are offered such as McKendrick's (1982) consumerist, Campbell's (1987; 1991) modernist and De Vries' (1975) exchangist analysis of consumer culture. Although there is not the scope (or need) to analyse these contributions in detail here, they do share some important commonalities; namely, the prominence they ascribe to promotion and hedonism, and their acknowledgement of the changing attitudes towards goods in seventeenth and eighteenth century Western Europe (for a detailed coverage of the anti-productionist analysis of consumer culture see Sassatelli, 2007). Nevertheless, there is no doubt that in the post-war period, for a number of reasons, the scale of consumer goods and access to them increased substantially and required a reaction from marketers (Ellis et al., 2011; Slater, 2004).

This period is one in which the marketing profession expanded at a rapid pace in order to meet the production, distribution and promotional needs of competing in such a competitive consumer landscape. This has been seen as a golden age for marketers and advertisers (Brookes & Palmer, 2004). Egan (2008: 7) claims that the 1950s represent a "watershed for marketing thought as the mainstream debate became steeped in science". (See also Ellis et al. (2011) for analysis of the debates surrounding marketing's position as a science and the development of competing paradigms). From this period onwards there was a substantial increase in the emphasis on marketing management, in order to meet and cultivate consumer demand. This focussed on the manner in which marketing should function, rather than explanations of how it was functioning (as had been the case in earlier managerially focussed work). The approach encouraged the integration of marketing activities and downward delegation of authority (Egan, 2008). Many concepts still taught and applied in modern marketing were developed and cemented through this approach (although they have often been shown by marketing historians to go back much further), such as the 4Ps Marketing Mix (McCarthy, 1960), market segmentation (Smith, 1956), and brand image (Gardner & Levy, 1955). The 1970s saw significant debates around broadening the definition of marketing to include non-consumer transactions (Kotler, 1972; 2005).

In much of the period following this, the marketing discipline has increasingly embraced a range of philosophical and methodological approaches beyond the more typical positivist, quantitative methods – although, again, there are significant early examples of this sort of work (Egan, 2008; Ellis et al., 2011). Many 'new' marketing approaches and concepts have been developed in the post-war period, such as social marketing, relationship marketing, critical marketing and the service-dominant logic, although historians of marketing thought are often found questioning their newness and showing that their foundations stretch back through much more complex histories (for example see Tadajewski (2008; 2009) and Tadajewski and Saren (2008) on the development of relationship marketing and Tadajewski (2010a; 2010b) in relation to critical marketing). Technological developments throughout the twentieth century have been of critical importance to diversifying the approaches and mediums through which marketers must now work. The Internet, social media and the digital world are of course crucial recent developments (Buchwitz, 2015), and are discussed in Chapters 4 and 6 of this book. However, through all of these debates and technological improvements, the fundamental goals and ideas of marketing have remained relatively unchanged (Shaw, 2016).

Case study: Chocolate and Cadbury's

Chocolate is a ubiquitous consumer product. The average person in the UK eats 11kg of chocolate, and spends $146 doing so, each year (Sedghi 2015; Statista 2016). Arguably, this rise to prominence has been underpinned by the development of the marketing system described in this chapter. The first use of cacao as a drink is estimated variously as by the Olmec and Mayan civilisations around 1000 B.C. (Guardian, 2007) if not the earlier Mokaya civilisations of 1900-1500 B.C. (Winterman, 2013). Cacao powder was also used in religious rituals as face paint and placed in the tombs of the dead, suggesting divine associations (Guardian, 2007). Brought to Europe by colonial travellers in the sixteenth and seventeenth centuries, chocolate became an increasingly popular alternative drink to tea and coffee in early eighteenth century London, tempered to European palates with the addition of sugar, another colonial import (Campos, 2009; Guardian, 2007; Robertson, 2009). A key development – technologically driven by the improvement of pressing techniques in Holland – was the invention of chocolate slabs or bars, which were again more palatable to the European consumer.

Cadbury was one of several British confectionery companies operating in the seventeenth and eighteenth centuries that successfully adapted to producing chocolate in solid form. Three such companies were started and run for many years by Quaker families, after whom they were named (Fry and Rowntree being the other two). Several important marketing developments allowed Cadbury to occupy a competitive position, despite Fry's selling two and a half times more product in 1870 (Fitzgerald, 2005). Between 1900 and 1939, Cadbury was able to occupy a dominant position in the British confectionery market, with their marketing capabilities "a primary cause of its commercial expansion" and "a formative influence on the nature of the confectionery industry" (Fitzgerald, 2005: 511). Their superior sales figures drove competing brand Rowntree's to introduce marketing developments of their own (Fitzgerald, 1989). Cadbury's marketing developments in this period came in three areas: production and management, mass selling, and branding and advertising.

First, they were able to exploit the advantages of large-scale manufacturing, and at the same time introduce changes to corporate structure which saw marketing develop as a functional and organisational capability. Production that favoured high standardisation and operational efficiency in creating a product with high consumer demand was crucial in the company's development. Second, they implemented "intensive, targeted and highly promoted mass sellers" (Fitzgerald, 2005: 512) allowing them to successfully meet the wishes of customers and consumers. Both of these innovations allowed Cadbury to gain a price advantage over competitors. Third, Cadbury invested substantial effort in branding and advertising which led to the creation of a national mass market for confectionery. Fitzgerald (2005: 512) writes that: "It is noteworthy that Cadbury honed its skills in production and in marketing simultaneously. It is the compatibility of the two functions within the company which provided its competitive advantage, exemplified by the strength of its value proposition to consumers."

Following a slowdown in development during the controlled production of World War Two, the company's marketing and production was increased with the building of a new factory in 1952, and the direction of the company altered through a merger with soft drink brand Schweppes in 1969 (Smith et al., 1990). The new company pursued a strategy based on acquiring other brands through the 1980s and 1990s, in pursuit of global dominance of the confectionery and soft drink markets. In order to ensure the enlarged company remained competitive, it introduced a programme called Managing for Value (MVF) in the late 1990s, which placed emphasis on ruthlessly focussed promotional support for those brands thought to be able to yield substantial profit. This was partly due to shareholder anxiety at the numerous mergers and acquisitions, and had significant consequences for Cadbury's marketers, who now had to prove that every new acquisition, product line and marketing initiative would be profitable. The company demerged in 2007 before being taken over by Kraft Foods, a US confectioner, in a £11.5 billion pound deal in 2010.

We can discern several trends from the general history discussed above. Colonial exploration and the development of new trade routes were key precursors in the development of a market for chocolate, as were technological developments, which allowed for product innovations, which were better suited to the wants and needs of European consumers. Following an expansion of the confectionery industry in the seventeenth and eighteenth centuries, an increasingly managerial approach to production and distribution allowed Cadbury to gain a price advantage in the early twentieth century. At the same time, increased attention to advertising and branding allowed for the creation of a national mass market. We've also seen elements not discussed in the chapter, such as the impact of mergers and acquisitions on marketing functioning, and had we explored the Quaker roots of the company in more detail we would have veered into the social responsibility of business and marketing. What this case study should illustrate is the vast importance of marketing over time in the case of just one company or product type, and the importance of understanding how marketing drives change across industries, companies and across wider society.

Review questions

1 Which of the following does Stearns (1998) suggest as reasons justifying historical study?
   A: It helps us understand people and societies
   B: It helps us understand change
   C: It is essential for good citizenship
   D: All of the above

2 It has been argued that trade dates back....(how long)?
   A: 400 years
   B: 4,000 years
   C: 40,000 years
   D: 400,000 years

3 Early trade was characterised by what?
   A: Bartering
   B: Shops
   C: Money
   D: E-commerce

4 In which ancient city does Shaw (2015, 2016) suggest the origins of marketing systems can be found?
A: Athens
B: Ostia
C: Pompeii
D: Sparta

5 Which three things does Shaw (2015, 2016) argue underpinned the development of a marketing system in the ancient period?
A: Coined money
B: Sedentary retailing
C: Central marketplaces
D: All of the above

6 According to Egan (2008) 'modern marketing' began, developed and flourished where?
A: Western Europe
B: China
C: Russia
D: USA

7 Which school of thought was influential on the early twentieth North American marketing scholars according to Jones and Monieson (1990)?
A: Functionalism
B: German historical school
C: French liberal school
D: Marxian economics

8 Marketing management thought in the later twentieth century was characterised by what kind of shift?
A: From how marketing functioned to how it should function
B: From how marketing should function to how it was functioning
C: From marketing's current functioning to its optimal function
D: From marketing's optimal function to its current functioning

9 Cadbury was sold to Kraft in 2010 for how much?
A: £115 billion
B: £11.5 million
C: £11.5 trillion
D: £11.5 billion

Further reading

There are two relatively new journals which exclusively publish historical research in marketing: the *Journal of Historical Research in Marketing* and the *History of Retailing and Consumption*. Other journals which have often featured pieces of historical research in marketing include (but are not limited to): *Journal of Macromarketing*; *Marketing Theory*; *Consumption, Markets & Culture*; *European Journal of Marketing* and *Journal of Marketing Management*.

The most freely accessible resource of marketing history research is perhaps the collections of proceedings of the Conference on Historical Analysis and Research in Marketing, available at http://charmassociation.org/. These pieces often have the advantage of being shorter in length than many journal articles, a feature of benefit to the busy student!

There are edited collections in both marketing history (Jones & Tadajewski, 2016) and the history of marketing thought (Tadajewski & Jones, 2008) which offer excellent introductions, and extensive bibliographies to guide further research. The history of consumption remains relatively under-researched within the field (Schwarzkopf, 2015) but chapters such as that by Witkowski (2016) offer a good starting point, and a 2015 special issue 'Marketing History from Below: bringing the consumer back in' of the *Journal of Historical Research in Marketing* is a useful contribution. There are numerous books looking at the development of 'consumer culture' or of 'consumer society', with Sassatelli (2007) offering an excellent historical summary and direction for further reading, as does Slater (2004). Interdisciplinary perspectives of much use theoretically are offered by the edited collections from Miller (1995) and by Schor and Holt (2000).

This chapter provides only a brief sketch of the history of marketing and consumption. The material above and that to which it points expands this story well beyond the bounds of this chapter. Historical research in marketing remains a field in its infancy, and as such contains many gaps. As a result, this chapter has not touched on many key issues in the history of any subject, providing a largely elite, male and white history. This is partly a result of the lack of scope available here and the lack of research in areas such as gender, the impact of people of colour, and the role of class in marketing's history and development. Some excellent work has begun to address this, for example Davis' (2016) analysis of the role of African-American women in the American advertising industry, and Witkowski's (2016) use of gender as one of his conceptual analysis of consumption in the US.

As historical research in marketing continues to grow, students, researchers and practitioners can look forward to learning more of the discipline's history.

References

Baines, P. (2004). *The Long 18th Century*, London: Arnold

Bartels, R. (1976). *The History of Marketing Thought* (2nd edition), Columbus, OH: Grid Publishing.

Brookes, R. & Palmer, R. (2004). *The New Global Marketing Reality*, New York: Palgrave Macmillan.

Buchwitz, L. A. (2015). 'A Model of Periodization of Radio and Internet Advertising History' in: Hawkins, R.A. (Ed.), *Crossing Boundaries, Spanning Borders: Voyages Around Marketing's Past: Proceedings of the 17th Conference on Historical Analysis and Research in Marketing* (pp. 14-29), CHARM Association, Long Beach, California.

Campbell, C. (1987). *The Romantic Ethic and the Spirit of Modern Consumerism*. Oxford: Basil Blackwell.

Campbell, C. (1991). Consumption: the new wave of research in the humanities and social sciences. *Journal of Social Behavior and Personality*, **6**(6), 57-74.

Campos, E.V. (2009). Thomas Gage and the English colonial encounter with chocolate. *Journal of Medieval and Early Modern Studies*, **39**(1), 183-200.

Carr, E. H. (1990). *What is History?* (2nd edition). London, England: Penguin Books.

Davis, J.F. (2016). *Pioneering African-American Women in the Advertising Business: Biographies of MAD Black WOMEN*. London: Routledge.

De Vries, J. (1975). Peasant demand patterns and economic development: Friesland, 1550-1750. In W. N. Parker & E. L. Jones (Eds.), *European Peasants and their Markets: Essays in Agrarian Economic History*. Princeton: Princeton University Press.

Egan, J. (2008). A century of marketing. *The Marketing Review*, **8**(1), 3-23.

Ellis, N., Fitchett, J., Higgins, M. Jack, G., Lim, M., Saren, M. & Tadajeski, M. (2011). *Marketing: A Critical Textbook*, London: SAGE.

Fitzgerald, R. (1989). Rowntree and marketing strategy, 1897-1939. *Business and Economic History*, **2**(18), 45-58.

Fitzgerald, R. (2005). Products, Firms and consumption: Cadbury and the development of marketing, 1900-1939. *Business History*, **47**(4), 511-531.

Fullerton, R.A. (1987). The poverty of ahistorical analysis: present weakness and future cure in U.S. marketing thought, in R. Bagozzi, N. Dholakia and A.F. Firat, eds., *Philosophical and Radical Thought in Marketing*, Lexington: Lexington Books, 97-116.

Gardner, B.B. & Levy, S.J. (1955) The product and the brand, *Harvard Business Review*, March-April, 33-39

Gori, K. & Perez-Vega, R. (2015). 'From archives to the Internet' in O'Gorman, K. & MacIntosh, R. (eds.) *Research Methods for Business & Management: A guide to writing your dissertation* (2nd edition). Oxford: Goodfellow (pp. 96-117).

Grossman, L.A. (1983). 'Business in the Bible: Marketing' in: Hollander, S.E. & Savitt, R. (Eds.), *First North American Workshop on Historical Research in Marketing* (pp. 136-140), Michigan State University, East Lansing, Michigan.

Guardian (2007). 'A brief history of chocolate', https://www.theguardian.com/lifeandstyle/2007/apr/07/foodanddrink. Accessed 16th August 2016.

Hobsbawm, E. (1962). *The Age of Revolution: Europe 1789-1848*, London: Weidenfeld & Nicolson.

Hobsbawm, E. (1975). *The Age of Capital: 1848-1875*, London: Weidenfeld & Nicolson.

Hobsbawm, E. (1987). *The Age of Empire: 1875-1914*, London: Weidenfeld & Nicolson.

Hobsbawm, E. (1994). *The Age of Extremes: The Short Twentieth Century 1914-1991*, London: Weidenfeld & Nicolson.

Hollander, S. C., Rassuli, K. M., Jones, D. G. B., & Dix, L. F. (2005). Periodization in marketing history. *Journal of Macromarketing*, **25**(1), pp. 32-41.

Jones, D. G. B. (2009a). 'Meet the editor of ... Journal of Historical Research in Marketing'. http://www.emeraldgrouppublishing.com/authors/interviews/jhrm.htm. Accessed 15th Januray 2016.

Jones, D. G. B. (2009b). Making (marketing) history! *Journal of Historical Research in Marketing*, **1**(1).

Jones, D. G. B. (2010). A history of historical research in marketing. In M. J. Baker & M. Saren (Eds.), *Marketing Theory: A Student Text* (2nd edition, pp. 51–82). London: Sage.

Jones, D.G.B. & Monieson, D.D. (1990). The early development of the philosophy of marketing thought. *Journal of Marketing*, **54**(1), 102-113.

Jones, D.G.B. & Tadajewski, M. (2016). *The Routledge Companion to Marketing History*, Routledge: London.

Kotler, P. (1972). A Generic Concept of Marketing. *Journal of Marketing*, **36**(2), 46-54.

Kotler, P. (2005). The role played by the broadening of marketing movement in the history of marketing thought. *Journal of Public Policy & Marketing*, 24(1), 114-116.

McCarthy, E. J. (1960). *Basic Marketing, A managerial approach*. IL: Richard D. Irwin.

MMcCracken, G. (1988a). The history of consumption: a literature review and consumers' guide. *Journal of Consumer Policy*, 10(2), 139-166.

McCracken, G. (1988b). *Culture and Consumption: New Approaches to the Symbolic Character of Consumer Goods and Activities*, Bloomington: Indiana University Press

McKendrick, N. (1982). Commercialization and the economy. In N. McKendrick, J. Brewer & J. Plumb (Eds.), *The Birth of a Consumer Society: The Commercialization of Eighteenth-Century England*. Bloomington: Indiana University Press.

Miller, D. (1995). *Acknowledging Consumption*. London: Routledge.

Mulvihill, D.F. (1983). 'Marketers in the New Testament' in: Hollander, S.E. & Savitt, R. (Eds.), *First North American Workshop on Historical Research in Marketing* (pp. 141-145), Michigan State University, East Lansing, Michigan.

Robertson, E. (2009). *Chocolate, Women and Empire: a Social and Cultural History*, Manchester: Manchester University Press.

Sassatelli, R. (2007). *Consumer Culture: History, Theory and Politics*. London: Sage.

Schor, J.B. & Holt, D.B. (2000). *Consumer Society Reader*. New York: The New Press.

Schwarzkopf, S. (2015). Marketing history from below: towards a paradigm shift in marketing historical research. *Journal of Historical Research in Marketing*, **7**(3), 295-309.

Sedghi, A. (2015). 'I should cocoa: which country spends the most on chocolate?', *The Guardian*: https://www.theguardian.com/news/datablog/2015/jul/19/which-country-spends-the-most-on-chocolate-bars. Accessed 16th August 2016

Shaw, E.H. (1983). 'Plato and the socio-economic foundations of marketing: an historical analysis in the development of macro-marketing thought' in: Hollander, S.E. & Savitt, R. (Eds.), *First North American Workshop on Historical Research in Marketing* (pp. 146-151), Michigan State University, East Lansing, Michigan.

Shaw, E.H. (1995). The First Dialogue on Macromarketing. *Journal of Macromarketing*, **15**(1), 7-20.

Shaw, E.H. (2015). 'On the origin of marketing systems' in: Hawkins, R.A. (Ed.), *Crossing Boundaries, Spanning Borders: Voyages Around Marketing's Past: Proceedings of the 17th Conference on Historical Analysis and Research in Marketing* (pp. 219-221), CHARM Association, Long Beach, California.

Shaw, E.H. (2016). 'Ancient and medieval marketing' In: Jones, D.G.B. & Tadajewski, M. (Eds.) *The Routledge Companion to Marketing History* (pp. 23-40), London: Routledge.

Shaw, E.H. & Jones, D.G.B. (2002). A history of marketing thought, in: Weitz, B.A. & Wensley, R. (Eds.) *Handbook of Marketing* (pp. 39-65), London: SAGE.

Slater, D. (2004). *Consumer Culture and Modernity*. Cambridge: Polity.

Smith, W.R. (1956) Product differentiation and market segmentation as alternative marketing strategies, Journal of Marketing, **21**(1), 3-8

Smith, C., Child, J., & Rawlinson, M. (1990). *Reshaping Work: The Cadbury Experience*, Cambridge: Cambridge University Press.

Statista (2016), 'Statistics and facts on the chocolate industry', Statista: The Statistics Portal, http://www.statista.com/topics/1638/chocolate-industry/, Accessed 16th August 2016.

Stearns, P. N. (1998). 'Why Study History?', American Historical Association, https://www.historians.org/about-aha-and-membership/aha-history-and-archives/archives/why-study-history-(1998). Accessed 7th August 2016.

Tadajewski, M. (2008). Relationship marketing at Wanamaker's in the nineteenth and early twentieth centuries. *Journal of Macromarketing*, **28**(2), 169-182

Tadajewski, M. (2009). The foundations of relationship marketing: reciprocity and trade relations. *Marketing Theory*, **9**(1), 9-38.

Tadajewski, M. (2010a). Critical marketing studies: logical empiricism,'critical performativity'and marketing practice. *Marketing Theory*, **10**(2), 210-222.

Tadajewski, M. (2010b). Towards a history of critical marketing studies. *Journal of Marketing Management*, **26**(9-10), 773-824.

Tadajewski, M. & Jones, D.G.B. (2008). *The History of Marketing Thought*, SAGE: London. (Three volume set).

Tadajewski, M., & Saren, M. (2008). Rethinking the emergence of relationship marketing. *Journal of Macromarketing*, **29**(2), 193-206.

Vennarucci, R.G. (2015). 'Marketing an urban identity: The shops and shopkeepers of Ancient Rome' in: Hawkins, R.A. (Ed.), *Crossing Boundaries, Spanning Borders: Voyages Around Marketing's Past: Proceedings of the 17th Conference on Historical Analysis and Research in Marketing* (pp. 135-158), CHARM Association, Long Beach, California.

Winterman, D. (2013). 'Chocolate: The rise of the cocoa purists', *BBC News Magazine*: http://www.bbc.co.uk/news/magazine-21847447. Accessed 16th August 2016.

Witkowski, T.H. (2016). 'A history of consumption in the United States', in Jones, D.G.B. & Tadajewski, M. (Eds.) *The Routledge Companion to Marketing History* (pp. 41-60), Routledge: London.

3 Money

Darren Jubb

Marketing requires the utilisation of a significant amount of organisational resources. Managing these resources in an efficient and effective manner is essential to achieve the desired objectives of marketing activities. One of the primary concerns of organisations is the financial implications of the resources required to conduct marketing activities, and is therefore an area that marketing managers must be familiar with. Engaging with the marketing budget, considering how marketing activities are measured both financially and non-financially, and being able to successfully report on their performance to the organisation are essential skills for a marketing manager in the contemporary business world. These issues are discussed in this chapter.

Marketing costs money

Marketing is without doubt an essential element in the continuing success of organisations. The importance of marketing is reflected in the substantial amounts of money that organisations dedicate to marketing activities. For example, it is now common for around 20-25% of the overall expenditure of an organisation to be focused on activities related to marketing (Stewart, 2009). With marketing costs representing a considerable percentage of the overall expenditure for organisations, marketing managers have come under increased pressure to justify their actions and to account for the contribution that marketing makes to the current and future financial success of the organisation.

Since the overall goal of a commercial organisation is primarily the maximisation of profit and generation of shareholder value, those running the organisation are often first and foremost concerned with the financial consequences of marketing activities. An important aspect of marketing management thus lies in considering the financial impact of the activities of marketing. It is important for marketing managers to be able to plan for, evaluate and report on marketing activities in financial terms. Recognition of the increasingly important role that marketing activities play within organisations, coupled with the increased significance of the cost of those marketing activities, has a number of impacts on marketing managers. From the point of view of the marketing manager, significant attention must be placed on considering both the financial costs of marketing activities and the contribution those activities are making to the overall value of the organisation. In order to do this the marketing manager must be familiar with the techniques of how the costs of marketing activities are assessed by the organisation, on the one hand, and how the overall success of the marketing function is assessed by the organisation, on the other.

Exercise 1

Think of some of the most common marketing activities within the marketing mix. Which of these activities will be the most financially significant for organisations?

How marketing budgets work

One of the first steps in undertaking successful marketing is establishing how much to spend and where to spend it. The costs associated with marketing must be budgeted for. A budget is a method of expressing, in financial terms, a proposed plan of action that is designed to assist in the coordination and control of an organisation over a set period of time. Typically a budget is prepared for a maximum of one year into the future with the annual budget often then divided into quarters and, in some instances, months. The exact period of the budget relates to the specific preferences of the organisation with respect to reporting, performance evaluation, and control. Based on organisational objectives for the period in question, the budget shows the expected financial revenues and costs associated with the expected activities during this period. As such, the purpose of a budget is to assist management in making judgements and decisions, as well as being a useful tool for planning and control, and it can act as a guide for the organisation to follow in the upcoming period. Once the budget for the organisation as a whole has been set, it can be split up into individual budgets for each separate division or function of the organisation. Each function of the organisation will have a set of budgeted figures relating to their activities. To achieve the goals that are set out in the organisation's overall budget, coordination between all of the functions of the organisation must be encouraged.

Exercise 2

Write down your own personal budget for the next month, including all expected income and expenditure. Reflect on how difficult this task is. What issues did you have when attempting to create your budget?

3

Budgeting is an essential operational function of an organisation. When used in an appropriate manner a budget is a useful tool that can assist in the management of organisations in a number of different ways. Table 3.1 discusses some of the most common roles that a budget plays within an organisation.

Table 3.1: Roles of budgeting.

Role	Description
Planning	Preparing a budget encourages management to bring together all aspects of the organisation through the process of formal financial planning. Budgets are prepared in coordination with each business function and in line with the overall objectives of the organisation.
Performance evaluation	Comparing the actual financial performance of activities at the end of a period with the budgeted financial performance allows the organisation to assess performance. Management attention is required for areas where actual results differ from expected results.
Communication	The budget can be used as a tool by management for bringing together the different business functions of the organisation. The budget is a means of communicating the objectives to be achieved in financial terms.
Motivation	Targeted levels of performance set by management can have a motivating impact but care must be taken. If a performance level is seen to be too difficult to achieve, the target may be viewed as unrealistic and employees could cease trying to achieve it. If a target is too easily achievable the organisation may be underperforming. A careful balance must therefore be struck.

Exercise 3

Consider again the personal budget that you created in Exercise 2. Think about how the above roles relate to that budget. How useful is the budget for planning? At the end of the month, has everything gone to plan?

■ Approaches to budgeting

Budgeting is an on-going process of first planning and then tracking the financial activities of the organisation. An important consideration for management concerns the method of preparation of the budget. At the most basic level, setting the budget involves management estimating the income and expenditure for the individual elements that make up the organisation, as well as the organisation as a whole. Some of the most commonly used approaches to budgeting are listed in Table 3.2. When considering what kind of approach to take with regards to budgeting it is important to carefully consider the complexity, cost and time involved with each approach.

Table 3.2: Approaches to budgeting.

Approach	Description
Periodic budgeting	With this approach to budgeting the plan for each financial period is set up front and rarely altered. If the budget period is one year then expenditure will be spread out evenly over that period, with the amount of expected income and expected expenditure of the year split into one-twelfth of the total and allocated to each month of the year.
Incremental budgeting	Occurs when the organisation prepares the budget for the next period by showing incremental effects based on past budgeted or actual results. In brief, this often means that the budget for the current period for a line item will be a set percentage higher or lower than the corresponding figure in the previous period.
Zero-based budgeting	Each area of the organisation starts with no allocated budget. Each of these business areas then creates their own budget from scratch for the appropriate period based on their anticipated activities. This can be time consuming and costly, and is often a difficult task.
Continuous budgeting	A continuous budget is one that is continually updated at the end of a specific period, typically one month with respect to an annual budget. The actual results are compared with the budgeted results and if there are any differences that are considered to be permanent, the remaining eleven months of the budget are updated to reflect this.
Flexible budgeting	The budgeted cost is adjusted in line with the level of activity achieved during the period of the budget. This is helpful when the budgeted level of activity is not the same as the actual level of activity. Differences in performance can arise not through efficiency savings or gains but through differences in volume.

■ Preparing the marketing budget

Once the overall budget for the organisation has been established, how much is to be allocated to the different functions, including marketing, is the next decision to be made by the organisation. The process of setting the marketing budget will of course vary depending on the approach to budgeting used by the organisation. The marketing budget stems directly from the strategic marketing plan. The purpose of the marketing budget is to summarise all the revenues and costs involved with marketing together into one place, although it should be noted that as the revenues generated from marketing activities are often difficult to track directly, marketing budgets often focus on the costs associated with marketing activities. Traditionally, the purpose of marketing has been to achieve success in sales, market share and gross margin in the marketplace (Weber, 2002). The marketing budget offers management the opportunity to keep a close eye on the costs associated with these marketing efforts. Typically the exact detail of the marketing budget is decided through a process of negotiation with the management of the marketing function. A number of approaches are commonly applied to setting the marketing budget. These are:

- **Percentage of sales**: In this instance the marketing expenditure is determined by calculating a set percentage of expected sales. This percentage is often rolled over from the previous year and set by people who work outside the marketing function. This approach is frequently used despite having no connection to the strategic objectives of the marketing department.

- **Affordable method**: This involves allocating the marketing expenditure based on what the organisation can afford to spend. Again the amount is not considered with reference to the objectives set out in the marketing plan but is arbitrarily decided upon by top management. This is often underpinned by the belief that increased spend on marketing leads to increased sales and thus whatever can be afforded should be spent.

- **Competitor comparison**: Amounts are allocated to the marketing expenditure based on what competitors in the market are spending. Following this approach is dangerous as different companies will have different strategies and objectives and the organisation should make sure that it is tailoring the marketing budget to these.

- **Objective and task**: Budgets are prepared on the basis of determining the resources that will be required to meet the objectives set out in the marketing plan. Thus, the creator of the budget must consider the cost of the strategies to be employed within this plan.

Of the above approaches, the objective and task method is the recommended method for preparing a marketing budget. In line with a zero-based budgeting approach, this would mean that every item of expenditure within the marketing budget is justified by management in each reporting period and is mapped to the strategic plan and objectives of the marketing functions on an on-going basis. The cost and complexity of this approach should be considered. The outcome of all of these approaches will be a quantified plan for a particular period. Table 3.3 highlights an example of a budget for advertising expenditure for a quarter.

Table 3.3: Example of marketing budget

	January	February	March	Total
	£'000	£'000	£'000	£'000
Advertising	100	100	100	300
Internet advertising	250	300	250	800
Direct to customer	40	40	40	120
Social media	100	100	100	300
Price promotions	75	75	85	235
Pricing	50	100	50	200
New product development	200	400	600	1,200
Sales force	1,250	1,250	1,250	3,750
Distribution	750	650	700	2,100
Sponsorship	20	13	14	47
Total	2,835	3,028	3,189	9,052

Measuring marketing performance

In recent years there has been an increase in the desire to establish a means for effectively measuring the value that marketing activities create. More and more often marketing managers are being asked to show how marketing expenditures result in the creation of shareholder value, and there is a greater emphasis on making marketing managers accountable for their actions. Marketing managers must therefore be able to measure and evaluate their activities. Successfully quantifying the value of products, customers and other marketing activities has become an important part of the role of the marketing manager, and has resulted in a range of marketing metrics being created and used. Ambler (2000: 61) provides a useful definition of marketing metrics:

A 'metric' is a performance measure that top management should review. It is a measure that matters to the whole business. The term comes from music and implies regularity: the reviews should typically take place yearly or half-yearly... Metric is not just another word for measure – while all metrics are measures, not all measures are metrics. Metrics should be necessary, precise, consistent and sufficient (i.e. comprehensive) for review purposes. Metrics may be financial (usually from the profit and loss account), from the marketplace, or from non-financial internal sources (innovation and employee).

Metrics will be calculated for each period, usually in conjunction with the budget period under review, and management will be interested not only in the metric as a stand alone result, but also in comparing the trend of that particular metric over time. By doing this, management can track the effectiveness, efficiency and productivity of marketing activities over time. Therefore, marketing managers will be assessed on the basis of such metrics and should be familiar with their composition.

The choice of which metrics are applicable will vary from organisation to organisation. It is important to note that there is no single perfect metric, and that a metric that successfully captures the performance of the marketing function in one organisation may not successfully capture the performance of the marketing function in another. Further, within organisations no one single metric can successfully capture the entire performance of the marketing function. Multiple measures must therefore be used and typically this involves a mixture of financial and non-financial measures that marketing managers can use to gain an increased understanding of how all the different elements of the marketing function. There are a number of different marketing metrics and measures available for managers to choose from. With this in mind, in this section the metrics discussed are some of the most common general financial and non-financial ones used by marketing managers to calculate the overall performance of marketing activities.

Financial metrics

It is often the case that the people in charge of running an organisation are most interested in how marketing activities are performing in financial terms, as well as assessing the contribution that marketing activities make to the overall financial performance of the organisation. It is common for top management to be interested in a range of general financial metrics to drive their assessment of performance. Some of the most commonly used general financial metrics are listed in Table 3.4.

Table 3.4: Short-term financial metrics

Metric	Description
Marketing spend	Simply the total amount of money that is spent on marketing activities within a certain period of time. Straightforward and easy to calculate.
Net profit and cash flow	These are the most commonly used measures for assessing the financial contribution that marketing activities make to an organisation. The reason for this lies in the simplicity of their calculation and the availability of the data. Information of both of these aspects is readily available within the organisation, and readily understood by management.
Return on investment (ROI)	Return on investment is a method of comparing between investments, primarily devised for the comparison of capital projects where an initial investment is made and followed by returns in subsequent years. This technique is useful where large initial investments have been made in marketing activities and future returns that are going to flow to the organisation as a result of these efforts can be measured. At its simplest, ROI is calculated as follows: $$ROI = \frac{(\text{Return from marketing investment})}{(\text{Marketing investment})}$$
Return on customer (ROC)	Can be used in addition to the return on investment approach in an attempt to ascertain, and subsequently maximise, the inflows that the organisation generates from its customers. ROC measures both the change in inflows and change in the underlying asset attached to marketing. Calculating return on customer is as follows (Peppers and Rogers, 2005): $$ROC = \frac{(\pi_i + \Delta CE_i)}{CE_{i-1}}$$ Where π_i = the cash flow for period i CE = customer equity.

The above approaches to assessing and measuring assesses the performance from a very short-term viewpoint, and fails to adequately consider the long-term value generating potential of many marketing activities. Moving beyond such single financial measures, a number of metrics have been developed with a view to combining financial and non-financial aspects, and a few of the most common of these are listed in Table 3.5.

Table 3.5: Long-term financial metrics

Metric	Description
Customer lifetime value (CLV)	A means to consider the profitability of individual customers through predicting the value that can be derived from the whole relationship with a particular customer. CLV is the present value of all future profits that will flow to the organisation from a customer through their entire relationship with the firm. CLV can be calculated as follows (Gupta et al., 2006). $$CLV= \sum_{i=0}^{T} \frac{(p_t - c_t)r_t}{(1 + i)^t} - AC$$ p_t = price paid by a consumer at time t, c_t = direct cost of servicing the customer at time t, i = discount rate or cost of capital for the firm, r_t = probability of customer repeat buying or being 'alive' at time t, AC = acquisition cost, and T = time horizon for estimating CLV.
Customer equity	A metric designed to calculate an optimal balance between the costs of acquiring customers and the costs of retaining those customers. From this viewpoint, customers are quantifiable as assets. Customer equity is the sum of all the current and future value of customers, calculated using the customer lifetime value calculation above. In this instance the asset is the relationship that the organisation has with the customer and the equity refers to the value of that asset (Perrson and Ryals, 2010).
Brand equity	Switches the focus from customers to brands, based on the notion that the brand is the most powerful tool that an organisation has. The organisation brand is viewed as an intangible asset that generates additional income and profits for companies, allowing companies to charge higher amounts for their products and services, and making it easier for the organisation to bring new products to the market (Clark, 1999). Brand equity can be measured both financially and non-financially. The calculation of brand equity is more complicated, but there are a variety of online tools available that will calculate this.

Exercise 4

Consider the above financial metrics. Which of these are the top management of organisations likely to be most concerned with?

■ Non-financial metrics

Whilst it is relatively straightforward to identify the financial costs attached to the activities of marketing, assessing marketing activities only as a cost to the organisation fails to recognise the positive contribution marketing activities make to the overall profitability of the organisation. Whilst it is initially important to recognise and budget for the expected cost of marketing activities, it is also important to consider the wider contribution that the activities of marketing make to the long-term success of the organisation. Moving from considering marketing as a mere cost of the organisation towards thinking about marketing as generating significant value for the organisation, results in the necessity for more novel means of capturing this contribution. Spending money on marketing activities results in the creation of marketing assets that will generate future value for the organisation. Marketing activities such as website creation and maintenance, to take but one example, will not necessarily generate returns immediately for the organisation but should instead be considered as a necessary investment that will drive sales and profits in future periods.

Marketing activities can influence the attitudes and behaviour of customers, which can impact on the future financial performance of the organisation, and it is now widely accepted that intangible assets are drivers of value for organisations. The actions of the marketing department create assets that contribute to the long-term productivity of a company. In addition to focusing on how marketing activities contribute to the overall financial performance of organisations, there has been an increase in marketing metrics that are based on measuring the non-financial aspects of marketing. An assessment of marketing performance is not complete if only financial measures and are being utilised. In some instances non-financial metrics can act as a sign of potential future financial performance. That being said, non-financial measures offer value in their own right. A number of the most commonly used non-financial metrics are listed in Table 3.6.

The metrics highlighted in this section are general metrics for assessing the performance of marketing activities, i.e. they are applied to marketing activities as a whole. With respect to individual activities within the marketing mix, there are specific marketing and financial metrics that will be applicable on a more micro level. For example, in the case of Internet marketing, managers might measure the performance of the marketing activity through an evaluation of impressions, page views and the click-through rate. Applying financial metrics to Internet marketing activities might involve calculating the cost per click or the conversation rate. There are therefore a great number of ways and means of evaluating the individual activities of the marketing function, and marketing managers should be aware of the metrics available to them and select the most appropriate financial and non-financial metrics applicable to their particular marketing activities (for more detailed information on this, including a list of metrics used at the individual level, see Mintz and Currim, 2013).

Table 3.6: Non-financial metrics.

Metric	Description
Market share	This shows the total percentage of a particular market that the organisation's products or services represent, measured in either revenue or units sold. Market share highlights how well an organisation is doing with respect to its competitors, and increasing total market share is often a target for management. The trend of market share over time, in particular, will often be carefully monitored.
Brand awareness	This attempts to capture how aware potential customers are of an organisation's available products and services. Surveys, tracking website traffic and tracking social media activities are commonly used means of assessing brand awareness and are most useful when compared to a benchmark level of awareness.
Customer satisfaction	Attempts to capture how satisfied customers are with the product or service they receive in relation to the product or service they were expecting to receive. The importance of customer satisfaction is linked to the continuing loyalty that is achieved from happy customers. Measuring satisfaction is not a straightforward endeavour, however. Ascertaining the true level of satisfaction amongst customers is difficult and the process is open to manipulation by management.
Customer loyalty	Developed as an extension to the concept of measuring customer satisfaction, this is a quantitative financial-based measure of the value of a particular customer base and is the origin of the idea of calculating the customer lifetime value (CLV), which was discussed in the preceding section.
Marketing audits	A means of assessing the effectiveness of the marketing function. Similar to a financial accounting audit, a marketing audit is a periodic systematic review of the entire marketing operation including the environment, strategy, operations, procedures, productivity and personnel within that function. Whilst this approach would provide a comprehensive evaluation of the marketing activities of an organisation, there are problems with seeking out suitably qualified professionals to conduct such audits, as well as issues surrounding the interpretation of the findings by top management.

Reporting marketing performance

An important part of being held accountable for the activities of marketing lies in reporting information on the financial costs and performance of marketing to interested parties. In this regard, reporting takes place across two main fronts: internal reporting and external reporting. Internal reporting concerns the giving of accounts within the organisation, whereas external reporting refers to the reporting of information to stakeholders outside of the organisation. Those in charge of organisations will seek information on the financial cost of marketing as well as information on the contribution that marketing has made to the overall organisational performance in order to hold marketing managers responsible for their activities. Traditionally, financial information and the results of marketing metrics have only been communicated within the organisation, although there have been recent calls for greater communication of this information to parties outside of the organisation.

■ Internal reporting

As part of the accountability surrounding marketing, marketing managers will expect to have to report to senior management of organisations on the performance of the marketing function. Performance is usually monitored and reviewed by organisation management on a regular basis – typically monthly, quarterly and yearly. It is important to be able to demonstrate knowledge on the performance of each aspect of the marketing mix. In particular, senior management will be most interested in the financial implications of marketing activities, and marketing managers therefore have to be prepared to provide this type of information. This starts from awareness of the financial parameters within which marketing activities take place in line with the marketing budget, but also concerns having a good understanding of the financial metrics stated in the previous section. Beyond this, reporting marketing performance to senior management and directors, who are often non-marketing professionals, can be a difficult task. With regard to reporting on the financial performance of activities, this is something that is more readily understood by the senior management of the organisation. However, the non-financial aspects concerning the technical marketing activities of the marketing function are more difficult to communicate but can be equally as important with respect to the future performance of the firm. It is therefore most common for the management of the organisation to assess the performance of the marketing function on the basis of a combination of financial metrics and non-financial metrics, as mentioned previously.

■ ## External reporting

The reporting of marketing performance to external stakeholders is an area that has been criticised for not developing beyond vague and generalised statements about the marketing activities that an organisation has undertaken during the financial year (Sidhu and Roberts, 2008). With respect to the reporting of general financial performance, this has typically come in the form of disclosure of the expenditure that the organisation has incurred in relation to the marketing function. However, the costs associated with marketing activities are no longer considered as something merely incurred by the organisation, but can be considered to give rise to an asset that generates value over the longer term. Despite this, accounting rules exclude the inclusion of internally generated intangible assets, such as those related to marketing activities, in the financial accounts of organisations, as it is considered too difficult to accurately assess whether future benefits will indeed flow to the organisation.

There have been recent calls for more communication between the fields of marketing and accounting to encourage greater marketing involvement in organisations' external reporting. One of the areas that could be considered for additional disclosure is customer equity, and Wiesel et al. (2008), in particular, make a case for including customer equity statements in the management commentaries of firms' financial reports. This would involve including the value of the customer base in the financial statements, including components of customer equity and changes in value over time. There is a belief that further disclosure of intangibles would be of value to external stakeholders and users of financial statements. In general terms, a recognition of the importance of marketing assets, as discussed in the preceding section of this chapter, has resulted in increased demand for these assets to be reporting to external stakeholders.

As things stand, very few companies actually disclose marketing activities and assets in their annual reports. Many companies provide general information about their brands and their general marketing activities but quantitative measures of marketing are restricted to internal use. A recent study by KPMG (Chapman and Vaessen, 2016) found that only 15% of the external reports of the 270 listed companies that they analysed provided information on measures related to the development of the brand or market share of the organisation. Even where information is provided, not enough detail is provided to external stakeholders to allow them to make an assessment of the on-going performance of the brand. One of the main reasons for organisations being unwilling to disclose information on the performance of their marketing function is, perhaps, concerns about commercial confidentiality and the sensitivity of the information.

Case study: Apex Hotels

Edinburgh-based Apex Hotels is a progressive company that owns nine high quality city centre hotels in a number of locations across the United Kingdom. Founded by former accountant Norman Springford and family, Apex Hotels was established in 1996 with the opening of the Apex International Hotel in the Grassmarket area of Edinburgh through the conversion of the Mountbatten Building, which was formerly owned by Heriot-Watt University. The hotel was extremely successful and since then the company has expanded its range of hotels to now run four hotels in Edinburgh alongside hotels in Dundee, Glasgow and London. The organisation is known for offering high quality customer service within all of their stylish city centre hotels.

Marketing at Apex Hotels

In recent years the marketing staff at Apex Hotels have switched the focus of their marketing efforts from more traditional marketing models towards placing an increased emphasis on digital marketing. Typically this has encompassed activities such as paid search and online display advertising whilst a significant amount of the business of Apex Hotels is currently generated through online travel agencies (OTAs) such as Booking.com. There are plans within the marketing department, however, to adopt an approach in the coming year that is much more geared towards direct acquisition of customers, particularly through driving direct bookings through the company website. Taking control of where business comes from is an important factor in the coming years for Apex Hotels.

At present, the majority of the costs of marketing within Apex Hotels occur in relation to digital marketing activities. In addition to this, a small amount of expenditure relates to other collateral items of marketing such as printing brochures and other paper-based advertising sources. A number of 'platform costs' are also present within the marketing department. These are costs which are necessary for the successful operation of the organisation, such as the costs associated with operating the website, but do not directly relate to revenue generation, instead supporting the other marketing activities that do. In order to move towards a marketing approach that places a greater emphasis on direct acquisition, the marketing department have to be able to justify why this approach will add value to the company overall, as well as providing evidence of the financial benefits this approach will bring. The financial justification behind this move is based on the premise that if the company is already spending a certain amount on paying commissions to OTAs and external affiliates for generating business, but an equivalent amount could be spent more efficiently on attracting customers through the website directly, then this would be a worthwhile trade-off and one that would yield greater profitability in the longer term. A change like this will be built into the marketing plan for the coming year, which is subject to approval by senior management.

Budgeting at Apex Hotels

The main opportunity for the marketing department to achieve approval for their plan for the year is during the annual setting of the budget. The budget setting process involves the marketing department submitting a breakdown of their planned expenditure for the year, broken down into monthly figures, for approval by the finance department. The budget for the current year is assessed and either approved or adjusted. Often this is done in comparison to the previous year's budget, with increases in levels of expenditure on the previous year's level having to be justified. Whilst the activities of marketing can be reasonably stable, this year, as previously mentioned, there was a pitch for a significant change in activities and thus additional financial justification was required. Importantly, this change represented a shift from a fixed commission model to a variable cost of acquisition dependent on advertising performance. In this instance, the marketing department successfully pitched for the change and the costs associated with this change were approved. It should be stressed, however, that despite this 'win', the setting of the budget is a fine balancing act. Whilst changes and increases in expenditure are approved for one area, the costs associated with another are maintained at previous levels or may even be reduced.

Beyond the setting of the budget for the coming year, every month the marketing department will review the actual results for the month in question and compare these results against the budget for that period. Should actual expenditure exceed what was budgeted for by a significant amount, then corrective action must be taken. Whilst the marketing department themselves are monitoring the financial results, the finance department also track the results. In addition to monitoring the budget, the efficiency of marketing expenditure is an important measure for the management of Apex Hotels. This involves capturing how much revenue was created as a result of marketing activities, and comparing that to the cost of marketing activities. Providing justification to management about the financial contribution that marketing activities will make to the organisation as a whole is therefore an important aspect of the accountability of the marketing department.

Review questions

1 In your own words, describe the role played by a budget in motivating employees.

2 When each area of an organisation creates their own budget from scratch, this is known as:

A. Flexible budgeting

B. Zero-based budgeting

C. Periodic budgeting

D. Parakeet budgeting

3 Describe the objective and task method for preparing a marketing budget.

4 What is ROI and how might it be calculated?

5 Describe three non-financial metrics in your own words.

6 Why might companies be unwilling to detail their marketing function's performance in external reports?

Summary

The preceding case study represents a real world example of the financial accountability associated with marketing activities. In particular it emphasises how those in charge of marketing activities have to be concerned with not only the marketing activities themselves but also the financial aspects relating to these activities. Beyond having an understanding of the costs attached to marketing activities, marketing managers have to be able to successfully plan for and justify these costs to senior management as well as managing and tracking the financial performance throughout the year. Whilst it is recognised that marketing activities add value to the organisation in a number of ways it is primarily financial accountability that senior management require evidence of, with a particular emphasis on ensuring that the costs associated with marketing drive revenue in an efficient manner.

References and further reading

Ambler, T. (2000). Marketing Metrics. *Business Strategy Review* **11**, 59–66.

Chapman, M. and Vaessen, M. (2016). Room for improvement. The KPMG Survey of Business Reporting, 2nd edition. https://home.kpmg.com/xx/en/home/insights/2016/04/kpmg-survey-business-reporting-second-edition.html. Accessed 10 May 2016.

Clark, B.H. (1999). Marketing performance measures: History and interrelationships. *Journal of Marketing Management* **15**, 711–732.

Gupta, S., Hanssens, D., Hardie, B., Kahn, W., Kumar, V., Lin, N., Ravishanker, N. and Sriram, S. (2006). Modeling customer lifetime value. *Journal of Service Research* **9**, 139–155.

Mintz, O. and Currim, I.S. (2013). What drives managerial use of marketing and financial metrics and does metric use affect performance of marketing-mix activities? *Journal of Marketing* **77**, 17–40

Peppers, D. and Rogers, M. (2005). *Return on Customer: Creating maximum value from your scarcest resource.* New York: Doubleday/Currency.

Persson, A. and Ryals, L. (2010). Customer assets and customer equity: Management and measurement issues. *Marketing Theory* **10**, 417–436.

Sidhu, B.K. and Roberts, J.H. (2008). The marketing accounting interface – lessons and limitations. *Journal of Marketing Management* **24**, 669–686.

Stewart, D.W. (2009). Marketing accountability: Linking marketing actions to financial results. *Journal of Business Research, Retailing Evolution Research* **62**, 636–643.

Weber, J.A. (2002). Managing the marketing budget in a cost-constrained environment. *Industrial Marketing Management* **31**, 705–717.

Weetman, P. (2013). *Financial and Management Accounting: An introduction*, 6th ed. ed. Pearson, Harlow, England.

Wiesel, T., Skiera, B. and Villanueva, J. (2008). Customer equity: An integral part of financial reporting. *Journal of Marketing* **72**, 1–14.

3

4 The Internet

Tom Farrington and Rodrigo Perez-Vega

"Cyberspace. A consensual hallucination experienced daily by billions of legitimate operators, in every nation, by children being taught mathematical concepts... A graphic representation of data abstracted from banks of every computer in the human system. Unthinkable complexity. Lines of light ranged in the nonspace of the mind, clusters and constellations of data. Like city lights, receding..."

William Gibson, *Neuromancer*, **1984**

The Internet provides a continually shifting and seemingly infinitely responsive context in which to create and develop innovative marketing strategies. As such, an understanding of how and why people use the Internet is crucial to creating strong and effective digital campaigns. While many readers will have a working knowledge of social media and online retail from the user side, the following pages offer practical insights into the facts and figures behind the interfaces. Beginning with a short biography of the Internet, the chapter then delves into the details of its usage in the 21st century, exploring the digital consumer, social media channels, and the ways in which all these terabytes of data are utilised.

What is the Internet anyway?

As any good introductory paragraph will tell you, the 21st century has thus far been one of increasingly rapid change and connectivity, driven by advances in technology that would seem the stuff of radical science fiction only a few decades earlier. Central to these developments is the Internet, the spread of which was described in alarmingly vivid detail by cyberpunk writer William Gibson (1984) in the 1980s, when social networking was a sort of dull card game played by businesspeople and a mouse was a very difficult creature to put to work. It's likely that you've already made use of the Internet at least twice by the time you've arrived at this sentence, and we don't blame you: it's really quite useful.

Yet, although many of us would feel thoroughly panicked without access to it, the vast majority of the roughly 3.2 billion Internet users (Sanou, 2016) have little or no knowledge of how the Internet actually works. We should also acknowledge that whilst the Internet is a significant technological development, more than half of the world's population does not have access to it. While Search Engine Optimisation (SEO) and Pay-Per-Click (PPC) might not be of significant interest to the average user (whoever that might be!), knowledge of such techniques is vital to the 21st century marketer. Going a little further back and stripping the Internet down to its most basic level allows us to appreciate not only the speed and extent of this phenomenon's development, but also the extraordinary social, political and economic benefits of a near-global, near-instantaneous, and predominantly decentralised communications network. And like the origin stories of all great superheroes of the modern age, this begins in the imagined fires of nuclear apocalypse.

■ The post-nuclear network

In its first iterations in the 1960s, the Internet was conceived as a response to impending nuclear conflict. Briefly, existing methods of person-to-person and person-to-computer communication relied upon switching facilities at their centre, and if this centre was destroyed in a nuclear attack, then the entire network would be lost. If communications were to have any chance of surviving a nuclear war, then this reliance on a control centre would have to be removed. Paul Baran's (1964) work, *On Distributed Communications Networks*, showed that a distributed (or decentralised) digital communications network would be significantly less vulnerable to nuclear attack than one with a central node (Tucker, 2014). You may already know (or have guessed) that such networks were being discussed as a resource for the American military, in the midst of the Cold War. Baran was part of a small network of scholars, which included Leonard Kleinrock and Donald Davies, working on this same theory (Blum, 2012), and even when these theoretical nodes were connected, it took significant technological advances to produce the computational infrastructure necessary to allow us to interact via the Internet in real time.

However, the utility of these networks to marketing was almost immediately apparent to Baran (1968), who presented his work, 'Some Changes in Information Technology affecting Marketing in the Year 2000' to the American Marketing Association just four years after his initial paper. This makes for fascinating reading, detailing predictions of personalised, Below-The-Line (BTL) advertising, streaming entertainment, online education and, not only the rise of online retail, but the precise hierarchy by which our 21st century online shopping experience would be organised.

As Baran (1968) notes, the prototypes for the equipment necessary for such an experience were being developed at the time of writing. Yet it was not until the early to mid-1980s that networked computers made significant forays into homes and offices, allowing a fairly small number of enthusiasts, academics, and government employees to exchange basic, textual information. Not only did equipment need to become more affordable, the Internet needed a serious image change. Perhaps surprisingly, this aesthetic shift was driven not by advances in technology, but by an evolution in language.

4

■ The elements of digital style

This new language was Hypertext Markup Language (HTML). Proposed by Tim Berners-Lee (1989) in the late 1980s, developed throughout the 1990s, and becoming an international standard in 2000 (ISO/IEC 15445:2000), HTML provides a (near) universal (and constantly evolving) language for writing web pages. Adapted from Standard Generalized Mark-up Language (SGML), the idea was that text could be marked up by a host behind-the-scenes into categories such as headings, lists, paragraphs etc., which would then be interpreted and displayed by a piece of software (e.g. a browser like Google Chrome). These categories are known as tags, pairs of which signal the beginning and end of a particular category of text, e.g. <p>Once upon a time in Paris</p> displays the enclosed text as a new paragraph. Add to this the links that navigate us from page to page, and we have the foundations for entirely new digital standards of expressing and experiencing information. Hypertext Transfer Protocol (HTTP) was also created by Berners-Lee and was the process used to move the HTML code from a host to an individual Internet user (often called a client). The interconnected hosts and clients were referred to as the World Wide Web (WWW), and this established convention of a common language and retrieval method laid the foundations upon which a global and ever-growing ecosystem of users and developers could be established.

Alongside the now-familiar HTTP and WWW Internet standards, the spread of HTML was once again facilitated by nuclear research. In 1993, CERN (the European Organisation for Nuclear Research, now better known for their Large Hadron Collider) popularised these standards which, co-inciding with the release of the very user-friendly early Web browser Mosaic, gave many non-experts their first glimpse of an online experience. Although it is beyond the scope of this chapter (or indeed this entire textbook) to provide a full history of the Internet, it is useful to note that these key stages work towards bringing this technology to as many people as possible. This democratisation of communication and information exchange is arguably the greatest feature of the Internet, yet is also the most controversial. Is there anything you've shared on the Internet that you'd rather you hadn't? Have you ever found certain pages inexplicably blocked? While the early days of what is often termed Web 1.0 were about the Few generating information and pushing this to the Many, the logic of decentralised and (re)distributed power that initially underpinned the Internet leads inevitably to a situation in which the Many are generating and sharing content for and amongst themselves. This is an example of how military and scientific endeavour often precipitate the development of new technologies that become part and parcel of our daily lives. Jet travel, which emerged after the Second World War, and mobile communications, which evolved from military activity during the 20th century, are both examples of this.

Exercise 1

What's the most dated-looking website that you can find online? Try looking at http://www.404pagefound.com/ if you're having difficulty. What are the features that make these websites look old-fashioned? How do they compare to the website of your favourite brand?

■ Web 2.0

Skipping forward into the 21st century brings us to Web 2.0, being the network of portable, connected devices (smartphones, tablets, watches) utilising sleeker, quicker browsers and a multitude of online apps. Advances in coding and integrative use of data allow these apps to compile and share information, creating smaller networks holding entirely personal, geo-locatable statistics that can be transmitted instantaneously to and stored indefinitely upon an anonymised server. The most recently available data in the UK tells us that 82% of adults make daily use of the Internet, with 70% accessing the Internet on a mobile device (Office for National Statistics, 2015). We'll look at what happens to all this data shortly, but with 77% of adults in the UK buying goods or services online in 2015/16, it is fair to say that digital marketing will be an active component of Web 3.0. The next section explores the practical implications of such statistics.

21st century marketing is a digital game

Just as marketing activities are underpinned by a good understanding of consumer behaviour, so it would be unwise to ignore the effects that digital technologies have had upon the marketplace, consumers and marketing practice. As noted above, the Internet has become one of the most important marketplaces for transactions of goods and services (Leeflang et al., 2014). In the UK, online spending in 2015 increased by 11% from the previous year to £114 billion (Rigby, 2016). Consumers are also spending more time online; Ofcom's Media Use and Attitudes Report (2015) found that Internet users aged 16 and above claimed to spend over 20 hours and 30 minutes online per week. In 2005, this figure was just below 10 hours (9 hours and 54 minutes). We are also becoming more dependent on our mobile devices to access the Internet. A survey found that on average Americans check their mobiles 150 times a day (KPCB, 2013): almost once every ten minutes! Spending more time online is also affecting the purchase decision process: how we recognise a need and become aware of different options (Hutter et al., 2013), how we search for information to fulfil that need, and the sources we use to justify our decisions (Chakravarty et al., 2010; Duan et al., 2008; Xiang and Gretzel, 2010). Purchase channels have also been extended to online retailers (e.g. Amazon, eBay) and there is an increasing opportunity for retailers to tap into mobile channels to market and sell products to consumers (Ström et al., 2014).

4

Exercise 2

If you make use of a smartphone, how much time do you spend using it to communicate with people you know? How much time do you spend browsing for or buying products? What are the last three things you searched for? Who are the last three people you communicated with?

Write a list of all the things (data points) that marketers could learn about you from this activity.

These changes have created several new opportunities for marketers and the businesses they work for. However, the rapid nature of these changes has also generated important challenges for marketing practice. Some of the challenges that marketing practitioners identified in relation to digital environments can be classified in four main themes: (1) explosion of data, (2) social media, (3) shifting consumer demographics / the digital customer, and (4) proliferation of channels (IBM Institute for Business Value, 2011). We will use these challenges to guide the following sections in this chapter.

■ Explosion of data

Every day 2.5 quintillion bytes of data (that's a figure with 17 zeros) are estimated to be generated in the world (VCloudNews, 2015). Consider the volume of data that you generate at a personal level if you are carrying a smartphone with you. You are constantly generating data in terms of your location, the pages that you navigate, the pictures that you send to your friends, etc. The volume and variety of data that is generated in the world exceed the capacity of manual analysis, and in many cases has also exceeded the capacity of conventional databases (Provost and Fawcett, 2013). Most commonly known as *big data*, companies and data scientists are still trying to make the most productive use of this to improve customer experiences and to increase profitability in organisations. Big data has caught the interest of marketing practitioners because it (arguably) allows them to uncover behavioural patterns of consumers and make more accurate predictions of their intentions (Michael and Miller, 2013). Imagine the potential of a detailed understanding of the processes taking place between an initial search for a product and the decision to purchase it. Locations, contexts, and even moods can be gleaned from social media posts. All this information can help marketers understand a consumer's purchasing preferences. If all this information is then aggregated and compared to purchases made by other consumers with similar behavioural profiles, then recommendations of what these others bought could also be retargeted to this consumer in the future.

This data can also be used in the pursuit of Search Engine Optimisation (SEO), through which a company attempts to have its website placed at the top of search results. The initial data gathering leads to an understanding of common search terms, from which are generated keywords to be placed strategically at certain parts of the page. Also of particular importance to Google's ranking algorithms are the age of the site, and the number of sites that link to a given page: these are seen as measures of a site's reliability and relevance. One fairly obvious method of growing links is by getting your page shared on already popular and trusted social media profiles.

Exercise 3

Conduct searches online for a popular product, musician, or charity, using at least two search engines (e.g. Google and Bing). Compile a list of sites that consistently feature on the first page of your search results. Are there any similarities in the ways in which the top sites display or structure the pertinent information?

Marketing professionals place a lot of faith this technology. While many companies still do not possess the mechanisms needed to leverage all this data into valuable information for improvements to their marketing programmes (Leeflang et al., 2014), companies are investing heavily to meet these needs (Columbus, 2016).

■ Social media

One of the distinctive phenomena in the digital world in recent years has been the arrival of the platform. Many new technologies refer to themselves as platforms, which implicitly identifies them as a technology that exists across multiple media. Most often, users can expect to interact with a platform on multiple devices such as a laptop, tablet, phone or smartwatch. Platforms are also named as such because they provide a specific space where different segments of a market with common interests can come together. The platform facilitates their interactions and creates some form of value, which is eventually leveraged by the platform to generate revenue. Amazon is a classic example of a market platform, where buyers and sellers are brought together and purchases are facilitated quickly and easily on behalf of the sellers. Amazon takes a cut of the sales revenue and the vendor does not have to worry about the cost and hassle of reaching their customers and then managing a transaction.

There are three main types of platform: a market platform, as already described, a product platform and an experience platform (Srnicek and Williams, 2015). A *product platform* is a space where new product development can take place with speed and efficiency by allowing contributors to share components and knowledge; an example of this is Software AG. An *experience platform* will be a familiar concept to most readers as social media platforms like Instagram, facebook, and snapchat are regarded as examples of this. An experience platform connects users together and offers a unique form of digital experience. Each digital experience and interaction enriches the platform's environment, making a perpetually developing space, whereby new experiences are built on the momentum of previous experiences. Crucially, other companies and developers can also create technology that 'plugs-in' to platforms, which helps them evolve and offer greater value. The unprecedented growth and success of platforms like Facebook has demonstrated the potential power and money-making ability of these technologies. Although Facebook doesn't sell anything to its users, all the data the platform gathers on its users relating to their relationships, interests, tastes and activities allows Facebook to sell targeted marketing opportunities to almost any business. This has led to advertising revenues in the billions of dollars in recent years for Facebook.

Social media platforms are a form of 'consumer-generated media', defined as a variety of new sources of online information that are created (or initiated), circulated and used by consumers intent on educating each other about products, brands, services, personalities, and issues (Mangold and Faulds, 2009). The impact of consumer-to-consumer communications has been greatly magnified in the marketplace. This chapter argues that social media is a hybrid element of the promotion mix, because in a traditional sense it enables companies to talk to their customers, while in a nontraditional sense it enables customers to talk directly to one another. The content, timing, and frequency of the social media-based conversations occurring between consumers are outside managers' direct control. This stands in contrast to the traditional integrated marketing communications paradigm whereby a high degree of control is present. Therefore, managers must learn to shape consumer discussions in a manner that is consistent with the organisation's mission and performance goals. Methods by which this can be accomplished are delineated herein. They include providing consumers with networking platforms, and using blogs, social media tools, and promotional tools to engage customers.

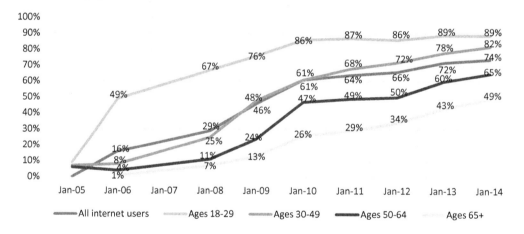

Figure 4.1: Social media use by age group over time. Source: (Wormald, 2013)

Despite the increasing adoption of social media by users of all age ranges (Figure 4.1), applications for organisational purposes, including marketing and knowledge management, are still at an early stage (Kane et al., 2014). McKinsey estimates that the economic impact of social media on business could exceed $1 trillion, most of which is gained from more efficient communication and collaboration within and across organisations, but also from an increase in customer engagement and marketing activities through these communication channels (Chui et al., 2012). The impact of social media on and for organisations, therefore, represents both a challenge and an opportunity for marketers and businesses. The challenge is represented by the amount of data that exists about any given market and market segment, meaning that making sense of the data in order for it to help marketing activities is difficult and complex. The opportunity is that never before has it been possible to identify, target and reach the people who you need to achieve your marketing objectives with such accuracy and reliability.

■ Digital customers

Shifting consumer demographics

A survey found that over 90% of people in the USA between 18 and 49 use the Internet and the only age group that has not widely adopted the use of this technology is the over 65s (Pew Research Center, 2013). According to the same survey (See Table 4.1), there are no significant difference in terms of use across gender, although income and education appear to be positively related to the use of the Internet.

Table 4.1: Internet usage demographics (US). Adapted from Pew Research Center (2013)

	Use of Internet
All adults	**87%**
Men	87
Women	86
Race/Ethnicity	
White	85
African-American	81
Hispanic	83
Age group	
18-29	97
30-49	93
50-64	88
65+	57
Educational level	
High school or less	76
Some college	91
College+	97
Household income	
Less than £30k a year	77
$30-$49k	85
$50-$74k	93
$75k+	99

Two themes are key to understanding some of the changes in consumption that businesses need to take into account when marketing to Internet users. The first is consumer empowerment, mainly underpinned by social media, which has levelled the playing field for interaction between consumers and brands. This has shifted some of the power that big companies and media had over the messages being distributed, and the meaning of brands themselves. The Internet has facilitated the co-creation of brand meaning, brand experiences, and brand value between the business and the consumer. Second, the hyper-connected consumer with multiple-screen media consumption is a phenomenon that is also reshaping how we market in the digital age. We are now going to examine these themes in more detail.

Consumer empowerment

Social media has levelled the field between brands, marketers and consumers, and consumers are feeling empowered by this shift (Kaplan and Haenlein, 2010). Consumers now understand the potential impact of their feedback on the reputation of a brand, for example through an online review, or a complaint on Twitter. Consumers are demanding that brands provide functional information through social media while remaining fun and playful (Jahn and Kunz, 2012). Some academics argue that social media is an environment that belongs to consumers, and therefore it is the role of marketing managers to adapt to this environment (Fournier and Avery, 2011). Either way, consumer empowerment can be beneficial, as this empowerment is also creating natural brand ambassadors that will loyally defend a brand under attack (Goodman et al., 2011), and who are keen supporters of brand activities – even if some are just there for the freebies (Jahn and Kunz, 2012). Consumer empowerment is also allowing companies to co-create brand meaning and even new offerings to consumers. An example of this would be the My Starbucks Idea website (http://mystarbucksidea.force.com/) where customers are encouraged to come up for ideas for the company. These can range from new combinations for beverages, to suggestions on how corporate social responsibility activities should be conducted.

The hyper-connected consumer

With smartphones allowing users to be connected to the Internet, this means that many consumers can now reach the digital world at almost any time, in almost any place. This has two major implications for companies. The first relates to pricing, and price transparency. Offline retailers now need to compete with online retailers for market share, and the convenience and price competitiveness that online shopping provides is making offline businesses struggle (Worstall, 2015). It is not uncommon for people to browse for things in shopping centres only to buy them online for a cheaper price – a phenomenon called *showrooming*. The second implication relates to how we consume media in a hyper-connected environment. Multi-screen media consumption took media outlets by surprise, with people commenting live on events by watching on their TV and engaging via smartphone or tablet. The use of hashtags to engage in conversation about TV shows is now common practice, and this provides the organisation with valuable information directly from consumers about their attitudes and feelings for the shows that they are watching. In fact, research has found that comments on social media for films being launched can influence intentions to watch that film and thus have an impact on its success or failure (Hennig-Thurau et al., 2014). Multi-screen media consumption has also extended to advertising. An example of this is an advertisement shown in the UK by the French carmaker Citroën, where the brand encourages its viewers to engage with the brand by using the Shazam app (an app that identifies music being played) to find out information about the song in the advert and, naturally, the car itself.

Channels

■ Proliferation of media channels

Technological developments have created new marketing communication channels; however, this is a challenge for companies as they need to consider a wider variety of alternatives when allocating marketing budgets, and must keep up with the number of new platforms and applications released in the marketplace. For example, a report found that on average 1,000 apps are submitted to Apple's app store every day by developers (Matthew, 2015). Many of them are unlikely to become mainstream, however, the rapid nature of this business demands marketers remain open and up-to-date with the latest platforms in order to assess their fit with the marketing strategy of a company. However, in general terms, digital channels can be classified into three major categories: owned, earned and paid media channels (Fill, 2009).

Owned media

Owned media refers to the channels that the company owns and over which it has full control. In the digital context, the most obvious example would be the company's website. However, the proliferation of channels (particularly social media) results in companies 'owning' other social channels such as a

Facebook Page or a Twitter account. This trend of extending owned media is becoming the norm among large and small organisations. According to Barnes et al. (2013), 77% of Fortune 500 companies were already using at least one type of social media website. Within the range of available social media platforms, Facebook is preferred by marketers (Figure 4.2), due to the critical mass that this platform has with consumers (1.13 billion daily active users on average in June 2016 according to Facebook).

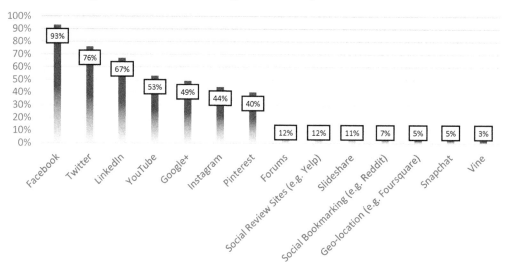

Figure 4.2: Social media platforms used by marketers. Adapted from (Statista, 2016)

However, marketers need to consider the implications of being present in several owned media platforms. Presence in each of the platforms has implications in terms of financial and human resources, therefore marketers should take a strategic approach to the proliferation of owned media and its alignment with their marketing objectives.

Earned media

Earned media in this context refers to mentions of the brand or company that were not paid for by the organisation but that can be found online. Examples of earned media include a blogger writing an unpaid review of their experience of a certain product or a film, or someone posting something about a product in their Facebook profile. Evidence suggests that online consumer-generated content such as online reviews (a type of earned media) can affect sales (Chevalier and Mayzlin, 2006). The motivations behind the generation of earned media have been widely studied, particularly in terms of engaging in word-of-mouth (WOM) activity (Allsop et al., 2007; Brown et al., 2005; Dichter, 1966; Sundaram et al., 1998). Altruism is one of the common motivations for both positive and negative WOM, as consumers want to share good experiences that they may have had with products, or spare others a bad experience. The level of involvement with a particular product or company can also affect the level of WOM activity. For example, Apple users are usually known to be highly involved with the brand, and tend to speak a lot about their products to others. Self-enhancement is another motivation to talk about a company or brand. If a person thinks that a brand association can improve the perception that others have of them, then that person is more likely to mention the brand publicly to others. An example of this might be when someone publicly checks into a place via Facebook. Of course, earned media is not always positive. Research shows that sharing negative reviews helps consumers cope with a bad experience by reducing levels of anxiety (Sundaram et al., 1998). Consumers may also take this a step further towards revenge, actively generating comments to damage the image of a brand.

Paid media

Paid media or advertising refers to media activity that is generated by the company in other websites. A common example would be a paid ad being display in a user's newsfeed on Facebook, or a blogger writing about a brand because they received a payment or a freebie. There is a proliferation of platforms in which companies can be present, however these can be classified in terms of search and display advertising.

- **Search advertising** refers to the ads that appear when a user is looking for something in search engines. The company bids for certain keywords and competes with other companies that also want to advertise when that particular keyword is searched by the user. This is a form of the Pay-Per-Click (PPC) advertising model, the most commonly used example of which is Google AdWords. PPC is used to understand the effectiveness of online marketing, and is calculated by dividing the cost of advertising by the number of clicks an advert generates. PPC is a cost-effective means of promoting your website because the website owner is only charged when their link is clicked, as opposed to buying a banner advert on a website, which is a more traditional form of selling advertising space.

- **Affiliates programmes** are another popular form of paid digital marketing, whereby an individual (or company) promotes goods or services on their website in exchange for commission on any sales generated through that advertising. For example, if you're reading a blog about GPS watches with links to purchase the specific models on Amazon, then the chances are that the blog is part of the Amazon

Affiliates programme, and earns money every time a reader makes an Amazon purchase via these links.

It is worth mentioning a key distinction here between Above-The-Line (ATL) and Below-The-Line (BTL) marketing, as the data made available by the Internet lends itself particularly well to the latter. ATL marketing targets a wide, general audience via mass media such as TV and radio, newspapers and magazines, and billboards. Meanwhile, BTL marketing works to appeal to smaller, more specific audiences, using data about consumer habits to make direct contact with those most likely to respond. Web 2.0 allows this targeting to become increasingly precise, down to an often eerily personal level, e.g. Facebook ads.

Exercise 4

Find at least one example of each of the following: owned media, earned media, paid media, PPC, and affiliate advertising.

■ Distribution channels and new business models

There are three types of businesses based on their distribution channels: online only, offline only and hybrid distribution.

- **Online only** organisations would be companies such as eBay or (until recently) Amazon that do not have an offline presence (i.e. bricks and mortar stores) and that rely completely on their website to sell their products.

- **Offline only** businesses would be businesses that do not sell their products through the Internet. They may still have a website, but this is used mainly for display purposes.

- Finally, there are **hybrid distribution** organisations. These organisations are normally 'traditional' companies that realise the potential of having an online distribution or that were pushed to the online environment due to external factors such as other competitors doing so, or by losing market share to online-only businesses. Examples of these types of hybrid organisations would be retailers such as Asda or Tesco, which have evolved to have both offline and online distribution channels.

However, the disruptive effect that the Internet is having on businesses goes beyond new distribution channels. The Internet allows for disruptive business models that were previously inconceivable. For example, the sharing economy has benefited greatly from the Internet, and it has generated well-established giants such as Airbnb and Uber. Available resources (e.g. a spare room, or time to drive someone around) are linked to demand through online-based applications. Other creative industries have also been reshaped by the Internet (e.g. the music industry with Spotify, or the film and TV industry with Netflix).

Social v commercial

The innovations in commercial digital marketing tools and techniques described above have been adopted in and adapted to the pursuit of social goals. A brief consideration of the implications of the Internet for those engaged in attending to social needs offers crucial insights into the social responsibilities of commercial marketers.

■ Social marketing defined

Dann's (2010: 151) review of the literature on social marketing offers the following definition:

> *"the adaptation and adoption of commercial marketing activities, institutions and processes as a means to induce behavioural change in a targeted audience on a temporary or permanent basis to achieve a social goal."*

Like most commercial marketing, social marketing seeks to understand and appeal to people in a way that motivates them to change their behaviour. Unlike most commercial marketing, social marketing understands this behavioural shift as an end in itself, rather than as an intermediary stage producing more engaged, loyal consumers, which leads ultimately to profit. Social marketing responds to social issues (such as domestic violence) and health risks (such as obesity), going beyond simple awareness-raising exercises to effect active changes in the way people act. Such campaigns are often known as 'interventions', which is helpful for understanding their social role. Examples of social marketing include television and radio campaigns to reduce speeding (such as Western Australia's 'Enjoy the Ride'), smoking cessation initiatives (such as WHO's World Tobacco Day), and anti-racism banners on football pitches ('Show Racism the Red Card' in the UK).

The UK's National Social Marketing Centre (NSMC, 2010) finds that successful social marketing:

1 Aims to change behaviour

2 Understands its audience through varied and robust research methods

3 Is informed by behavioural theory

4 Identifies insights that lead to action

5 Assesses costs v benefits

6 Considers competitors

7 Tailors interventions according to nuanced segmentation

8 Employs a mixture of methods in enacting behavioural change

■ How does a social marketing intervention work?

The NSMC suggests a successful social marketing intervention should follow six stages, shown below in Figure 4.3:

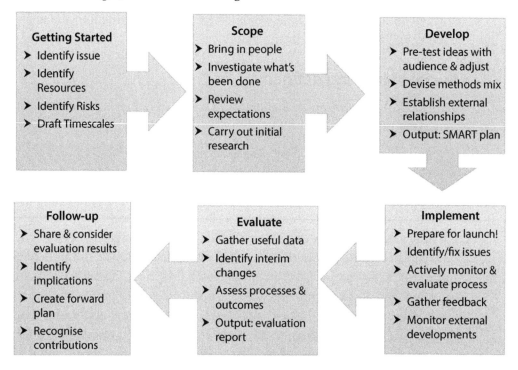

Figure 4.3: Adapted from NSMC (2010)

■ What can commercial marketing learn from its social kin?

A major challenge for digital marketers is finding ways to gather and utilise data without leaving people feeling pestered. Viewing individuals simply as consumers who are more likely to buy something if it's constantly thrust in front of them shows a clear lack of insight into the human condition. Although the rise of social media platforms mean people are now more likely to publicly share information about themselves, with the opportunity and power to act upon this data comes significant responsibility. If 21st century digital marketers take a more nuanced and respectful approach to their research and practice, then they might build the sort of genuine trusting relationships that will prompt a willingness in people to both inform marketers of their true needs, and listen to the proffered commercial solutions. In appealing to increasingly well-informed and cynical populations, commercial marketing that takes heed of successful social marketing interventions by identifying and responding to human or social needs (rather than creating consumer wants) may well be the sustainable stuff of the future.

Case study: Give your home a profile

4

"Give your home a profile" is Vuzii's ethos. This Scottish based start-up was founded by three entrepreneurs from the UK and Norway in September 2015. Vuzii aims to become the leading collaboration platform

for the interior design community worldwide. Vuzii relies on user generated content (UGC) such as pictures that users post of their homes, and information they share about it. Users can then get inspiration from other members on how to decorate their places, what furniture to buy and even earn a commission as an affiliate for the brands they tag in their photos. Vuzii relies on earned, owned and paid media to reach their members and to invite other Internet users to join their community.

Task (20 minutes)

As the freshly appointed marketing manager at Vuzii, your tasks are to:

- Map out the company's current online blueprint by listing all the different media channels in which the company has presence. Once you have finished, classify the different channels that the brand uses.

- Examine the content being shared and devise a list of objectives that the brand may have in mind for that particular channel.

- Create a list of other platforms under each type of media channel that the brand could consider using and that could help reach the objectives that you previously listed.

Directed further reading

The Internet

Kitchen, P. (2013). The *Dominant Influence of Marketing in the 21st Century: The Marketing Leviathan*, Palgrave Macmillan UK.

Teigland, R., & Power, D. (2013). *The Immersive Internet: Reflections on the Entangling of the Virtual with Society, Politics and the Economy*, Palgrave Macmillan UK.

Digital marketing

Baines, P., Fill, C., & Page, K. (2011). *Marketing*, OUP Oxford.

Chaffey, D., Smith, P. R., & Smith, P. R. (2012). *Emarketing Excellence: Planning and Optimizing Your Digital Marketing*, Routledge.

Social and humanistic marketing

Hastings, G. (2007). Social Marketing: Why should the Devil have all the best tunes? : Elsevier Science.

Varey, R., & Pirson, M. (2013). *Humanistic Marketing*, Palgrave Macmillan UK.

Multiple choice questions

1 What was the Internet initially conceived as protecting communications from?
A: Satellite interference
B: Nuclear war
C: The language barrier
D: Flooding

2 Which now common technological innovations did Baran predict in the late 1960s?
A: Online retail
B: Streaming entertainment
C: Online education
D: All of the above

3 Surveys have found that on average some Americans check their mobiles:
A: 30 times a day
B: 70 times a day
C: 150 times a day
D: 200 times a day

4 How often have UK Internet users claimed to spend online per week?
A: 20 hours and 30 minutes
B: 8 hours and 20 minutes
C: Approximately 24 hours
D: 6 days

5 How many bytes of data are estimated to be generated globally per day?
A: 180 billion
B: 2.5 quintillion
C: 48.8 trillion
D: 1024 quadrillion

6 What does SEO stand for?
A: Streaming Entertainment Online
B: Strategic Engagement Operations
C: Site Embedded Optionality
D: Search Engine Optimisation

7 On average, how many apps are submitted to Apple's app store every day?
A: 1000
B: 2000
C: 3500
D: 4250

8 Which of these is a form of paid media? There may be more than one answer.
A: Unsolicited product reviews
B: Facebook check-ins
C: PPC (Pay-Per-Click) advertising
D: Amazon Affiliated blog posts

9 Which of these are examples of social marketing?
A: Enjoy the Ride (campaign to reduce speeding)
B: World Tobacco Day
C: Show Racism the Red Card
D: All of the above

4

References

Allsop, D.T., Bassett, B.R. and Hoskins, J.A. (2007). Word-of-mouth research: principles and applications. *Journal of Advertising Research* **47**, 398.

Baran, P. (1964). On distributed communications networks. *IEEE Transactions on Communications Systems,* **12**(1), 1-9.

Baran, P. (1968). *Some Changes in Information Technology Affecting Marketing in the Year 2000.* Santa Monica, CA: RAND Corporation.

Barnes, N.G., Lescault, A.M. and Wright, S. (2013). 2013 Fortune 500 are bullish on social media. University of Massachusetts, Dartmouth.

Berners-Lee, T. (1989). Information management: A proposal. https://www.w3.org/History/1989/proposal.html.

Blum, A. (2012). *Tubes: A Journey to the Center of the Internet.* Ecco Press.

Brown, T.J., Barry, T.E., Dacin, P.A. and Gunst, R.F. (2005). Spreading the word: Investigating antecedents of consumers' positive word-of-mouth intentions and behaviors in a retailing context. *Journal of the Academy of Marketing Science* **33**, 123–138.

Chakravarty, A., Liu, Y. and Mazumdar, T. (2010). The differential effects of online word-of-mouth and critics' reviews on pre-release movie evaluation. *Journal of Interactive Marketing* **24**, 185–197. doi:10.1016/j.intmar.2010.04.001

Chevalier, J.A., Mayzlin, D. (2006). The effect of word of mouth on sales: Online book reviews. *Journal of Marketing Research* **43**, 345–354. doi:10.1509/jmkr.43.3.345

Columbus, L. (2016). 51% of enterprises intend to invest more in big data - Forbes. www.forbes.com/sites/louiscolumbus/2016/05/22/51-of-enterprises-intend-to-invest-more-in-big-data/#4194fdb53ad0. Accessed 8/16/2016.

Dann, S. (2010). Redefining social marketing with contemporary commercial marketing definitions. *Journal of Business Research,* **63**, 147-153. doi: 10.1016/j.jbusres.2009.02.013

Dichter, E. (1966). How word-of-mouth advertising works. *Harvard Business Review* **44**, 147.

Duan, W., Gu, B. and Whinston, A.B. (2008). Do online reviews matter? – An empirical investigation of panel data. *Decision Support Systems* **45**, 1007–1016.

Fill, C., (2009). *Marketing Communications: Interactivity, Communities and Content.* Pearson Education.

Fournier, S. and Avery, J. (2011). The uninvited brand. *Business Horizons* **54**, 193–207.

Gibson, W. (1984). *Nueromancer.* Ace Books: New York

Goodman, M.B., Booth, N. and Matic, J.A. (2011). Mapping and leveraging influencers in social media to shape corporate brand perceptions. *Corporate*

Communications: An International Journal **16**, 184–191.

Hennig-Thurau, T., Wiertz, C. and Feldhaus, F. (2014). Does Twitter matter? The impact of microblogging word of mouth on consumers' adoption of new movies. *Journal of the Academy of Marketing Science* **43**(3), 375–394. doi:10.1007/s11747-014-0388-3

Hutter, K., Hautz, J., Dennhardt, S. and Füller, J. (2013). The impact of user interactions in social media on brand awareness and purchase intention: the case of MINI on Facebook. *Journal of Product & Brand Management* **22**, 342–351. doi:10.1108/JPBM-05-2013-0299

IBM Institute for Business Value, (2011). From stretched to strengthened: insights from the global chief marketing officer study, executive summary. http://economictimes.indiatimes.com/photo/10652961.cms. Accessed 8/10/2016.

Jahn, B. and Kunz, W. (2012). How to transform consumers into fans of your brand. *Journal of Service Management* **23**, 344–361. doi:10.1108/09564231211248444

Kane, G.C., Alavi, M., Labianca, G. (Joe) and Borgatti, S.P. (2014). What's different about social media networks? A framework and research agenda. *MIS Quarterly* **38**, 275–304.

Kaplan, A.M. and Haenlein, M. (2010). Users of the world, unite! The challenges and opportunities of social media. *Business horizons* **53**, 59–68. doi:10.1016/j.bushor.2009.09.003

KPCB (2013). 2013 Internet Trends. www.kpcb.com/blog/2013-Internet-trends. Accessed 8/16/2016.

Leeflang, P.S.H., Verhoef, P.C., Dahlström, P. and Freundt, T. (2014). Challenges and solutions for marketing in a digital era. *European Management Journal* **32**, 1–12. doi:10.1016/j.emj.2013.12.001

Mangold, W.G. and Faulds, D.J. (2009). Social media: The new hybrid element of the promotion mix. *Business Horizons* **52**, 357–365. doi:10.1016/j.bushor.2009.03.002

Matthew, J., (2015). Apple App Store growing by over 1,000 apps per day. *International Business Times UK.* www.ibtimes.co.uk/apple-app-store-growing-by-over-1000-apps-per-day-1504801. Accessed 8/10/2016.

Michael, K. and Miller, K.W.,(2013). Big data: New opportunities and new challenges [guest editors' introduction]. *Computer* **46**, 22–24.

National Social Marketing Centre (2010). Available at www.thensmc.com/sites/default/files/benchmark-criteria-090910.pdf

Ofcom Media Use and Attitudes (2015). Time spent online doubles in a decade. consumers.ofcom.org.uk/news/time-spent-online-doubles. Accessed 8/10/2016.

Office for National Statistics (2015). *Internet Access - Households and Individuals: 2015,* http://www.ons.gov.uk/peoplepopulationandcommunity/

householdcharacteristics/homeInternetandsocialmediausage/bulletins/ Internetaccesshouseholdsandindividuals/2015-08-06.

Pew Research Center (2013). Internet User Demographics. Internet User Demograhics. http://www.pewInternet.org/data-trend/Internet-use/latest-stats. Accessed 8/16/2016.

Provost, F. and Fawcett, T. (2013). Data science and its relationship to big data and data-driven decision making. *Big Data* **1**, 51–59. doi:10.1089/big.2013.1508

Rigby, C. (2016). UK online spending rises by 11% to £114bn in 2015, and by 12% to £24bn over Christmas: IMRG. InternetRetailing. http://Internetretailing. net/2016/01/uk-online-spending-11pc-up-at-114bn-in-2015-and-12pc-up-at-24bn-over-christmas. Accessed 8/10/2016.

Sanou, B. (2016). *ICT Facts and Figures 2016*, International Telecommunications Union, http://www.itu.int/en/ITU-D/Statistics/Pages/facts/default.aspx

Srnicek, N. and Williams, A. (2015). *Inventing the Future: Postcapitalism and a world without work*. Verso Books.

Statista (2016). Social media platforms used by marketers worldwide 2016 | Statistic. Statista. http://www.statista.com/statistics/259379/social-media-platforms-used-by-marketers-worldwide. Accessed 8/10/2016.

Ström, R., Vendel, M. and Bredican, J. (2014). Mobile marketing: A literature review on its value for consumers and retailers. *Journal of Retailing and Consumer Services* **21**, 1001–1012. doi:10.1016/j.jretconser.2013.12.003

Sundaram, D.S., Mitra, K. and Webster, C.,(1998). Word-of-mouth communications: a motivational analysis. *Advances in Consumer Research* **25**, 527–531.

Tsai, H., Huang, H., and Chiu, Y. (2012). Brand community participation in Taiwan: Examining the roles of individual-, group-, and relationship-level antecedents. *Journal of Business Research* **64**, 676-684. doi: 10.1016/j.jbusres.2011.03.011

Tucker, A. (2014). *Interfacing with the Internet in Popular Cinema*: Springer.

VCloudNews (2015). Every day big data statistics – 2.5 quintillion bytes of data created daily. http://www.vcloudnews.com/ every-day-big-data-statistics-2-5-quintillion-bytes-of-data-created-daily/

Wormald, B. (2013). Social Media Use by Age Group Over Time. Pew Research Center's Internet & American Life Project. http://www.pewInternet.org/data-trend/social-media/social-media-use-by-age-group. Accessed 8/3/2014.

Worstall, T. (2015). The Shopping Malls Really Are Being Killed By Online Shopping. Forbes. http://www.forbes.com/sites/timworstall/2015/01/04/the-shopping-malls-really-are-being-killed-by-online-shopping. Accessed 8/16/2016.

Xiang, Z. and Gretzel, U. (2010). Role of social media in online travel information search. *Tourism Management* **31**, 179–188. doi:10.1016/j.tourman.2009.02.016

5 Customers

Matthew Alexander

Introduction

■ Why the concern about relationships in marketing?

The word 'relationship' is ubiquitous in modern society. Apart from the social relationships we have with family and friends (from distant to extremely intimate), there are a whole range of more spurious relationships which we have (or are told we have) with other focal objects. From politicians to firms to inanimate objects our relationships are central and, seemingly, essential to our modern lives. But it did not always seem this way. This chapter explores the birth, growth and metamorphosis of relationships in marketing. The notion that firms and customers can instigate, develop or break off socio-economic relationships with each other is of vital importance to marketers, but our understanding of the term is constantly evolving. This chapter explores the birth and development of relationship marketing in the latter half of the 20th century and early years of the 21st. In this period a range of new concepts such as customer relationship management, customer loyalty, customer lifetime value, customer equity and, more recently, customer engagement all suggest the growing importance of the customer to organisations and a growing need to understand how these relationships can be influenced and maintained.

The definition of marketing set down by the American Marketing Association (AMA) in 1985 gives no indication of the importance that relationships would have only a few decades later (Gundlach, 2007):

"The process of planning and executing the conception, pricing, promotion, and distribution of goods, services, and ideas to create exchanges that satisfy individual and organisational objectives"

Here we see marketing's economic and transactional roots writ large. The purpose of marketing is to establish what to sell, who to sell it to, at what price and to ensure that customers buy it in order that the firm can make money (note that the customer is not included in the definition). By 2004 the definition had changed substantially:

"Marketing is an organisational function and a set of processes for creating, communicating, and delivering value to customers and for managing customer relationships in ways that benefit the organisation and its stakeholders"

Here we see the impact of relationship marketing's evolution. Gone is the stricter exchange focus to be replaced by two references to the customer and the use of the word relationships. The next section will explore how this change occurred.

■ The roots of transactional marketing

The roots of marketing lie in economics, and it is in the development of macro and micro economic theory and the concepts of 'the market' and 'supply and demand' that we see the earliest shoots of marketing. In the early part of the 20th century a greater focus on the interaction between supply and demand allowed early marketers to create lists of variables which would inform the marketing process (Harker & Egan, 2006).

These lists of variables inspired Neil Borden to develop the *marketing mix*, which he referred to throughout his research in the 1940s and 50s (Borden, 1964). Originally a list of 12 variables which "the marketer would have to consider in any given situation….[and]…would blend the various ingredients or variables of the mix into an integrated marketing program." (Grönroos, 1994: 350). These 12 variables, in turn, were reduced down to the now familiar 'four Ps' (Price, Product, Promotion and Place) by McCarthy (1960). After World War 2, marketing management and the marketing mix, combined with growing economies in the western world and increases in disposable incomes, saw an exponential growth in marketing activity. The huge domestic US economy with its homogenous customer base, shared culture and media with a rise in standardised products and services meant that the simple approach associated with the four Ps had free rein (Harker & Egan, 2006).

■ Problems with the dominant model and birth of relationship marketing

The latter decades of the 20th century saw problems emerging with the traditional marketing mix model which had so successfully underpinned the boom years of the post WWII era. Increased competition (both national and international) and growing customer interest and involvement meant firms had to do more than simply apply the 4Ps to any given situation. Harker and Egan (2006: 220) note that "whereas the transactional marketing paradigm sought to 'bend' the customer to fit the product, what was required was theory and practice that would shape the product to the consumer". Additionally, the rise of both services and business to business (B2B) marketing in the late 1970s gave academics two settings where the relationship between a firm and its customers was central to its success. It was, seemingly, Berry (1983: 25) who first coined the phrase 'relationship marketing' and that this should involve "attracting, maintaining and – in multi-service organisations – enhancing customer relationships". The idea of balancing attraction and maintenance (more commonly known as retention) has become a dominant narrative in relationship marketing. This is perhaps best represented by the notion of marketing relationships being like a leaky bucket (Ehrenberg, 1988).

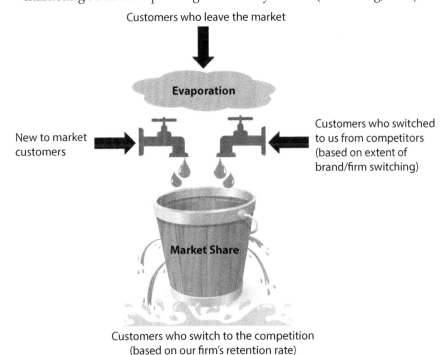

Figure 5.1: The leaky bucket (Ehrenberg, 1988)

The leaky bucket model (which has seen some adaptation over the years) consists of a number of constituent parts:

- **New to market customers** – these are new customers attracted to our organisation through marketing efforts (new water from the tap)

- **Customers who switch to the competition** – this is water leaking from the bucket (also known as defection)

- **Customers who switch from the competition** – (more water added)

- **Market share** – this is the water in the bucket

- **Evaporation** – these are customers who leave the market for reasons which an organisation cannot control

This is a powerful model for marketers, a scenario where failure to maintain the bucket (your relationships with customers) causes leaks which despite a reasonable attraction rate could cause an organisation to become unprofitable. It is the desire of firms to retain customers, prevent defection and, in doing so, maintain market share that has fuelled the relationship marketing revolution. The first stage for many firms in the relationship marketing process is learning about their customers, the subject of the next section.

Getting to know your customers

■ What is customer relationship management (CRM)

"RM is often comprehended as a firmer grip on the customer, much like the fisherman's relationship to the fish; more sophisticated equipment and techniques make it less probable that the fish will get off the hook" (Gummesson, 1994: 9)

The growth in relationship marketing in the 1980s and 1990s was mirrored by huge technological developments which would have a significant effect on the ways in which firms managed their relationships with customers. In the 1990s, sophistication of technology and its application within the management world enabled firms to begin to gather information on customers and store this within databases. Increasingly sophisticated algorithms combined with customer purchase data at an individual customer level meant that firms could learn about customer choices, purchase patterns and trends and use this data to select products, choose displays, and, more importantly, target specific customers with specific offers. This strategy came to be known as customer relationship management (CRM).

However, ambiguity and debate over the meaning of CRM is evident between business and academic worlds and the extent to which it should be seen simply viewed as a technological tool to aid marketers or embedded at a strategic level within organisations. Additionally, in recent years, the way that firms make use of CRM data has been under greater scrutiny with the outputs of CRM being given new labels such as spam or junk mail. Definitions of CRM within academic literature are varied and suggest a lack of consensus (Payne & Frow, 2005). Gummesson (2008: 5) sees a delineated relationship: "CRM is the values and strategies of RM – with special emphasis on the relationship between a customer and a supplier – turned into practical application and dependent on both human action and information technology"; whereas Parvatiyar and Sheth (2000) suggest that the terms RM and CRM are often used interchangeably. It is perhaps this blurring of the lines between RM and CRM that has created many of its perception problems. The list below suggests that CRM activity is heterogeneous, albeit connected directly to a firm's ability to gather information from customers and store it in an electronic database.

Types of CRM activity[1]

- Direct mail/email

- Loyalty card scheme

- Database

- Help desks and call centres

- Populating a data warehouse and data mining

- E-commerce

- Internet personalization

■ CRM gone wrong: "You don't know the power of the dark side!"

CRM initiatives around the world represent a large commitment in financial terms with investment expected to increase (Fournier & Avery, 2011). However, many CRM practices manifest behaviour or outcomes which may damage or even permanently destroy relationships. Research by Frow et al. (2011) suggests that 35-75% of CRM initiatives fail in some way suggesting, perhaps, that firms are getting it wrong. Fang et al. (2011) note that the 'dark side' of relationships emerges when imbalanced tensions appear in relationships, and other authors see favouritism and differential treatment of customers as the root cause, where some customers are advantaged and others disadvantaged

---

1   These types of CRM were suggested by marketing practitioners and reported by Payne and Frow (2005)

by the initiative (Nguyen & Simkin, 2013). Alternatively, a lack of clarity around purpose or definition may lead to tactical errors in implementation. At its most extreme Frow et al. (2011) suggest that some maliciously motivated suppliers may deliberately abuse the relationships they have with customers using CRM technology and other tactics. These tactics coalesce around three main areas: communication based dark-side behaviour, alternative manipulation and side effects. The various sub-types of behaviours are discussed in Table 5.1 below.

Communication	
Information misuse	Collection and use of data by firms either with individual customer tracking or by making use of data brokers who buy and sell customer data, often without the permission of individual customers.
Customer confusion	Use of misleading or confusing information by firms or hiding of relevant information from customers which could benefit them. For example, complex and constantly changing pricing structures making it difficult for customers to understand the best option.
Dishonesty	This would include such practices as 'up' and 'cross' selling. Seen by firms as legitimate tactics but can result in customers paying for things they do not need.
Privacy invasion	Considers incidents where the information flowing to firms is misused. Customers are not aware of what information about them is being recorded. Some hotel companies ask staff to record information about a guest– without their knowledge
Alternative manipulation	
Customer favouritism	CRM requires customer segmentation based on characteristics of buying behaviour; this can result in them being treated differently to other customers who have paid the same price for the product or service.
Customer lock-in	Occurs where firms introduce switching barriers which make it difficult for customers to switch to other providers. Switching barriers could include cost and learning barriers.
Relationship neglect	Firms may take advantage of customer inertia and essentially ignore them. Better prices and new deals are focussed around new customers.
Financial exploitation	Relates to additional fees which firms include in small print and which are then used to generate additional revenue these could include late payment fees or surcharges not clearly advertised.
Side effects	
Spill-over effects	One of the most irritating outcomes of CRM practices is where data relating to some customers spills over to others through TV advertising, unsolicited junk mail or unwanted email promotions.
Ecological impacts	Developing strong customer relationships (and increased sales) may lead to negative ecological impacts on the environment or public health.

Table 5.1: CRM dark side practices (based on Frow et al. 2011)

It is easy to see how some of the practices in Table 5.1 might be seen by firms as legitimate strategies with positive outcomes on the bottom line. The hotel firm that asks staff to record details about customers (books they have in their room, drinks they consume, the fact that they always arrive from the airport in the evening) might see this as building relationships with customers by learning their habits, likes and dislikes. But, if the customer has not given permission, then there is a danger of privacy invasion. Similarly, firms may think it a positive strategy to reward customers who exhibit certain purchase behaviours without considering the impact on others (see Figure 5.2 for an example of 'dark side' practices).

In 2015 the UK energy market was publicly scrutinised for using 'Deliberately confusing' energy bills as a tactic to discourage customers from shopping around for the best deal. This was in spite of government led efforts to shake up the sector and promote switching. A report from the think tank Centre Forum identified a decline in switching between 2008 and 2012. The report highlighted a "confusing plethora of tariffs and the inhibiting way in which information is presented. Customers frequently complain about receiving too much information, and having too much choice, rather than too little. Bills are complex and like for like comparisons difficult." This is a clear case of customer confusion which prevents customers from making a decision and results in increased profits for energy firms.

Figure 5.2: Customer confusion in the energy sector. Based on Martin and Hill (2015)

In most cases, CRM initiatives fail because companies lose sight of the human element of the relationship over the position a customer holds on a database. Additionally, firms can be somewhat one-dimensional in their relationships with customers despite the heterogeneous nature of relationships (Fournier & Avery, 2011).

For CRM to work more effectively, Payne and Frow (2005) believe it needs to be implemented at a strategic level with a cross-functional integration of capabilities across the organisation. An integrated process suggests a more enlightened approach to CRM, perhaps not one that all firms might aspire to. However, given the wider reach and greater impact of negative word-of-mouth it is likely that more firms will seek to avoid dark side practices, with a view to building mutually productive relationships with customers.

Customer loyalty: The quest for the Holy Grail

At its simplest level customer loyalty is about creating and maintaining a successful offering which customers want to purchase over an extended period. A glance at lists of companies with strong performance on customer loyalty[2] offers up a perhaps unsurprising list of names of high profile firms with a strong reputation for quality. That said, customers also seek additional benefits associated with purchasing from an organisation, such as:

- **Confidence benefits:** purchasing this product/service is a safe option with less risk

- **Social benefits**: being known and recognised by a provider and

- **Special treatment**: where customers with a repeat purchase pattern get additional benefits such as special deals or enhanced service levels.

Achieving high levels of loyalty can be seen as both a defensive (protecting an existing customer base) and offensive strategy (aiming for increased sales, margins and profitability). Additionally, the use of loyalty programmes relates strongly to firms' use of CRM techniques, whereby customers signed up to the programme provide important purchase data (e.g. supermarket loyalty cards). Carefully applied, loyalty programmes can also create competitive advantage within the marketplace, particular through differentiation of offering and effective targeting of offering.

■ Background to loyalty research

Customer loyalty is not a new term in marketing, but its meaning has changed significantly over the last 60 years. Early marketing thought saw loyalty as simply a pattern of repeat purchase, i.e. an observable behavioural pattern (for example, buying the same newspaper from the same shop every day for 20 years). This repeat purchase was seen as stochastic (an undetermined repeat purchase) (Oliver, 1997). However, the rise of relationship marketing saw researchers challenging this dominant idea. Research in the 1970s introduced attitudinal elements to our notion of loyalty. Jacoby and Keyner (1973: 2) defined loyalty as a "non-random purchase over time of one brand from a set of brands, by a customer using a deliberate evaluation process". This important definition suggested an attitudinal element to loyalty which had at that point not been considered and suggested that loyalty could be a state of mind as well as a behavioural trait. The importance of understanding loyalty through multiple stages of belief, affect (liking) and intention continued until

2   see http://brandkeys.com/portfolio/customer-loyalty-engagement-index/

the 1990s (see Dick & Basu, 1994) when Oliver (1997: 392) presented a more unitary definition:

> "A deeply held commitment to rebuy or repatronize a preferred product/service consistently in the future, thereby causing repetitive same-brand or same brand-set purchasing, despite situational influences and marketing efforts having the potential to cause switching behaviour"

Critically, Oliver supplements the focus on attitudinal forms of loyalty with an additional behavioural element suggesting a strength of character around loyalty where the customer resists alternatives due to a deeply held commitment to rebuy. The definition forms the basis of a four stage model of loyalty (Figure 5.3). The model envisages the customer moving through loyalty stages as their level of commitment increases.

■ Loyalty stages

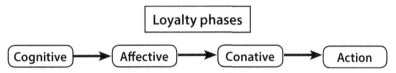

Figure 5.3: The four stage model of customer loyalty (Oliver, 1997)

- The cognitive stage is the weakest form of loyalty, in fact Oliver suggests that loyalty is not even really a consideration for the customer. Here the customer simply likes the brand offering and is aware that they do so.

- The affective stage is where loyalty becomes more encoded in the customer's mind. In this phase repeated cognitive episodes combined with prior attitude and future satisfaction create a stronger bond with the brand offering.

- In the conative phase customers' affect becomes intention, a commitment to rebuy from an organisation.

- This attempt to pursue action represents a stronger form of loyalty. However, Oliver (1997: 393) notes that this intention may be 'anticipated but unrealized'. Oliver's contribution was the inclusion of action loyalty. This is represented by a state of readiness to act and desire to overcome obstacles to continue to buy from the same organisation.

A summary of the model is found in Table 5.2.

Loyalty research also highlights that it is a vulnerable state and dependent on customers' switching and defection behaviours. Switching relates to a customer's motivation to buy from an alternative provider. Oliver (1999) highlights that the four stage model has significant vulnerabilities in all stages, but strongest in the cognitive and affective stages. In all stages customers could switch because of poor product or service performance but customers are also vulnerable to attractive offers from competitors. Firms can react to switching vulnerabilities through switching barriers. These could include financial costs associated with changing providers, learning costs associated with a new system of payment, website or electronic device or effort costs of searching for information. Additional switching barriers might be associated with loyalty cards which are discussed in the next section.

Stage	Identifying marker	Sustainers	Vulnerabilities
Cognitive	Loyalty to information such as price, features etc.	Costs Benefits Quality	Actual or imagined better features or price through advertising or experience Deterioration in brand features or price Variety seeking and voluntary trial
Affective	Loyalty to a liking: "I buy it because I like it"	Satisfaction Involvement Liking Preference Cognitive consistency	Dissatisfaction Enhanced liking for competitive brands Deterioration in brand features or price Variety seeking and voluntary trial
Conative	Loyalty to an intention: "I am committed to buying it…"	Commitment Cognitive consistency	Induced trial of competitive brands Deterioration in brand features or price
Action	Loyalty to action inertia, coupled with overcoming obstacles	Inertia Sunk costs	Induced unavailability Deterioration in brand features or price

Table 5.2: Four stage loyalty model wth sustainers and vulnerabilities (based on Oliver, 1997/1999)

■ Loyalty programmes – buying loyalty

The rise of the loyalty programme (or scheme) is not perhaps as recent as you might think. In the 1960s Tesco introduced their famous 'Green Shield Stamps' which was a precursor to many contemporary loyalty programmes. The premise was that for every purchase you earned a certain number of stamps which could be saved and redeemed against gifts and goods at a later date.

In the 1980s Esso fuels launched a similar scheme and few homes were without an Esso glass or two in the cupboard for the next decade (people received glasses as a symbolic reward for loyalty). However, the investment in such schemes is significant and neither of the above have stood the test of time.

In the 1990s technology growth had seen the rise of CRM (see above), and this meant that not only could firms begin to learn from customers, but also use the information gained to customise their offerings to different customer groups. Most loyalty programmes work along similar premises. A customer signs up for the scheme and is given a card (or purchases are recorded online) and they receive benefits related to the type (or quantity) of purchases. Benefits might be financial (such as cash back, points or air miles), non-financial (such as priority in queuing or upgrades), but customers may also seek (or firms offer) higher level bonds which deepen the relationship the customer has with the firm (Lovelock & Wirtz, 2011):

- **Social bonds** – giving the customer personalised levels of service (e.g. use of name)

- **Customisation bonds** – meeting customers' individual needs (e.g. type of pillow in a hotel)

- **Structural bonds** – aligns customer needs with those of the firm more closely (e.g. an SMS about flight status or a customised account)

Variations include schemes where purchase volumes result in customers moving up levels within the scheme (most commonly associated with airlines). Higher level customers (say moving from a Silver to a Gold status) receive increased benefits such as increased luggage allowance, lounge access and upgrades on board.

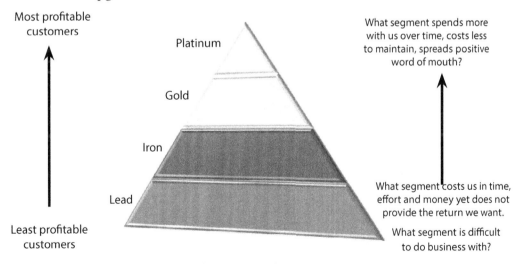

Figure 5.4: Customer pyramid; based on Zeithaml, Rust, & Lemon (2001: 471).

This tiering effect focusses firm resource on customers who have higher spending/usage patterns and allows the firm to consider different customer groups' expectations (see Figure 5.4).

However, some authors have challenged a seemingly unquestioning approach to customer loyalty programmes and cards. Indeed anecdotal evidence suggests many firms would avoid them if they could but feel them necessary to keep up with the competition (Uncles et al., 2003). Customer use of loyalty cards may actually represent a more nebulous relationship with a brand, with customers holding multiple cards both within and between product categories. This type of polygamous loyalty is often called 'programme loyalty' with 'coupon loyalty' a similar concept. This form of loyalty is structurally weak with customers attached to the benefits associated with loyalty and not to the firm itself. To utilise some kind of loyalty programme a firm must ensure that loyal customers are always more profitable than those making one-time transactions as the investment associated with a loyalty programme is vast and could be invested elsewhere and/or customers could perhaps be attracted by other, cheaper, promotional expenditure (see the Tesco case study).

Additionally, there is no guarantee that revenues would increase over time for all customers and firms need to consider the effect of the loyalty programme across the customer life cycle (see next section). Research by Evanschitzky et al. (2012) explored the relative effects of programme loyalty and company loyalty (more of an attitudinal form of loyalty) on future sales to customers, willingness of customers to pay a price premium, share of wallet (how much spend on a particular purchase type goes to a brand) and share of visits (how often does a customer visit one brand over others). The research found that programme loyalty is a stronger predictor of future sales but company loyalty is a better predictor of price premium, share of wallet and share of visits. This research suggests that benefits associated with loyalty cards are more or less transient and are vulnerable to changes in customer behaviour and socio-economic factors. This leads us to consider why firms are still so fond of these schemes. The next section considers the long-term benefits of loyalty and the tantalising promise of customer retention.

Case study: Tesco and Clubcard, time for a change?

(Based on Ruddick, 2014)

UK supermarket retailer Tesco's Clubcard was one of the key retail innovations of the 20th century. Launching in 1995 it allowed Tesco to rise to become one of the biggest retailers in the word. Clubcard (and associated database) allowed Tesco to gather a huge amount of detail about their customers and their shopping habits. However, in recent years competition from European discount supermarket chains such as Aldi and Lidl has resulted in falling sales for Tesco and a reduced market share leading to suggestions that it might be time to axe Clubcard, a decision that would have seemed ridiculous less than 5 years ago.

Problems stem from two areas: first, customers have become cynical about points-based schemes with some estimates suggesting less than 5% of points are ever redeemed; second, the shopping habits of consumers have changed, with shoppers buying little and often from multiple retailers rather than relying on the large weekly shops as they had in the past. This in turn means the data Tesco receives is perhaps less valuable than in the past. One response has been to offer discounts on key product lines rather than attempting to tempt shoppers to switch brands.

The scheme still has around 16 million users (some of them still enthusiastically collecting points) but estimates suggest the scheme costs £500 million per year, money that might be invested elsewhere, for example in price cuts and tempting new shoppers into the store. Scrapping Clubcard would require a brave decision, not least due to the loss of data the company would suffer.

Q: What advice would you give the board of Directors at Tesco about Clubcard?

Staying the distance: long term relationships

The growth of research on customer loyalty made organisations and academics alike start to wonder about the extent to which having loyal customers would actually create any return on investment (ROI). In fact so critical was this notion that the term return on relationships (ROR) is often used to indicate the financial benefits from relationship marketing activity. In essence the benefits of managing customers over time must be clear to firms, otherwise a more transactional approach is arguably more sensible, with reduced costs and complexity surrounding the business model. Models such as 'the leaky bucket' (Figure 5.1) are often used to show how firms' extensive investment in marketing activity appears to simply be pouring down the drain as marketing is mainly viewed as a vehicle for attracting customers to your organisation. Figure 5.5 visualises how the balance between attraction and retention might play out within an organisation. Firms that are good at attraction have no problem gaining customers however, the matrix suggests these might not all stay and may defect to the competition (leaks in the bucket). Alternatively, firms that are good at retaining customers but cannot attract new ones suffer a slow death as customers gradually leave the market (evaporation from the bucket). The recommended approach is to balance both strategies so that new customers replace old ones and improved retention reduces leaks.

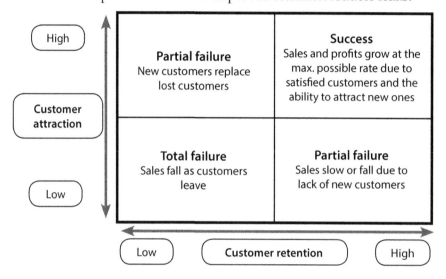

Figure 5.5: Balancing attraction and retention

Firms began to realise that both offensive (marketing activity) and defensive (loyalty/retention) measures were needed to combat defection (the term given to customers who leave the market). In 1990 a crucial research study showed dramatically the impact that reducing defection could have on the bottom line. Reicheld and Sasser (1990) indicate the range of reasons customers might have for defecting which include:

- **Price**: Customers who defect when a cheaper price is available elsewhere.
- **Product**: Customers who switch to a supplier with a superior product
- **Service**: Customers who switch suppliers due to poor service.
- **Market**: Customers who switch markets because of failure or business relocation
- **Technological**: Defection due to a technological advance in the sector (could be a switch outside the industry)

- **Organisational**: Customers within larger organisations may be forced to switch supplier due to political decisions within an organisation.

Whilst some of the above (market and organisational for example) are often unavoidable (and represent evaporation from the bucket) customers who can be retained after product or service failure, for example, could provide a firm with additional return on investment over a longer term. Indeed Reicheld and Sasser (1990) report the case of the credit card firm MBNA which focussed efforts on improving retention in the 1980s and as a result increased profits 16 fold. This kind of powerful effect on the bottom line can be explained through the cumulative effects which firms can gain through retaining customers (see Figure 5.6). What this figure indicates is that in the short term customers are unprofitable (due to marketing and other initial costs). In the first year customers earn the firm a base profit only through sales. Subsequent years are much more profitable as customers spend more (perhaps through increased trust). Retained customers often cost the firm less (e.g. customer inertia), provide referrals and recommendations to others (word of mouth/social media) and in some cases can often be willing to pay a price premium for the firm's products and services.

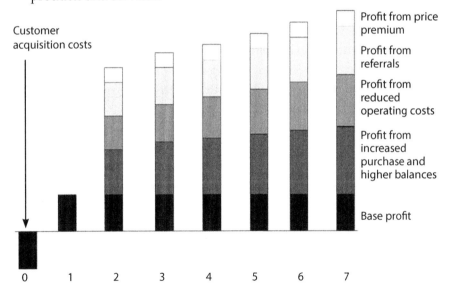

Figure 5.6: Customer profitability over time. (adapted from Reichheld & Sasser Jr, 1990)

This increased value over time is often referred to as customer lifetime value (CLV). This is a formula that firms can use to calculate the value of customers over a particular lifetime horizon. The formula compares the sales a firm's gains from a customer, the cost of maintaining the relationship and multiplies this by a discount rate (to recognise that future profits are not worth as much in today's money as present profits). Using the formula allows firms to assess their ROI from marketing activity. Use of CLV alongside theories of customer equity (essentially the sum of all individual customers' CLV) can give firms valuable insight into the long term effects of marketing decisions (see Rust et al., 2004 for additional insight into the effects of ROR). Ultimately, a greater focus on retention and ROR can benefit a firm in a range of ways. Firms can reduce marketing costs as retention increases; loyal customers often have lower price sensitivity and are retained despite occasional dissatisfying experiences.

Conclusion

In recent years academic research has given greater attention to relationship marketing and considering its place within the wider marketing sphere (where customers are increasingly knowledgeable and willing to take on an enhanced role in exchange see Chapters 6 and 7). Harker and Egan (2006) observe that there is no common *lingua franca* for RM which suggests heterogeneity in interpretation and lack of a unifying theoretical framework. Additionally, the apparent unidirectional nature of marketing relationships, where firms control and are the main beneficiary from the relationship (Oliver et al., 1998), means that customers are increasingly suspicious of firm's actions with regard to relationship marketing efforts. Additionally, customer activity and effort outside of normal transactions – recently termed 'customer engagement' (Jaakkola & Alexander, 2014; Van Doorn et al., 2010) – suggests that the aforementioned unidirectionality of relationships is being challenged by customers willing to co-develop or augment the offerings of a firm or influence the attitudes and behaviours of other customers towards a focal offering. However, the continuing dominance of CRM (total worldwide CRM software revenue totalled $18 billion in 2012, up 12.5% from $16 billion in 2011[3]) suggests that investment into customer relationships shows no signs of abating and that the holy grail of loyalty and retention still enthrals.

Review questions

1   What are the various factors that could be said have precipitated the growth of relationship marketing?

2   How does the 'leaky bucket' model help us understand the way that firms manage customer relationships?

---

3   http://www.gartner.com/newsroom/id/2459015

3   What the benefits and drawbacks of CRM for firms?

4   Why is it important for firms to engender loyalty in their customer base?

5   How does the four stage loyalty model help us understand how customers build relationships with firms?

6   Why is it important to consider the benefits of relationship marketing over time?

7   What possible uses could social media offer for a professional?

References

Berry, L. L. (1983). Relationship marketing. In L. L. Berry, G. L. Shostack, & G. D. Upah (Eds.), *Emerging Perspectives on Services Marketing* (pp. 25-28). Chicago: American Marketing Association.

Borden, N. H. (1964). The concept of the marketing mix. *Journal of Advertising Research,* **4**(June), 2-7.

Dick, A. S. and Basu, K. (1994). Customer loyalty: Toward an integrated conceptual framework. *Journal of the Academy of Marketing Science,* **22**(2), 99-113.

Ehrenberg, A. (1988). *Repeat-Buying: Facts, theory and applications.* London: Edward Arnold.

Evanschitzky, H., Ramaseshan, B., Woisetschläger, D. M., Richelsen, V., Blut, M. and Backhaus, C. (2012). Consequences of customer loyalty to the loyalty program and to the company. *Journal of the Academy of Marketing Science,* **40**(5), 625-638.

Fang, S. R., Chang, Y. S. and Peng, Y. C. (2011). Dark side of relationships: A tensions-based view. *Industrial Marketing Management.* **40**, 774-784.

Fournier, S. and Avery, J. (2011). Putting the relationship back into CRM. *MIT Sloan Management Review,* **52**(3), 63-72.

Frow, P., Payne, A., Wilkinson, I. F. and Young, L. (2011). Customer management and CRM: addressing the dark side. *Journal of Services Marketing,* **25**(2), 79-89.

Grönroos, C. (1994). From marketing mix to relationship marketing: towards a paradigm shift in marketing. *Management Decision,* **32**(2), 4-20.

Gummesson, E. (1994). Making relationship marketing operational. *International Journal of Service Industry Management,* **5**(5), 5-20.

Gummesson, E. (2008). *Total Relationship Marketing.* Oxford: Butterworth-Heinemann.

Gundlach, G. T. (2007). The American Marketing Association's 2004 definition of marketing: Perspectives on its implications for scholarship and the role and responsibility of marketing in society. *Journal of Public Policy & Marketing,* **26**(2), 243-250.

5

Harker, M. and Egan, J. (2006). The past, present and future of relationship marketing. *Journal of Marketing Management,* **22**(1-2), 215-242.

Jaakkola, E. and Alexander, M. (2014). The role of customer engagement behavior in value co-creation a service system perspective. *Journal of Service Research,* **17**(3), 247-261. doi:1094670514529187

Jacoby, J. and Kyner, D. B. (1973). Brand loyalty vs. repeat purchasing behavior. *Journal of Marketing Research,* **10**(1), 1-9.

Lovelock, C. and Wirtz, J. (2011). *Services Marketing: People, Technology, Strategy* (Vol. 7th (International Edition)). Upper Saddle River, New Jersey: Pearson.

Martin, K. D. and Hill, R. P. (2015). Saving and well-being at the base of the pyramid: implications for transformative financial services delivery. *Journal of Service Research,* **18**(3), 405-421. doi:10.1177/1094670514563496

McCarthy, E. J. (1960). *Basic Marketing.* Homewood: Irwin.

Nguyen, B. and Simkin, L. (2013). The dark side of CRM: advantaged and disadvantaged customers. *Journal of Consumer Marketing,* **30**(1), 17-30.

Oliver, R. L. (1997). *Satisfaction: A behavioral perspective on the consumer.* United States: McGraw-Hill.

Oliver, R. L. (1999). Whence consumer loyalty? *The Journal of Marketing,* **63**, 33-44.

Oliver, R. L., Rust, R. T. and Varki, S. (1998). Real-time marketing. *Marketing Management* **7**(4), 28–37.

Parvatiyar, A. and Sheth, J. N. (2000). The domain and conceptual foundations of relationship marketing. In J. N. Sheth & A. Parvatiyar (Eds.), *Handbook of Relationship Marketing* (pp. 3-38). Thousand Oaks, CA: Sage.

Payne, A. and Frow, P. (2005). A strategic framework for customer relationship management. *Journal of Marketing,* **69**(4), 167-176.

Reichheld, F. F. and Sasser Jr, W. E. (1990). Zero defections: quality comes to services. *Harv Bus Rev,* **68**(5), 105-111.

Ruddick, G. (2014). Clubcard built the Tesco of today, but it could be time to ditch it. *The Daily Telegraph,* 16th January.

Rust, R. T., Lemon, K. N. and Zeithaml, V. A. (2004). Return on marketing: using customer equity to focus marketing strategy. *Journal of Marketing,* **68**(1), 109-127.

Uncles, M. D., Dowling, G. R. and Hammond, K. (2003). Customer loyalty and customer loyalty programs. *Journal of Consumer Marketing,* **20**(4), 294-316.

Van Doorn, J., Lemon, K. N., Mittal, V., Nass, S., Pick, D., Pirner, P. and Verhoef, P. C. (2010). Customer engagement behavior: theoretical foundations and research directions. *Journal of service research,* **13**(3), 253-266. doi:10.1177/1094670510375599

Zeithaml, V. A., Rust, R. T. and Lemon, K. N. (2001). The customer pyramid: creating and serving profitable customers. *California Management Review,* **43**(4), 118-142.

6 Consumers

Tom Farrington

"Consumerism is the one thing that gives us our sense of values. Consumerism is honest, and teaches us that everything good has a barcode."

J.G. Ballard, *Kingdom Come* (2006)

Understanding the thoughts and practices of contemporary consumers is at the heart of what marketing practitioners and researchers do. The following pages briefly chart the historical development of the consumer, and introduce academic debates over consumer culture and identity, before looking at several manifestations of consumer power in contemporary marketing practice: crowdsourcing, blogs, and viral marketing. We'll conclude with a look into what makes consumers truly happy.

Introduction

In the academic world, extended forays into etymology can often deflect serious scholarship, but the historical development of the word 'consumer' offers a striking and perhaps surprising perspective from which to initiate the somewhat critical agenda of this chapter. You may have seen the word 'consumption' used as a synonym for tuberculosis, and this is derived from the earliest definitions of resources being used up, wasted or squandered. Here, the disease wastes the mental and physical resources of the body. These negative associations went right to the top, with several centuries of pre-modern European and American governments explicitly regulating the ways in which their citizens consumed. 'Sumptuary' laws restricted gifts of cutlery in 16th century Italy, while women were jailed for wearing scarves in 18th century Germany (Trentmann, 2016). Although such laws would be laughable in modern-day Europe, the thinking behind them seems remarkably contemporary: money spent on fancy foreign goods was money lost from local producers and, in turn, local treasuries.

Over the next two hundred years, the negative connotations of consumption were gradually shifted through various arguments developed in science, theology, and philosophy, in which the pursuits of newness and luxury were reconfigured as divinely inspired and the mark of civilised nations. Economics provided a significant push in William Stanley Jevons's *Theory of Political Economy* (1879), in which Jevons argued that it was consumer wants that determined the value of an object, rather than the materials and work that produced it. Jevons (1879: 40) observed that "[e]very manufacturer knows and feels how closely he must anticipate the tastes and needs of his customers: his whole success depends upon it; and, in like manner, the theory of Economics must begin with a correct theory of consumption." These observations may also sound remarkably modern to the marketing scholar familiar with the work of Vargo and Lusch (2004) into Service-Dominant Logic and the co-creation of value.

Any investigation into the history of the consumer, however brief, must surely acknowledge the role of the slave trade in increasing the availability of luxury goods such as cotton, sugar, rum, and tobacco from the mid-1600s to the mid-1800s. These consumer goods originated in often British and Dutch-owned plantations in the Americas, where people (largely forcibly removed from Africa) were enslaved, sold as goods, and suffered brutal violence and unimaginable loss of life in order to satiate growing consumer demands (Cain & Hopkins, 1986). While slavery is now officially illegal across the world, the slave trade continues in various forms, such as human trafficking, forced marriage, and child labour. This returns us to the negative physical connotations of consumption, and highlights the growing need for transparency in supply chains, in order that the consumer can be informed of the conditions under which their goods are produced.

Fast-forwarding to the early twentieth century, the ability to more efficiently extract and store energy in the form of fossil fuels spurred the production of a dizzying array of commercial consumer goods. Consumer demand for luxury in the decades following the relative austerity of the First and Second World Wars saw the rise of consumerism in earnest across the UK and USA. While it is beyond the scope of this chapter to tread further into the historical landscape of politics, revolution, and counter-revolution against which the contemporary 'consumer' is formed, a definition of consumerism will prove useful to the discussions that follow. Sklair (2010: 136) defines:

> *"the culture-ideology of consumerism [as] a set of beliefs and values, integral but not exclusive to the system of capitalist globalization, intended to make people*

believe that human worth is best ensured and happiness is best achieved in terms of our consumption and possessions."

We shall return to the question of happiness at the end of the chapter. For now, let us take a look at how technological developments in twenty-first century consumer culture have offered empowerment to individuals, and what this empowerment means for marketing.

How the power has moved into our hands

Marketing to consumers has traditionally been something of a prescriptive process, in which consumers passively buy what the market offers. The marketing firm would make use of the available forms of mass media to promote prefabricated goods to a carefully researched segment of the population at a fixed price point. Consumer choice in this scenario is limited: To buy or not to buy? Although this represents an oversimplification, the wide spread of Internet access and connected devices has created and normalised significant alternatives to this process. Now with access to an incredible volume of information, the consumer is thus empowered with a new and ever-changing set of decisions and choices prior even to engaging with a company. Which site do we trust to offer quality products? Which channels do we know that host advertising from companies aligned with our personal values? Is it better to buy online or head to the shops? Which customisation options have been suggested to offer the best performance?

Leaving aside for the moment the question of whether this really represents empowerment, Wathieu et al. (2002) discuss the following abilities now available to the consumer in making their choices:

- **Control over the composition of the choice set**: the ability of the consumer to specify and adjust the choice context.

- **Progress cues**: the ability of the consumer to repeatedly assess progress during the overall process of choice.

- **Information about other consumers**: the ability of the consumer to learn how other consumers have approached the same choice, and the outcomes of their decision.

In disputing the traditional conception of empowerment, Shankar et al. (2006: 1025) note that "[e]mpowering consumers is often equated in practice to giving people more and more choice", with the idea that "consumers can be, should be or even need to be empowered appear[ing], at least at face value, to be foundational to any organisation purporting to have a marketing orientation and to the effective and efficient operation of advanced industrialized economies."

Whether or not consumer empowerment is illusory, it is clear that marketers are no longer able to simply put something in front of people and hope they like it; they must actively understand and appeal to the specific cultures and subcultures created by consumers. To make matters more complex, contemporary marketing scholars now largely concur that we are living in a consumer culture, whereby the dominant values of society are organised through and defined in relation to our consumption practices, so what we consume is the ultimate reference point for how we see and understand the world. In this situation, consumption may even take precedence over (and strongly influence) religious or spiritual culture, professional culture, national culture and so on. Slater (1999: 23) explains that "there is high anxiety because every choice seems to implicate the self: all acts of purchase or consumption, clothing, eating, tourism, entertainment, are decisions not only about how to act but who to be."

Consumer Culture Theory (CCT) explores the relationships that operate through this arrangement, where an individual's sense of identity and selfhood is constructed and enacted through the use of marketplace offerings, both material and symbolic (Arnould & Thompson, 2005). This may initially sound highly abstract and inconsequential but, put simply, the research associated with CCT often offers striking glimpses into the way people use products to express who they are and where they fit in their community. While it is true that CCT research tends to assert the multiplicity of consumer identities and the ability of many individuals to slip easily between cultural categories, the ultimate goal is understanding who consumes what, and why and when they do it. Embracing the complexity of consumer aspirations and motivations may not be a straightforward task, but the detailed insights offered by such investigations can only lead to a more critical and diligent twenty-first century marketer or scholar.

One way of understanding this is to consider the extent to which discovering the political values of a company or brand can attract you to or repel you from purchasing something associated with them, even when nobody else need know (Shah et al., 2007). If the company openly supports a political candidate to whom you are vehemently opposed then you may think twice about purchasing from that company. Part of this may stem from the concern that your money might eventually fund an aspect of that candidate's campaign, but there is also the more profound, emotive sense that this company's products no longer fit with your political identity (Matos et al., 2017).

Exercise 1

Think of an area of your social life, e.g. university, sport, religion, politics. Now note down five goods or services that can be consumed in relation to each. What are the values associated with the consumption of these goods or services? How does the use of these goods or services modify the way in which you understand the original area of your social life?

Contemporary debates over the consumer's relation to culture make one thing very clear: it is vital that at some level consumers are recognised as individual persons, each with a unique personality and perspective. As individuals we all have bad days and good days. Humans have yet to find a way of capturing and transmitting the exact thoughts, feelings, and impulses of one individual to another; these are all tangled up in a dense, irreproducible, and ever-changing web of perspectives and experiences that is unique to each person.

For example, even at the same time, on the same day, in the same year, a young female citizen of the Spokane Tribe of Indians studying medicine in California will interpret the same marketing communication about a credit card company from a perspective that is probably quite different to that of a retired female professional golfer now living in Florida, currently eating an overpriced sandwich. That same message will be interpreted and integrated according to perspectives formed from unique sets of experiential reference points, both conscious and subconscious. Scholars and practitioners must be aware that their potential to influence is always already mediated by the mental and physical state of the individual. Research suggests that the waking mind is wandering onto thoughts other than the process at hand around 47% of the time (Killingsworth & Gilbert, 2010). The fact that people are so easily distracted could mean that they'll be distracted by your marketing, but it could also mean they'll get distracted again, before the message gets through. In practical terms, this emphasises the broader appeal of clear and simple marketing communications.

The next section explores a phenomenon that embeds the consumer-as-creator ever more deeply into the marketplace: crowdsourcing.

Crowdsourcing

In name and practice, crowdsourcing is a combination of crowds with out-sourcing, defined by Howe (2006) as "the act of a company or institution taking a function once performed by employees and outsourcing it to an undefined (and generally large) network of people in the form of an open call."

Crowdsourcing has been differentiated into two general operational types: selective or integrative (Djelassi & Decoopman, 2013).

- **Integrative** crowdsourcing sees the company collecting various (and hopefully complementary) resources from the network. In other words, contributors from the crowd can offer pieces of the solution, which are gathered by the organisers in order to solve the overall problem; like getting different pieces of the jigsaw from different places to form a complete picture. An example of integrative crowdsourcing can be found in one of the earliest forms of crowdsourcing: the Longitude rewards offered by the British Government in 1714. Rewards worth between £1m and £3m in today's money were offered to anyone who could determine a ship's longitude (east-west position) at sea. The sum of money increased relative to the precision with which the ship's longitude was measured. Such rewards are known as inducement prizes.

- Meanwhile, **selective** crowdsourcing involves multiple responses to the open call, with the company selecting the best solution. Essentially, this is a 'winner takes all' format where the organisers rely on the competition among members of the crowd to drive them towards creating an optimal solution. The UK's 2014 Longitude Prize (running from 2015-2019) is an example of selective crowdsourcing. Run in the spirit of (but otherwise unconnected to) the seafaring crowdsourcing of 1714, this offers a £10 million reward to anyone that can create a diagnostic test to solve the problem of global antibiotic resistance.

Crowdsourcing can also be broken down into four types, corresponding to the aims of the activity: crowdfunding, crowd labour, crowd research, and creative crowdsourcing. We'll now look at each of these in detail.

■ Crowdfunding

According to the UK Crowdfunding Association (UKCFA, 2017), crowdfunding is "a way of raising finance by asking a large number of people each for a small amount of money." These appeals to potentially millions of funders thus differ from traditional financing for businesses or other projects, where typically a relatively small number of people are each asked for large financial investments. Social media is used to promote the crowdfunded project, with the hope that crowdfunding is big in the UK. The UKCFA defines three sub-types of crowdfunding:

- **Donation/reward crowdfunding**: Here people donate money without any expectation of return. While rewards may be offered, such as credits or exclusive material on a video project, the rewards are understood to be bonuses, with the motivation to donate stemming from a will to help others towards success.

- **Debt crowdfunding**: Also known as Peer-to-Peer (p2p) lending, here funders typically expect to receive their money back, and may even gain some interest on top. This allows people to realise a project without having to negotiate a loan from a bank.

- **Equity crowdfunding**: This looks a little more like traditional investment, where funders exchange their money for shares or a stake in the project, the value of which could go up or down relative to the success of the venture.

Examples of crowdfunding sites include Kickstarter, Patreon, and GoFundMe. In some cases, the total financial assistance will have to be declared and fully pledged within a set timeframe, before any money is transferred from the crowd. From a consumer perspective, it is worth bearing in mind that on some crowdfunding sites there is little protection for funders should the projects they fund fail to produce the goods promised.

Crowd labour

This involves the recruitment of often unidentified individuals contributing work to very specific tasks through virtual labour markets, for example, Amazon Mechanical Turk or fiverr. Jobs are matched to individuals by the site, by the person or company looking for the task to be completed, or by the person looking for work. This can be very useful for small, labour-intensive tasks for which computers cannot be used, e.g. graphic design work. While this can be a convenient and productive arrangement for the company and the worker, crowd labour can raise several ethical, practical and legal issues:

- Companies that *can* afford to pay for expertise may simply use crowdsourcing to cut costs and maximise profits.

- Unqualified or actively malicious worker contributions could have negative impacts on product quality.

- There may be an emphasis on speed over care, again leading to poor work.

- The problem may be too complex, with insufficient expertise available to complete it.

- There may be a lack of continuity over the course of a project, as the crowd sourced at the beginning may be entirely reconstituted many times during the project.

- Limited interactions between the crowd sourced and the client could quickly lead to a lack of clarity over purpose.

- Limited interactions between crowd participants may lead to replication; there may not be a forum through which to share ideas and build upon each other's knowledge and achievements.

- Crowd labour may be resisted by organised professionals who collectively refuse to outsource their services due to the associated devaluing of their expertise.

- There is no guarantee of minimum wage, no employee rights, and the potential for requestors to withhold payment indefinitely until work meets their standards (which may be entirely unrealistic). There is likely to be no recourse to legal action on either side.

Crowd research

This is a form of market research that gathers opinion from target demographics. While cheap, quick, and easy systems of crowd research such as online voting may be unduly influenced by a minority of voters, or produce a self-selection bias (Brabham, 2010), more costly, longer-term, cross-cultural or carefully targeted crowd research projects have the potential to produce reliable data through the establishment of market research online communities (MROCs) (Patino et al., 2012), and improve forecasting of business outcomes (Lang et al., 2016).

Creative crowdsourcing

Creative crowdsourcing stems from idea competitions or innovation contests, in which the consumer contributes original ideas, products, or content relative to a particular challenge. Examples of this include competitive programming events such as Google Code Jam (where teams of software engineers compete to write code in response to a particular brief), and hacking contests such as Google Code-In and Hack the Pentagon (hackers are invited to break through the cybersecurity technologies of organisations that rely on secrecy, such as Google and the US.Government).

The techniques detailed above can also be utilised to inform and enhance marketing practices. For instance, crowds can be employed to share advertising material at specific times in specific locations, provide continuous, bespoke, brand-related imagery, or even compose fake positive reviews, continually click on advertisements, and stream particular songs or shows on multiple devices at multiple locations.

American funk band, Vulfpeck, famously recorded an album where each track was simply silence. The album was available on the Spotify music streaming platform and the band used creative crowdsourcing to get their fans to stream the silent tracks on repeat over night in order for the band to earn royalties from Spotify. Spotify rewards artists with royalties based on how many times their music has been streamed. Luckily for Vulfpeck, the story went viral and they were able to recruit a crowd that far exceeded their normal fanbase. Ultimately, the royalties earned allowed the band to go on tour again. And what was the name of this album of silence?...*Sleepify*.

6

Collaborative consumption, platform capitalism, and the sharing economy

Facilitated by the rise and continued evolution of the mobile Internet, collaborative consumption offers consumers opportunities for self-expression without ownership of a resource changing hands. There are various examples of this sort of business model, such as Uber, Lyft, and Airbnb. Belk (2014: 1595) notes two common features of these businesses:

1 "their use of temporary access non-ownership models of utilizing consumer goods and services and

2 their reliance on the Internet, and especially Web 2.0, to bring this about."

While the traditional marketplace brings together supply and demand between a consumer and a producer, subject to externally-enforced market regulations, platform capitalism operates at a level over and above the marketplace (the 'platform'), bringing together supply and demand between the consumer and anyone with spare resources who wants to make some money. This potentially global space is accessible by anyone with a device connected to the Internet, and largely unregulated by external forces (e.g. governments, national legislation). As such (at least initially), the platform capitalist sets the rules of the game, and can net serious profits through this intentional blurring of the boundaries between employment, freelancing, and sharing resources.

As Pasquale (2017) explains, we are told that platform capitalism is a good thing because it:

- Enables low-cost entry into markets for providers
- Reduces discrimination through increased service provision
- Promotes economic growth through employment
- Offers flexibility to users and providers
- Increases volume and availability of data, allowing more accurate tailoring to needs
- Ultimately makes for more choice.

Reflecting Foucault's (1977) investigations into 'counter-memory,' Pasquale (2017) tempers this positive story with a counter-narrative, highlighting the potential for platform capitalism to:

- Further embed occupational inequalities by disempowering workers through auctioning of skills (with sale to lowest bidder)

- Reinforce systemic discrimination through rating systems, in which users may discriminate based on a worker's profile picture

- Undermine economic growth through wage reduction

- Force workers to be always on-duty, awaiting work (much like zero-hour contracts)

- Effectively price traditional service-providers out of existence, thereby reducing choice.

As such, some manifestations of this business model have attracted considerable criticism for the adverse social effects of their unethical business practices (Slee, 2016), with Airbnb's short-term letting service blamed for restricting the availability and affordability of long-term housing, and Uber accused of exploiting drivers through low pay and dangerously long working hours (Barnes & Mattsson, 2017). A potential alternative to this situation can be found in the Platform Cooperativism movement, which according to Pasquale (2017: 317) aims to combine the "best aspects of old and new consumption and labor models [towards] promoting more streamlined services while respecting fair labor practices and community norms and obligations."

It is worth noting that no matter the scenario, certain consumers will be unwilling to share, given, for example, a profound emotional identification with a particular product or place, a predilection for customisation, or a need to retain exclusive, personalised access (Barnes & Mattsson, 2017). A crucial aspect for those entering this area of marketing to understand is the motiva-

tions for a consumer to engage in the various types of transaction that characterise the sharing economy. Such investigations are at the current forefront
of related research.

The next section considers an often highly effective medium through
which consumer motivations may be understood and influenced: the blog

The blogosphere

A blog (derived from the phrase web log) is a site that consists of short 'posts'
of text, typically displayed in reverse chronological order. Recent data suggests that the global 'blogosphere' (all blogs connected) is populated by just
under 200 million bloggers (Kerr et al., 2012), and that although the rapid
growth of blogs has largely tailed off in relation to the rise of microblogging
(e.g. Twitter), blog posts remain widely read and highly influential (Universal
McCann, 2012). Blogs can function as online diaries (e.g. Richard Herring's
Warming Up: richardherring.com/warmingup/), known as *personal blogs*
and discussing a wide range of subjects, but the most influential are often
organised around a particular topic or theme, and are known as *topical blogs*.
For example, the blog might bring new musical acts to public attention (neon.
gold, pigeonsandplanes.com, popjustice.com); test and rank sports gear
(dcrainmaker.com, runblogger.com); digest medical research (badscience.net,
blogs.bmj.com/bmj/category/richard-lehmans-weekly-review-of-medical-
journals/); or keep readers up-to-date with the latest tech news (techcrunch.
com, gizmodo.com).

In contradistinction to the way in which traditional marketing reaches
the consumer (exposure by mass media), Kerr et al. (2012) note that blogs
empower consumers through four strategies (originally proposed by Denegri-
Knott, 2006):

- **Consumer control over the marketing relationship**: bloggers and blog
  consumers are able to block material that they do not wish to see using
  browser plug-ins and email filters, or download and disseminate material
  that they enjoy.
- **Availability of information**: the blogging community is able to
  interpret individual marketing campaigns in relation to vast swathes of
  information online, and in relation to the views of other consumers. This
  leads to...
- **Aggregation**: whereby like-minded consumers unite online to talk about
  particular marketing campaigns, where even inconclusive discussions

6

can lead to perceptibly positive or negative overall impressions. Such discussions may lead to the formulation of groups specifically opposed to a brand, working to investigate their business practices.

■ **Participation**: through which consumers can actually create content, which may satirise the marketing campaign, or highlight its merits.

Huang et al. (2007) find five motivations for people to become bloggers: self-expression, life documentation, commenting, forum participation, and information seeking. The most influential blogs are convenient, interactive, specialised, easily accessible, and highly personalised (Chiang & Hsieh, 2011). While marketers will have difficulty controlling blogging activity, this is clearly a pro-active community that it is vital for marketers to reach. Providing bloggers with information is crucial to harnessing their considerable influence. The next section looks at one way of getting the right information out there quickly and effectively: viral marketing.

Exercise 2

Choose a particular interest of yours and find some good quality, influential blogs that discuss this. Note down some of the techniques they use to make the presentation of their news/views eye-catching and informative. What is it that makes this blog more influential? Who is being influenced by this blog, and how? Do some further digging, and try to find out if the blog is entirely independent, or owned/sponsored by a larger company. Does this change your opinion of the content?

Viral marketing

Perhaps the most well-known variant of electronic word-of-mouth (e-WOM) marketing, viral marketing campaigns rely on p2p communication of messages initially sent out to a relatively small group of consumers (Pescher et al., 2014). The idea is that the message then spreads exponentially, like the replication of a virus through living organisms. Viral marketing relies on the idea that consumers are more likely to pay attention to and trust information communicated to them by other individuals than by advertisers (Schulze et al., 2014). In order for maximum distribution and redistribution, it is thus vital that each recipient values the message enough to forward it on to others.

Viral marketing campaigns are attractive as they are cost-effective and have the potential to influence vast numbers of people very quickly. One of the earliest successful examples of this was the promotion of Hotmail in 1996, which signed up over 12 million new users in less than a year and a half by attaching a short marketing message at the bottom of outgoing emails, at a cost of only $500,000 (Krishnamurthy, 2001). More recently, games on Facebook such as FarmVille and CityVille took mere weeks to gain 100 million monthly users (Schulze et al., 2014). Research into viral marketing campaigns shows an influence on consumer preferences and purchases (East et al., 2008), and identifies satisfaction, customer commitment, and product-related aspects as frequently cited reasons for consumer participation (Pescher et al., 2014). Krishnamurthy (2001) notes the importance of:

- **Choosing the right initial recipients**: they should have access to a large social network, the ability to persuade others, and sufficiently represent your target market.

- **Carefully composing the message**: the message must clearly and simply communicate the value proposition with a consistent brand image, and be easy to pass on.

- **Control mechanisms**: you'll need to make sure that the right message is being spread, and keep tabs on who is spreading it. This is useful to measure impact, but also keeps you aware of any backlash.

6

Case study: Pepsi and the viral spiral

The inability to control the potential backlash noted above is the central disadvantage of viral marketing. A particularly vivid example of this is the almost universally negative reaction to Pepsi's *Join the Conversation* commercial, released on the 49th anniversary of the assassination of Martin Luther King and featuring Kendall Jenner, in which the millionaire model becomes the de facto leader of a public protest, and achieves the unstated sociopolitical aims of the 'movement' by offering a drink to a member of the assembled police force. Immediate criticism of this ostensible co-opting of legitimate protests against systemic racism led to the multimillion dollar campaign being withdrawn (and an apology issued) within hours of its initial release.

Pepsi's failure to step back and think critically about this much-maligned campaign meant that the advert went viral for all the wrong reasons. This negative spiral was driven by the individuals and communities to whom the campaign was designed to appeal, who variously accused the advert of racism, exploitation, and the commodification of protest. This meant that much of the target audience first received and viewed the advert in an entirely negative context.

It's worth noting that attempts to associate a brand with socially progressive politics don't necessarily always fail. For example, Coke's *I'd Like to Buy the World a Coke* campaign from 1971 (in which a culturally diverse choir sings a song of togetherness and harmony) was widely admired, spawned a couple of hit singles, and for many still positions Coke as a brand symbolic of an experience shared the world over, no matter where or by whom. Is this difference in reception a consequence of timing? Does this demonstrate the power of brand leader (Coke) over brand competitor (Pepsi)? Or was Coke's message somehow more clear and authentic than Pepsi's? In the contemporary marketplace, timing, positioning, and communication can make or break even the most expensive campaigns.

A variant of viral marketing is 'buzz marketing', through which the company hires brand ambassadors within the target demographic to influence their peers, often identified for their ability to harness extensive social media connections. This immediately presents clear ethical and legal problems, in that these (typically young, often under-16) brand ambassadors may feel uncomfortable about, or be actively discouraged from, disclosing the financial reasons for their endorsements, thereby rendering the advertising unidentifiable so potentially illegal (Ahuja et al., 2007). While some social media sites require users to clearly state that they are engaged in promotion, many have no such restrictions, and this remains a grey area for legislators.

Exercise 3

If you use Instagram, log on and head to the search function. You may not notice it at first, but many of the suggestions appearing are likely to be examples of viral and/or buzz marketing. Try to find examples of users (brand ambassadors/influencers) demonstrating, wearing, or holding products. Note the contexts, poses, and outfits, and note the function of the brand within the carefully constructed 'lifestyle' depicted.

What are some of the techniques used to attract the viewer, and to make them share the communication, in this very specific form of marketing?

So what makes consumers happy?

Understanding the relationship between consumer and product is of primary importance for marketing practitioners and scholars, and in pursuing this understanding, it is worth briefly reflecting on the relationship between consumption and happiness. Recent research shows that buying material goods produces a marked spike in happiness, but that this soon returns to pre-purchase levels. While these momentary increases can be returned to with repeated use of the product (Weidman & Dunn, 2016), the intensity of happiness is never as high as during purchased experiences, like concerts and dining out (Gilovich et al., 2015). They conclude that purchasing experiences (or experiential consumption) makes people happier because:

"(1) Experiential purchases enhance social relations more readily and effectively than material goods; (2) Experiential purchases form a bigger part of a person's identity; and (3) Experiential purchases are evaluated more on their own terms and evoke fewer social comparisons than material purchases." (2015: 152)

While the anticipation, purchase, and consumption of experiences will make you happier than buying products, and for longer, it is spending or donating money for the benefit of other people (known as 'prosocial spending') that offers the most significant, long-lasting elevation of happiness levels (Dunn et al., 2008; Dunn et al., 2011). This extends across a vast range of cultures, countries, and levels of wealth, and is so powerful that even just recalling a moment of prosocial spending or behaviour delivers a swift increase in happiness (Aknin et al., 2013).

The relationship between happiness and consumption is important for marketers and marketing scholars to consider because it throws into sharp relief the ultimate goals of what we do. Are we working to maximise profit or happiness? If it is possible for our work to do both, then which is the most important to us, as people? These are significant and tricky questions for all those who seek to earn money by doing or making, and the answers will shift and grow with individual experience. Happily, by purchasing, reading, and perhaps buying a friend a drink while discussing this book, you may well be experiencing a heady mixture of material, experiential, and prosocial happiness in this very moment!

Review questions

1 What was the initial definition of consumption?
A: used up
B: wasted
C: squandered
D: All of the above

2 What was restricted in 16th Century Italy?
A: Gifts of cutlery
B: Rope
C: Trousers
D: Internet access

3 What are given as examples of modern slavery?
A: Human trafficking
B: Forced marriage
C: Child labour
D: All of the above

4 What is the traditional relationship between consumer and producer?
A: Passive consumer/active producer
B: Young producer/quiet consumer
C: Passive producer/active consumer
D: Noisy consumer/quiet producer

5 According to Wathieu et al. (2002) what is one of the features of consumer empowerment?
A: Fossil fuels
B: Information about other consumers
C: Food blogs
D: The USA

6 What does CCT stand for?
A: Consumer Crafting Team
B: Colouring with Crayons Together
C: Consumer Culture Theory
D: Cadbury's Crème Turnip

Directed further reading

Elias, A. S., Gill, R., & Scharff, C. (2017). *Aesthetic Labour: Rethinking Beauty Politics in Neoliberalism*, London: Palgrave Macmillan UK.

Horkheimer, M., Adorno, T. W., & Noeri, G. (2002). *Dialectic of Enlightenment*, Stanford University Press.

Klein, N. (2000). *No Logo*, London, Flamingo.

Slater, D. (1997). *Consumer Culture and Modernity*, London: Wiley.

Srnicek, N. (2016). *Platform Capitalism*, London: Wiley.

Sundararajan, A. (2016). *The Sharing Economy: The End of Employment and the Rise of Crowd-Based Capitalism*, MIT Press.

References

Ahuja, R. D., Michels, T. A., Walker, M. M. & Weissbuch, M. (2007). Teen perceptions of disclosure in buzz marketing. *Journal of Consumer Marketing,* **24**(3), 151-159.

Aknin, L. B., Barrington-Leigh, C. P., Dunn, E. W., Helliwell, J. F., Burns, J., Biswas-Diener, R. & Norton, M. I. (2013). Prosocial spending and well-being: Cross-cultural evidence for a psychological universal. *Journal of Personality and Social Psychology,* **104**(4), 635.

Arnould, E. J. & Thompson, C. J. (2005). Consumer culture theory (CCT): Twenty years of research. *Journal of Consumer Research,* **31**(4), 868-882.

Barnes, S. J. & Mattsson, J. (2017). Understanding collaborative consumption: Test of a theoretical model. *Technological Forecasting and Social Change,* **118**, 281-292.

Belk, R. (2014). You are what you can access: Sharing and collaborative consumption online. *Journal of Business Research,* **67**(8), 1595-1600.

Brabham, D. C. (2010). Moving the crowd at Threadless. *Information, Communication & Society,* **13**(8), 1122-1145. doi:10.1080/13691181003624090

Cain, P. J. & Hopkins, A. G. (1986). Gentlemanly capitalism and British expansion overseas. The old colonial system, 1688-1850. *The Economic History Review,* **39**(4), 501-525.

Chiang, I. & Hsieh, C.-H. (2011). Exploring the impacts of blog marketing on consumers. *Social Behavior and Personality: an international journal,* **39**(9), 1245-1250.

Denegri-Knott, J. (2006). Consumers behaving badly: deviation or innovation? Power struggles on the web. *Journal of Consumer Behaviour,* **5**(1), 82-94.

Djelassi, S. & Decoopman, I. (2013). Customers' participation in product development through crowdsourcing: Issues and implications. *Industrial Marketing Management,* **42**(5), 683-692.

Dunn, E. W., Aknin, L. B. & Norton, M. I. (2008). Spending money on others promotes happiness. *Science,* **319**(5870), 1687-1688.

Dunn, E. W., Gilbert, D. T. & Wilson, T. D. (2011). If money doesn't make you happy, then you probably aren't spending it right. *Journal of Consumer Psychology,* **21**(2), 115-125.

East, R., Hammond, K. & Lomax, W. (2008). Measuring the impact of positive and negative word of mouth on brand purchase probability. *International Journal of Research in Marketing,* **25**(3).

Foucault, M. (1977). *Language, Counter-memory, Practice,* Cornell University Press.

Gilovich, T., Kumar, A. & Jampol, L. (2015). A wonderful life: Experiential consumption and the pursuit of happiness. *Journal of Consumer Psychology,* **25**(1), 152-165.

Howe, J. (2006). Crowdsourcing: A definition. http://crowdsourcing.typepad.com/cs/2006/06/crowdsourcing_a.html. Accessed 11/04/2017.

Huang, C.-Y., Shen, Y.-Z., Lin, H.-X., & Chang, S.-S. (2007). Bloggers' motivations and behaviors: A model. *Journal of Advertising Research,* **47**(4), 472-484.

Jevons, W. S. (1879). *The Theory of Political Economy,* Macmillan and Company.

Kerr, G., Mortimer, K., Dickinson, S. & Waller, D. S. (2012). Buy, boycott or blog: Exploring online consumer power to share, discuss and distribute controversial advertising messages. *European Journal of Marketing,* **46**(3/4), 387-405.

6

Killingsworth, M. A. & Gilbert, D. T. (2010). A wandering mind is an unhappy mind. *Science,* **330**(6006), 932-932.

Krishnamurthy, S. (2001). Viewpoint. *The Journal of Services Marketing,* **15**(6/7), 422.

Lang, M., Bharadwaj, N. & Di Benedetto, C. A. (2016). How crowdsourcing improves prediction of market-oriented outcomes. *Journal of Business Research,* **69**(10), 4168-4176. doi:10.1016/j.jbusres.2016.03.020

Matos, G., Vinuales, G. & Sheinin, D. A. (2017). The power of politics in branding. *Journal of Marketing Theory and Practice,* **25**(2), 125-140.

Pasquale, F. (2017). Two narratives of platform capitalism. *Yale Law & Policy Review,* **35**(1), 11.

Patino, A., Pitta, D. A. & Quinones, R. (2012). Social media's emerging importance in market research. *Journal of Consumer Marketing,* **29**(3), 233-237.

Pescher, C., Reichhart, P. & Spann, M. (2014). Consumer decision-making processes in mobile viral marketing campaigns. *Journal of Interactive Marketing,* **28**(1), 43-54.

Schulze, C., Schöler, L. & Skiera, B. (2014). Not all fun and games: Viral marketing for utilitarian products. *Journal of Marketing,* **78**(1), 1-19.

Shah, D. V., McLeod, D. M., Kim, E., Lee, S. Y., Gotlieb, M. R., Ho, S. S. & Breivik, H. (2007). Political consumerism: How communication and consumption orientations drive 'lifestyle politics'. *The Annals of the American Academy of Political and Social Science,* **611**(1), 217-235.

Shankar, A., Cherrier, H. & Canniford, R. (2006). Consumer empowerment: a Foucauldian interpretation. *European Journal of Marketing,* **40**(9/10), 1013-1030.

Sklair, L. (2010). Iconic architecture and the culture-ideology of consumerism. *Theory, Culture & Society,* **27**(5), 135-159.

Slater, D. (1999). *Consumer Culture and Modernity,* Wiley.

Slee, T. (2016). *What's Yours is Mine: Against the Sharing Economy,* Or Books.

Trentmann, F. (2016). How humans became 'consumers': A History. The Atlantic. /www.theatlantic.com/business/archive/2016/11/how-humans-became-consumers/508700. Accessed 11.05/2017.

UKCFA. (2017). What is crowdfunding?. UKCFA. www.ukcfa.org.uk/what-is-crowdfunding/. Accessed 11.05/2017.

Universal McCann (2012), Wave 6 - The Business of Social, www.universalmccann.de/wave6/downloads/wave6_insights_international.pdf. Accessed 11.05/2017.

Vargo, S.L. and Lusch, R.F., (2004). Evolving to a new dominant logic for marketing. *Journal of Marketing,* **68**(1), pp.1-17.

Wathieu, L., Brenner, L., Carmon, Z., Chattopadhyay, A., Wertenbroch, K., Drolet, A., & Ratner, R. K. (2002). Consumer control and empowerment: A primer. *Marketing Letters,* **13**(3), 297-305.

Weidman, A. C., & Dunn, E. W. (2016). The unsung benefits of material things. *Social Psychological and Personality Science,* **7**(4), 390-399.

7 Services

Andrew MacLaren

"Be our guest,
 Be our guest,
 Put our service to the test,
 Tie your napkin 'round your neck, Cherie,
 And we provide the rest.
 Soup du jour,
 Hot hors d'oeuvres,
 Why, we only live to serve,
 Try the grey stuff, it's delicious,
 Don't believe me? Ask the dishes…"

(Lumiere, *Beauty and The Beast*)

Services are part and parcel of today's globalised, diversified, augmented and extended economy. You can't function in developed society without engaging in a service encounter, nor could you function 2000 years ago. Services are evident all around us and we need to understand their characteristics, the effective means of managing them and indeed how to cope when they go wrong…which they often do.

Introduction

Business concepts have tended to polarise the behaviours of the market between two spheres: production and consumption (Smith, 1776). This was appropriate at the time of the industrial revolution when factories produced goods (production) and people within the household consumed them (consumption); the world was rather simple.

We begin this chapter, by looking at the nature of services. We will start by paying attention to the scope and definition of services – what it is and how the term is used and applied, and then look at the four underpinning characteristics. Service encounters are considered next, exploring the dynamic exchange that takes place between a service provider and a customer. Following this, these elements are considered in relation to the 4Ps model of the marketing mix, and an extended marketing mix concept is presented (the 7Ps). The final section of the chapter explores how services are managed and measured. The chapter finishes with a case study from the hospitality industry.

So, why bother with services? Why are they so important that the subject gets its own chapter in this book? We don't have a chapter on car marketing, for example, so why are we picking on services? The answer is that services are a very big part of global contemporary business. You are over three times more likely to be working for a services company than a manufacturing company when you leave university: the vast majority of jobs in the developed economy are in services.

As the complexity of the market-driven economy has developed, notions of consumption have evolved into a variety of different distinct concepts. Take for example the music streaming platform, Spotify; if you pay for a premium subscription on Spotify you can download and enjoy the music you like wherever and whenever you choose, but what exactly are you buying? You don't own the copies of the music you listen to, and if your subscription ceases you can no longer download your favourite music. In reality you are buying the privilege to access a vast array of music and related content, so it is *access* that is the value proposition of Spotify as a business. Therefore, from a production/consumption perspective, you are not consuming the Spotify product, because the product itself is really a vehicle through which you get access to another product (the music). Equally, Saren (2015) argues that it is theoretically challenging to even consume music since some of the enjoyment of music is in its interaction with your personal emotions, memories, and mood so you in fact have an active role to play when you listen to music; what it means is specific and unique to you.

What Saren (2015) is pointing out is that the traditional approach of polarising market activities between consumption and production is an outmoded way of thinking, and we should be careful about how we use the term 'consumption'. This is where things like Spotify are important in our understanding of contemporary marketing, because it is a business that offers software as a service (SaaS). Most of those clever apps on your smartphone are using software to create a service that somehow improves your life or your state of mind. Understanding how service works and why you must treat it as a stand-alone concept will help you make sense of and work with contemporary marketing activities in a useful way.

The characteristics of services

Service Dominant Logic is the term that represents the move away from polarised marketing concepts to a more nuanced understanding of the role of service. Vargo and Lusch (2008) define this by saying that rather than being categorised as either producing or consuming products, we are actors mobilising resources within networks. This idea of networked actors in the marketplace allows us to acknowledge that we all have roles to play, and very often the 'product' we are 'consuming' in contemporary contexts is not physically tangible, nor is it owned, nor is it a passive experience; we have to contribute in order to get the value from it – we have to perform as customers.

Services cover such industries as wholesale and retail, for example shops and warehouses, transportation and communication. They cover financial intermediation – banks, building societies and insurance companies. They include public administration – city councils, the civil service, and education – health and social services. Significantly, services include the leisure, hospitality and tourism sector – for example pubs, nightclubs and holidays. This is one of the largest economic sectors in the world and employs more people than any other sector. Also, in the not-for-profit sector most organisations have a large element of service delivery as part of their operations.

In economic terms, a service is the non-material equivalent of a good. That is an inverse definition, which is often not very helpful as a definition – it is like saying a cat is a non-dog equivalent of a four-legged mammal. In more useful definitions, service provision has been defined as an economic activity that does not result in ownership (e.g. psychotherapy) and this is what makes it different from providing physical goods (e.g. a pair of socks, a shirt).

When someone buys a car it becomes theirs to keep – but when they pay to get it repaired or serviced, they do not own the garage mechanic. There is a clear distinction regarding ownership in the context of services. It is also claimed that a service is a process that leads to some sort of benefit by facilitating a change in a customer, a change in their physical possessions (as with a car service) or a change in their mood. By going to watch your favourite band in concert, your attendance facilitates a change in your sense of well-being, or indeed, if you go for a massage at a spa, then the relaxation and peacefulness is part of the outcome you are looking for as a customer, and that outcome represents a change of state in you as the customer.

Goods can vary according to heir physical presence. What this shows is that most products do have some combination of physical good and service. All goods and services, therefore, exist on a continuum, with pure goods at one end and pure services at the other. There is a vast array of different products across this spectrum, which have a mixture of goods and services as part of their offering. At one end of the spectrum there are goods that require minimal service in order for them to be consumed, for example a chocolate bar, which we could purchase from a vending machine. In many contexts we will buy chocolate through a retailer, who will add value by potentially offering information, comparisons, and facilitating the purchase in an easy way. Service at this end of the spectrum is an added, non-essential element. As the complexity of the product sought increases so does the requirement for and involvement of a service element. Buying a car is a far more involved and complicated purchase and we are likely to require some form of service assistance to complete the purchase. At the opposite extreme of the continuum, we see products where the core benefit being purchased is the experience itself, for example, a visit to a theme park or engaging in education. At this end of the spectrum the customer is paying for the facilitation of a change in mood or state.

Unlike goods, services cannot be manufactured and stored before or after the experience. They have a very brief life. You cannot store the empty seats on an aircraft on one flight and then use them on another day to make more money when there is higher demand; the seats expire when the aircraft takes off. Managing supply and demand is important for managers of services. In the short term we can try to meet excess demand by putting on an extra flight when the demand is high but it is difficult to manage in the long term and with a fixed asset such as an aeroplane, the manager's job is to maximise sales of seats at all times. One of the key techniques to manage supply and demand is by price – so, for example, high demand services or peak times will cost more than other times and we may even offer discounts to tempt customers to purchase our service at off-peak times. As consumers we are used to price fluctuations based on demand, and it is a marketer's job to monitor, analyse, and forecast demand so as to set the price in the sweet spot between demand, competition and value. For example, peak train fares are in force during rush hour periods where demand for using the service from commuters is high. Gyms often offer 'off-peak' memberships, which are popular among retired people who are able to use the gym at quieter times during the day.

Services are produced and consumed simultaneously, just like the empty seats on the aeroplane cannot be stored; the service provided for those occupying the filled seats is being produced by the cabin crew simultaneously as the passengers consume it. The same goes for getting your hair cut. What you are paying for is the hairdressing professional to cut and style your hair; they have to do that in your presence. This is entirely different from buying this book or a cheese sandwich: the product can be manufactured and packaged elsewhere in a dedicated facility with quality controls and system protocols, whereas the hairdresser needs the person who will consume their product to be present right in front of them as they produce it – it is a simultaneous exchange.

We are also at the mercy of the service provider's mood, our own mood and several other contextual factors, all of which make any service experience unique. This makes services heterogeneous; they are changeable, unpredictable and hard to consistently produce in the same manner.

Characteristic	What that means	Example
Intangibility	You can't touch it or take it home	Hopefully, you will come home from a theme park feeling exhilarated, but that feeling is intangible.
Heterogeneity	It's different every time	Getting on a 6am flight because you're going on holiday will feel different to getting on a 6am flight to fly somewhere for a business meeting. Both customers and providers' roles make it difficult to make services experiences consistent.
Inseparability	The production and consumption happen at the same time	You have to be present to get a haircut, and so does the hairdresser.
Perishability	Services have a very specific shelf-life	You can't stay in a hotel 7 days ago, the empty bedrooms the hotel had 7 days ago have perished and can no longer be sold.

■ Intangibility

Intangible means that the item/good is not solid – it is unable to be touched. This creates some challenges for us as consumers because we cannot use the senses in the same as we do when we buy a product like an item of clothing. Clothes can be picked up, the fabric can be felt, they can be tried on for size and fit, other clothes can be compared directly and even if you decide to buy something, it can be returned to the shop if you change your mind. Conversely, you cannot sample a meal before you order it, you cannot return it afterwards if you find a better one.

To help customers buy a service, marketers provide tangible cues to help the customer make a the right decision before purchasing. The tangible cues are the variables of the services marketing mix : the 7 Ps – which are discussed late in the chapter.

Exercise 1

Think about how you use tangible cues to help you make decisions in a service situation: imagine you are trying to choose a restaurant for lunch. What are the tangible cues that you may use and which senses to use in each case? Using sight for example you may read the menu, note the prices, look at the décor, see if the restaurant is busy. You may use smell – does it smell nice? When you are inside you may see how the staff greet you and show you to a table, or do they ignore you? You may go in and hear that they play really bad music and you want to go somewhere quiet...you might also look online at the restaurant's star rating and read some reviews...these are also tangible cues because they are somewhat measurable.

The intangibility of services makes them a risky purchase for customers, so the more tangible marketers can make a product feel, the more they reduce the risk for the customer. Brands are very important in the services industry because brands help to introduce a sense of tangibility. This is why you will often see an advert for a hotel chain focussing on tangible things such as the quality of their comfortable beds or their hot and powerful showers.

■ Heterogeneity

Heterogeneity means that a service has the potential to be different every time we consume it – services are very difficult to standardise. This arises from the fact of inseparability, which means that customers and service providers have to interact with each other. The nature of this interaction means that there are a lot of factors which are outside the control of the service provider. What if your normally cheerful hairdresser is in a bad mood? How might this affect your service experience? What if, to get over a bad mood, you are looking to have a complete image make-over? How might this affect your service experience?

Other customers can also affect our service experience. Imagine a crowded airport when there are serious delays due to weather, suddenly the departures space has to accommodate three times as many people as it is designed for. This means your experience will be negatively impacted by the other customers sharing the space. Another example would be of a nightclub that is half empty; in this instance the absence of other customers would negatively impact on the service experience. There are many examples, both good and bad: if your favourite celebrity is in the same restaurant as you, then it will likely improve your service experience; if the person sitting beside you on an aeroplane is so overweight that they are taking up some of your personal space then it is likely that you will not enjoy the flight.

The impact of other customers is part of the *servicescape*, conceptualised by Bitner (1992). The servicescape takes into account all environmental factors in a service setting both from an employee perspective and a customer perspective, helping identify areas where friction, inconsistency or failure could occur. The elements that Bitner (1992) takes into account range from internal emotional responses to the environment, to external physical responses to the environment. The servicescape is a useful framework for developing service blueprints, mentioned later in the chapter, and demonstrates the complexity that can be present in a service environment.

The important point to make is that the heterogeneity of services makes them difficult to manage. By its very nature, changeability is difficult to predict and plan for. In many cases companies focus on operating systems and procedures and, in particular, staff training to ensure consistency. In addition, companies expect problems to occur, but make sure that systems are in place to allow the business to learn from mistakes and to correct the problem quickly. This is why you will see complaints procedures and feedback opportunities in service settings, because the business recognises that issues do occur and they need a channel the customer can use to address the problems they experience.

Inseparability

Inseparability means that the service itself cannot be separated from the customer. In practice, that means that for at least some the service experience the consumer has to be present while the service is being produced. In the case of getting a haircut you have to be there. Inseparability means both the service provider and the service customer have to be in contact for the service to take place – a service encounter. This differs from manufacturing where a good can be made a long time before the customers buys it.

Perishability

Perishability simply means a service cannot be stored. Just like the aeroplane seats discussed earlier in the chapter, you cannot sell the seats on yesterday's flight to Barcelona today, they have perished. In services that means that supply and demand have to be keenly understood and the business's yield must maximise the potential earnings in relation to demand. Software systems help service businesses forecast demand and manage pricing accordingly so that yield is maximised. This software comes from the original internation-alisation of hotel and air travel businesses, where they linked their computer systems to integrate bookings and ensure profitability was maintained across a larger and more complicated network. This process is called yield manage-ment and it is fundamental to service business management.

Exercise 2

Go onto a low-cost airline website and search for a flight for two people from Edin-burgh to Faro in Portugal. Have a look at the price point. It will likely tell you how many remaining seats are available at the current price: that is yield management in action! If you exit the website and return later, the price may now appear higher because the system has recognised increased demand due to your earlier enquiry. This is a blessing and a curse of digital technology, airlines can now exercise yield management in real time, they can see how many people are looking at a flight and using statistical modelling they can work out the maximum price they can charge at any given time, making it harder for the consumer to find a real bargain.

Due to perishability and lower predictability of demand, service busi-nesses are well known for employing flexible operating methods in order to minimise the impact of fluctuating demand. Service businesses are thus more likely to have a greater number of part-time, flexible or zero-hours workers in order to reduce the costs in times of low demand. Employees are also often required to be multi-skilled so that they can offer value to the business even during off-peak times. The waiting staff in a restaurant in a seasonal resort may also be the painters, decorators, builders and maintenance team in the off-season, which allows them to maintain employment all year round.

Service encounters

Building from the characteristics of service, we can understand the consump-tion of a service to be an 'encounter'. An encounter is a meeting, exchange or interaction between people, so by considering service consumption as an encounter we acknowledge the roles the customer and the provider play. Another important word here is 'roles'; this indicates the performative nature of service consumption. In a service encounter both sides are performing a role: the role of the provider and the role of the customer. We know these are roles and not fixed identities because it is only in that moment (when the provider is on-duty and working as a service provider and the customer is in need of the service) that their exchange becomes as service encounter. This means that a service encounter is defined by the context in which it takes place and is a social construction between the parties involved. So a service encounter is intangible – it emerges from the exchange between the involved parties; it is heterogeneous – it is dependent on how the people performing the roles are feeling in that moment and what is happening in their surroundings; it is inseparable – the two parties need to be actively involved in the exchange for it to happen and it is defined by its surrounding context; finally, it is perishable – it expires and ceases to exist after the encounter has finished.

This is why service encounters are particularly useful to understand in the study of marketing. They represent the essence and complexity of the subject, because we are required to understand and conceptualise the exchange between two perspectives (consumer and producer) and understand that exchange in terms of both sides. We cannot focus simply on what makes a salesperson good at their job without considering the people they are selling to. The two sides must encounter each other in order for a sale to take place; therefore our attention is focussed on the process of the exchange rather than the individuals themselves. Solomon et al. (1985) call a service encounter a social situation.

The extended marketing mix

Following our understanding of the characteristics of services and service encounters, there are three additional elements to the marketing mix that are used to supplement the 4Ps .

■ People

We need to think of strategies that we can use to make sure that people impact positively on the service experience and that includes staff *and* customers. Many CEOs of large service-based businesses will tell you that their frontline service staff are the most valuable asset within the company, because the amount of training and development that takes place in order to ensure that they produce and deliver a consistent and valuable service is considerable. Equally, in the purest sense, the people are the product in a service setting so they must be taken care of and be considered carefully.

■ Physical evidence

Physical evidence is represented by the cues that can be used to make the service more tangible. Tangible cues reduce consumer decision-making risk. Physical evidence includes essential evidence and peripheral evidence.

- **Essential evidence** is key to the service and an important contributor to the customer's decision making;

- **Peripheral evidence** is less central but may reinforce brand values or augment the service experience in a positive way, such as free souvenirs given at a themed restaurant. Look no further than the toy that children find inside a McDonald's Happy Meal.

■ Processes

These are the operating processes that take the customer through from ordering to the delivery of the service. Some processes will take place only when the customer first buys the service, for example the process of opening a bank account, while others will be repeated on a regular basis as the customer uses the service, for example, booking-in to your weekly yoga class at your gym.

You also get sub-categories of processes within service organisations.

- **People processing**: People have to be physically present and a system must exist to move them through the experience. This can be anything from a queueing system at Disney World to the waiting room in your dentist's practice – these are basic examples of facilities for people processing. An example of obvious and well-considered people processing can be found at any IKEA store, where the entire servicescape has been designed with people processing in mind...there are arrows everywhere telling you where to go next!

- **Possession processing**: Our valuable possessions are likely to break down or need maintenance. Here the quality of the repair service is not dependent on the owner being present whilst the service operation takes place. Possession processing is a valuable part of the automobile industry; when we buy a car, the sales representatives are not only thinking about the price agreed for the sale, they are thinking about all the repeat business they can get from you when your car needs to be serviced in the future.

- **Mental stimulus processing**: Particularly in the experience economy, understanding of how to facilitate and deliver mental stimulus processing is a core part of service delivery. Casinos are examples of businesses in which the environment is designed to engender an immersive and absorbing atmosphere for players.

■ **Information processing**: This is the 'admin' side of services. If you want to book a holiday, the chances are that your passport and bank details will be required. Services must have efficient channels for information processing, otherwise they may lose customers. Online information processing has become easier in some ways because we can manage many of our own transactions via our portable devices. However, the most common point for an online customer to abort a transaction is at the checkout stage where all the information processing is due to take place. Any complications or ambiguity at this point leads to people deciding to give up. Therefore, information processing is a part of the overall service design that must be well resolved. Advances in technology have enabled information processing to become quicker, more accurate and more frequent. This often happens at the expense of the need for people processing. For example, we book flights through the Internet and can access our boarding passes automatically without speaking to any customer service representatives.

7

Managing and measuring expectations: Blueprints, scripts and beyond

■ SERVQUAL

As services have become more sophisticated and management has emerged as a vital part of delivering effective service products, so too has the need to structure and control the elements of the product. Parasuraman et al. (1988) map out the service process in order to allow the points of friction, error or failure to be identified and addressed. The model they developed to measure service quality is called the SERVQUAL model.

Marketing actions, word of mouth and prior experience lead to the customer forming expectations of what a service will be like. As consumers, we gather information through multiple channels (some from the business itself and some from things like social media, review platforms or via traditional broadcast media), and this information helps us form expectations of a service.

When we proceed to experience a service product we then assess (often unconsciously) our experiences in relation to the expectations we formed prior to the experience. Satisfaction is achieved if the experience meets or surpasses the prior expectations.

The SERVQUAL model represents a continuous loop of expectation form-ing and then interpreting following new experiences, therefore, one of the most important factors influencing the expectations we form prior to an experience is the influence of previous experiences. If we have consistently experienced good service at a restaurant, then our expectations will be elevated based on previous encounters with that product. Therefore, it is always important for a business to recognise how dissatisfaction and satisfaction feed back to adjust customers' expectations.

The SERVQUAL model leads to the identification of points of friction or 'gaps', as presented below:

Gap	Definition
Gap 1 - Service providers' misconception of the customer	The gap between what the customer expects/perceives and what the management thinks the customer expects/perceives
Gap 2 - Inadequate resources	The gap between what is provided and what is required to match consumer expectations
Gap 3 - Inadequate or inconsistent service delivery	The gap between the service design and service delivered.
Gap 4 - Exaggerated promises	The gap between the service delivered and the service advertised
Gap 5 – Jumping to conclusions	The gap between what service staff think is the right course of action in delivering the service and what the customer would actually like to happen.

The effectiveness of models like the Parasuraman et al. (1988) SERVQUAL model is in their ability to distil and break down complex systems into a form that makes them measurable and more predictable. This is helpful to those whose job it is to manage services on a day to day basis and these models are genuinely useful in practice, however Arnould and Price (1993) note that models such as SERVQUAL are based on the idea of disconfirmation (i.e. establishing to what extent the delivery of a service did not meet a customer's expectations). This is effective so long as we assume that customers actually formed any expectations in the first place and that they would purely measure satisfaction in terms of those expectations (such as expected speed of service or expected price). What Arnould and Price (1993: 26) say is that some experi-ences emerge from "the dynamic interaction of participants" and therefore, we cannot always be certain what our expectations are in advance of experi-encing something that is the product of our own performative interactions.

■ Blueprinting and scripting

The larger a service based organisation is, the more likely it is that elements of the service design are blueprinted or scripted. This is a process that George Ritzer (2009) famously called 'McDonaldization' – referencing the way in which McDonald's fast food chain were the pioneers of scripting and controlling every aspect of service delivery. Service work can be blueprinted loosely by way of zoning service areas and drafting orders of service delivery and role descriptions for different team members, but it can also be highly and myopically scripted and structured to the extent employees may be penalised or disciplined for failing to meet 'brand standards' of service delivery. Some contemporary examples of this include the messages you hear from flight attendants on board aircraft…

> *"Ladies and gentlemen, as the captain prepares for take-off, please ensure you have stowed your carry-on luggage underneath the seat in front of you or in an overhead locker. Please take your seat and fasten your seat belt. And also make sure your seat back and folding trays are in their full upright positions.*
>
> *If you are seated next to an emergency exit, please read carefully the special instructions card located by your seat. If you do not wish to perform the functions described in the event of an emergency, please ask a flight attendant to reseat you.*
>
> *We remind you that this is a non-smoking flight. Smoking is prohibited on the entire aircraft, including the lavatories. Tampering with, disabling or destroying the lavatory smoke detectors is prohibited by law.*
>
> *If you have any questions about our flight today, please don't hesitate to ask myself or one of cabin team. Thank you."*

Scripts are all around us in service environments and their role covers a range of requirements from simply controlling the staff all the way to ensuring compliance with certain laws has been achieved. Beyond the law, some scripts also look to mitigate against potential safety risks and even to cope with potential customer misbehaviour (such as reminding people that smoking on a flight is not allowed).

Service blueprinting has become an integral part of developing a service offering since the contemporary adoption of advanced technologies by both consumers and businesses. As Patrício et al. (2008: 319) note:

> *"The infusion of technology into services has created many opportunities for developing new offerings, but to take full advantage of these capabilities, technology and customer perspectives must be completely integrated into service design and management."*

7

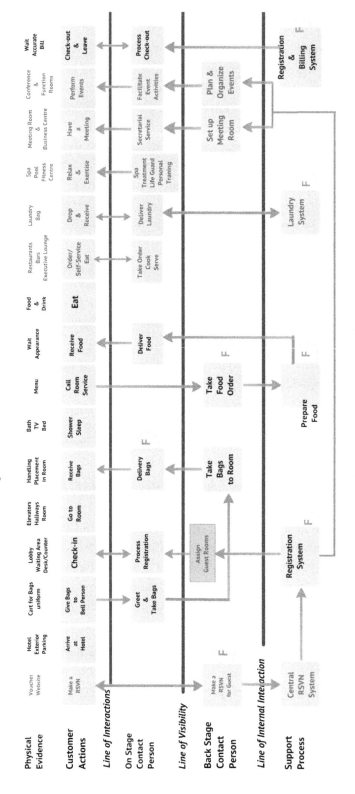

Figure 7.1: The a service blueprint for a Hilton Hotel. Source: https://prezi.com/g9v6md2zetle/service-blueprint-ritz/

As the relationship between service providers, customers, and technologies becomes more integrated and complex, so we see the increasing necessity of service design. The Hilton Hotels Corporation was a famous pioneer of blueprinting and measuring all aspects of its service design in order to maximise profits and management effectiveness (Hilton, 1957). To the present day, the marketing departments of Hilton Hotels are responsible for the service blueprinting and they assimilate all aspects of the Hilton Brand into the service design. Figure 7.1 is a snapshot of what a service blueprint looks like for a Hilton Hotel.

Hilton International's efforts are focussed on excellent service; "Delivering the brand experience is the principal marketing tool we have, and is the beginning and end of what we do." (Ashton, 2006: 1). Hilton's service blueprint outlines the ideal guest experience. The marketing team outlines requirements for recruitment, training and development, which allows them to monitor and evaluate service levels, and address issues of service failure and recovery. Service failure and service recovery are inevitable processes that service businesses must plan for and contend with effectively in order to sustain success (Miller et al., 2000).

■ The experience economy

As service delivery and management have become more sophisticated and we as consumers have become more discerning in what we seek to gain from consuming them, the experience economy has developed to become an established part of the services landscape. Pine and Gilmore (1998: 97) originally conceptualised the experience economy using the analogy of birthday cake:

> *"How do economies change? The entire history of economic progress can be recapitulated in the four stage evolution of the birthday cake. As a vestige of the agrarian economy, mothers made birthday cakes from scratch, mixing farm commodities (flour, sugar, butter, and eggs) that together cost mere dimes. As the goods-based industrial economy advanced, moms paid a dollar or two to Betty Crocker for premixed ingredients. Later, when the service economy took hold, busy parents ordered cakes from the bakery or grocery store, which, at $10 or $15, cost ten times as much as the packaged ingredients. Now, in the time-starved 1990s, parents neither make the birthday cake nor even throw the party. Instead, they spend $100 or more to 'outsource' the entire event to Chuck E. Cheese's, the Discovery Zone, the Mining Company, or some other business that stages a memorable event for the kids – and often throws in the cake for free. Welcome to the emerging experience economy."*

Pine and Gilmore's (1998) assertion is that services can be built upon in order to use them as a stage for creating an experience. A traditional example of this would be a cruise ship; the basic service is moving people to holiday destinations, but the ship itself is augmented into a diversified arena in which multiple layers of experiences are staged. The evolution from selling basic commodities to staging experiences is shown in the Figure 7.2.

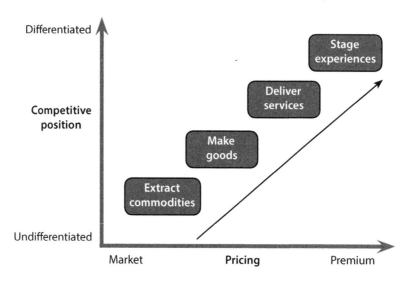

Figure 7.2: The evolution of staged experiences, adapted from Pine and Gilmore (1998)

The importance of experiences to service-based businesses has become part of the marketing lexicon in contemporary business. Particularly in the retail and in the leisure, hospitality and tourism sectors, developing an experiential element to the service delivery has been found to differentiate the product from competitors and stimulate a deeper and more profound level of engagement between customers and the brand. Van Doorn et al. (2010) found that positive experiences led customers to be more motivated to spread positive word of mouth and perhaps start fan or community pages on social media. Brakus et al. (2009) have taken this to the next level, suggesting it is possible to have a 'brand experience' as part of a range of other experiential dimensions such as feelings, fantasies and fun. This resonates with the ideas presented by Arnould and Price (1993) noted above, reflecting the emergent and personal nature of service experiences. The evolution of services delivery into experience facilitation relates closely to the content covered in Chapter 5, where we saw the changing nature of the role customers play in businesses and the more collaborative approach taken. The experience economy has been able to develop as a result of this evolutionary change in the dynamic between brand and customer.

Case study: Creating Value for the Ritz-Carlton Hotel Group

Ritz-Carlton Hotels are renowned for their level of service and the relationships they develop with their customers, who are some of the most loyal in the industry. The average customer lifetime value of a Ritz-Carlton customer is calculated to be $250,000. Several marketing processes inform the effective way in which Ritz-Carlton achieves this standard. Starting with the company's mission statement: "We are ladies and gentlemen serving ladies and gentlemen", it is apparent that the company's culture acknowledges the degree of sophistication and respect that is espoused by the employees of the company as well as their wealthy customers.

Ritz-Carlton seeks to differentiate its product through the intangible elements of service. This makes their challenge more complicated due to the difficulties in consistently delivering a service that copes with heterogeneity, perishability, and the simultaneous and intangible nature of services. One of the critical elements of their service design is that all employees have a high degree of service empowerment, meaning they are entitled to act as they see fit to either create an extra special 'wow' moment with a customer or to rescue a service encounter that has gone wrong or failed in some way. Each employee, from the laundry staff to the restaurant managers, is entitled to make a gesture to the value of $2000 without seeking any approval from their superior in an effort to ensure guest satisfaction. This means that if things go wrong then customers do not have to wait or make extra effort to seek a resolution through a manager who has elevated authority to solve the issue; the staff member who is directly involved has the authority to expedite a solution and ensure continued satisfaction. If you remember the chapter on customers, you will recognise how this process will achieve the development of a relationship-based exchange with the customer. This is important when you consider that $250,000 CLTV figure, because although $2000 seems like a lot of money, it is in fact less than 1% of the value of what that customer is worth to the business over their life time.

This is a high risk/high reward approach for the business, as it relies on the level of quality of service to be maintained across the board, and they do not focus on some of the easier, more tangible benefits of staying at Ritz-Carlton hotels such as the amazing bedrooms or the top class cuisine in the restaurants. The marketing agenda here is to focus on something they know their competitors will struggle to replicate, therefore ensuring a unique selling proposition.

The interesting thing about the achievements of Ritz-Carlton is that their satisfaction levels among guests and staff alike are industry-leading. When a new hotel was being opened in Berlin, people were queueing around the block to be considered as applicants for the hotel's staff.

Review questions

1 What are the four core characteristics of services?

2 Define a service encounter.

3 When discussing services, we can refer to the marketing mix being extended, what are the three extra Ps?

4 Name two kinds of Processing that occur in service products.

5 The SERVQUAL model identifies five service gaps – name them.

6 How much money is a Ritz-Carlton employee allowed to spend on a customer to ensure satisfaction?

Directed further reading

Alexander, M., MacLaren, A., O'Gorman, K., & White, C. (2012) Priority queues: Where social justice and equity collide. *Tourism Management,* **33**(4), 875-884.

Parasuraman, A., Zeithaml, V. A., & Berry, L. L. (1988). Servqual: A multiple-item scale for measuring consumer perc. *Journal of retailing,* **64**(1), 12.

Pine, B. J., & Gilmore, J. H. (1999) *The Experience Economy: Work is theatre & every business a stage*, Harvard Business Press.

Vargo, S. L., & Lusch, R. F. (2008). Service-dominant logic: continuing the evolution. *Journal of the Academy of marketing Science,* **36**(1), 1-10.

References

Arnould, E. J., & Price, L. L. (1993). River magic: Extraordinary experience and the extended service encounter. *Journal of Consumer Research,* **20**(1), 24-45.

Ashton, M. (2006). B2B marketing: How trusted are you? *Campaign,* October.

Bitner, M. J. (1992). Servicescapes: The impact of physical surroundings on customers and employees. *The Journal of Marketing,* **56**, 57-71.

Brakus, J. J., Schmitt, B. H., & Zarantonello, L. (2009). Brand experience: what is it? How is it measured? Does it affect loyalty? *Journal of Marketing,* **73**(3), 52-68.

Hilton, C. N. (1957). *Be My Guest*, Simon and Schuster.

Miller, J. L., Craighead, C. W., & Karwan, K. R. (2000). Service recovery: a framework and empirical investigation. *Journal of Operations Management,* **18**(4), 387-400.

Parasuraman, A., Zeithaml, V. A., & Berry, L. L. (1988). Servqual: A multiple-item scale for measuring consumer perceptions of service quality. *Journal of Retailing,* **64**(1), 12.

Patrício, L., Fisk, R. P. & e Cunha, J. F. (2008). Designing multi-interface service experiences the service experience blueprint. *Journal of Service Research,* **10**(4), 318-334.

Pine, B. J. & Gilmore, J. H. (1998). Welcome to the experience economy. *Harvard Business Review,* **76**, 97-105.

Ritzer, G. (2009). *McDonaldization: the reader*, Pine Forge Press.

Saren, M. (2015). 'Buy buy Miss American Pie' The day the consumer died. *Marketing Theory*, 565-569, doi: 10.1177/1470593115607943.

Smith, A. (1776). *An Inquiry into the Nature and Causes of the Wealth of Nations*, Edinburgh.

Solomon, M. R., Surprenant, C., Czepiel, J. A., & Gutman, E. G. (1985). A role theory perspective on dyadic interactions: the service encounter. *The Journal of Marketing,* **49**, 99-111.

Van Doorn, J., Lemon, K. N., Mittal, V., Nass, S., Pick, D., Pirner, P. & Verhoef, P. C. (2010). Customer engagement behavior: Theoretical foundations and research directions. *Journal of Service Research,* **13**(3), 253-266.

Vargo, S. L. & Lusch, R. F. (2008). Service-dominant logic: continuing the evolution. *Journal of the Academy of marketing Science,* **36**(1), 1-10.

7

8 Small Business Marketing

Elaine Collinson

"There's nothing wrong with staying small. You can do big things with a small team."

Jason Fried, Digital Entrepreneur

Introduction

This chapter discusses marketing in the context of the small firm. It begins with a look at what constitutes a small to medium sized enterprise, identifying the key characteristics and how this context impacts on the marketing function. The area of entrepreneurship is also discussed, towards an explanation of entrepreneurial marketing.

Although small firms are now almost universally regarded as a vital element of prospering economies, this view is of fairly recent origin. In the 'big is best' era from the late 1930s to the early 1970s, small firms were regarded with only peripheral interest by economists and business analysts. During this period the decline of the small business sector was seen as a sign of economic progress: "…as industrial societies matured, it was asserted, the small business sector gradually withered before the advance of the super-efficient large firms enjoying ever more increasing economies of scale" (Curran & Blackburn, 1991: 1). The evolution of the way small businesses were viewed occurred as a result of changes in the broader orientations of economic theory, especially where these changes permeated popular perceptions, as occurred following the Oil Crisis of 1972 and after the publication of popular and pioneering works, such as *Small is Beautiful* (Schumacher, 1973). This evolution was supported by a better understanding of the characteristics of small firms and reinforced by the associated decline in Europe and North America in both popular and governmental confidence in the integrity and capacity of large scale business structures to sustain growth, employment and wealth.

The last three decades have seen an expansion in the number of small firms in many advanced economies, stimulated by changes in the industrial infra-structure and the commitment of various governments to encouraging new forms of economic enterprise. Throughout the 1980s there was a widespread increase in confidence in the potential of small firms to contribute to economic regeneration, encompassed by the ideological formulation of the 'Enterprise Culture'. In the UK, interest in the small business sector essentially dates from the publication in 1971 of the report of the Committee of Inquiry on Small Firms chaired by John Bolton. The *Bolton Report* (Bolton, 1971) was the first to offer a multi-perspective assessment of the statistical profile of the small firms sector and was a significant turning point in the contemporary understanding of small businesses (Carter & Collinson, 2002).

Small and medium sized enterprises – A definition

Small to medium sized enterprises (SMEs), make up the highest proportion of firms operating in most countries across the globe. In the US there are currently over 28 million small firms, employing nearly 56 million people (Small Business Administration, 2015). In 2013 over 99% of the 4.9 million businesses in the UK were SMEs, employing 14,424,000 people. The European Commission's SME Performance Review estimates the Gross Value Added of SMEs as €473 billion or 49.8% of the UK economy (Ward & Rhodes, 2014).

In addition to the country level statistics, information relating to small firms is collected each year via the Global Entrepreneurship Monitor, now in its 17th year and analysing a total of 62 economies. It includes areas such as societal values about entrepreneurship, self-perception relating to entre-preneurship, age, gender, economic setting and an overall evaluation of total entrepreneurial activity for each country. This comprehensive study has ena-bled governments across the globe to both learn from each other and identify benchmarks for success in the area of small firm creation. (Kelley et al., 2016).

One of the issues with comparing small businesses across the globe is how these are defined. Within the UK and Europe a small firm is any business employing fewer than 250 people, whereas in the US the figure is 500. Size is also dependent on sector since a construction company employing 200 people can be considered small in the global marketplace but a hairdresser employing 200 people would be considered a significant player in the sector. In this chapter a small firm will be deemed as one employing fewer than 250 people.

SME characteristics and impact

Small firms are intrinsically different in make-up from their larger counterparts. These basic differences affect the planning process, the management structure and the way in which marketing is implemented (Carson et al., 1995; Carson & Cromie, 1989; Liu, 1995; Stokes 1995). This fluid management approach is just one of the characteristics of small firms. Key to small firm growth is the motivation of the owner manager(s) in starting the business. Many people who start their own business are driven by a desire to work independently and do something different. This issue of freedom is key to their motivation and covers all aspects of the firm such as decision making, product development, target marketing and growth. The creative industries and third sector, e.g. social enterprises, who often offer a product or service designed for a specific social need, are examples of firms where freedom plays a key role in start-up. Motivation for start-up will also impact on the following:

- Growth
- Willingness to diversify/ change
- Levels of investment
- Financial management

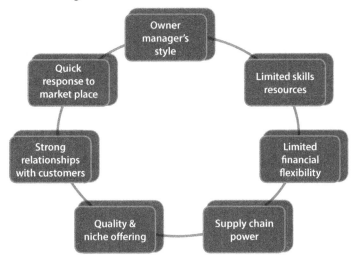

Figure 8.1: SME characteristics

In many small firms, resistance to change and fear of losing control (both financially and in decision making) result in them remaining small in size, with limited growth aspirations.

■ Owner's management style

In a small firm, decision making is clearly aligned to the owner's management style – if they are risk averse or open to taking risk, participative in their approach to management, open to new ideas etc. – all will impact on both how decisions are made and how customers are managed. With a charismatic owner manager, the focus can often be on building strong relationships with the customer base, leading to customers expecting this level of interaction even once the business has grown. This sense of closeness and strength of personal relationship between the customer and core members of the business is more difficult to retain as the business grows. Transitioning to sustained success for a business that has built its value based on these strong personal ties can be challenging.

■ Limited skills and resources - size

A key characteristic in discussing small firms is that of size, both in wealth generation, employment levels and company growth. Recent decades have seen the emergence of small IT based firms whose natural size is small, offering a bespoke and specialised service or product. Traditionally, size has often been perceived as weak but this is not the case in the niche specialised setting. Many small high tech firms are extremely profitable, often being bought by larger corporations once they achieve a certain level of growth.

Case study : Optos – improving profitability

Optos Ltd. is a small business operating in Scotland, manufacturing high end retinal imaging laser technology to support practitioners diagnosing and treating ocular pathology. The company was successful in its niche market but recognised that internal functions required improvement to increase efficiency and enhance productivity. Through a period of re-organisation they introduced a programme of change, empowering the workforce in their decision making processes, ensuring efficient warehousing of stock, improved labelling of goods and more collaborative management. The result over a 3 year period was an increase in profitability of 29% and a reduction in waste of both commodities and staff hours.

This programme of internal operations made the firm more profitable and focused on enhancing both product quality and innovation. This resulted in this small business being bought in 2016 by Nikon. Despite now being part of a larger group, the firm is still run as a self-contained business in order to maintain its creative environment.

Exercise 1

In the Optos case study above, can you identify three things the company was able to do because it was small that would have been difficult to do in a large firm?

Think about the relative costs of doing some of the things they did, and what proximity the management had to production in order to diagnose areas for improvement.

The focus on employment generation at the government level has often limited small firms who do not want to grow the business, since certain levels of funding become available to firms only once they have reached a certain size. For example, in the UK, a 'high growth firm' is identified by the government support agencies as one which has grown from zero to twenty five employees in a period of five years.

Government agencies also offer support to start-up firms who have aspirations of going global from the outset. The Start Global Programme, offered by Scottish Enterprise, provides support to new and early stage firms in the form of:

■ Workshops

■ Entrepreneurial training

■ One-to-one support

■ A market visit to explore opportunities

(See http://www.scottish-enterprise.com/services/support-for-entrepreneurs/start-global-programme/overview.)

The government support context within which small firms are launched will have a direct impact on areas such as funding for expansion, access to expertise, mentoring opportunities, access to micro credit systems and networking. The Global Entrepreneurship Monitor mentioned earlier in the chapter provides a global analysis of different support networks and its impact on total entrepreneurial activity (TEA) (Kelley et al., 2016).

■ Limited financial flexibility

One of the key characteristics of many small firms is the fact that they operate within tight financial budgets. In addition to the impact on skills resources mentioned in the previous section, this also impacts on growth potential, expansion into new markets, launching of new or improved products and long term survival. Despite small firms making up a large percentage of many economies, there is still a high failure rate in the sector, often attributable to lack of financing at the correct time. Successfully managing cash flow is crucial at all stages of growth.

Many small firms are launched when a market opportunity is identified or a creative entrepreneur takes their idea to market, often with limited funds and expertise in the area of finance. If a small firm is very successful and grows quickly in its first few years, this can often put an additional financial and managerial burden on the founders, whilst at the same time attracting competition to the emerging market.

Figure 8.2: Factors affected by firm size

■ Supply chain power

Access to both financial and skills resources is limited by a firm's size. Small firms are not likely to have personnel dedicated entirely to procurement or negotiations in the supply chain. This lack of both expertise and buying power in the supply chain can often lead to an acceptance of lower margins on sales and being controlled by larger partners in the chain.

One example of this issue is in the retail sector. In the UK the market is largely controlled by six large retailers, namely Sainsburys, Morrisons, Waitrose, M&S, Asda and Tesco, with low-cost retailers such as Aldi and Lidl making a strong impact in recent years. With the increased focus on high quality and locally produced food, the retailers source many ranges from small local producers. This is excellent for the SME, given the size and value of the order, but can often see them relinquishing a lot of their control in the process. Retailers will often dictate ingredients, volume and timing of orders.

Working with large retailers also requires small firms to be approved by the British Retail Consortium who will annually audit their processes for quality control and manufacturing processes. This level of structure and reporting is often difficult for small firms to manage and the over-reliance on large orders can place firms in a precarious position. The cost of compliance with industry standard audits can be prohibitively expensive for small firms since they do not operate on the scale where it is justifiable and thus this often prevents them from being able to grow.

Power in the supply chain can be enhanced if the small manufacturer is selling a branded product via a retailer, but if they are producing under the retailer's brand, then the control shifts. This results in a lack of freedom in both decision making and in how they wish to develop the product range, with many retailers requiring an integrated supplier relationship in order to monopolise production. Owner managers have limited freedom in this scenario, which is often different to how they perceived running their own business when they started out.

Quality and niche offering

American businessman, Steve McIntyre-Smith famously said: "Niche or be niched." A niche is a small market segment formed by a defined group of customers that share similar characteristics. From a marketing perspective, a niche is not usually well served, the competitors in the segment are limited and therefore customers' needs are not always satisfied. Niche customers have a distinctive and complete set of requirements, for which they are often willing to pay a premium price. Serving a niche implies going after high margins and attracting large shares of a specific group of customers, in order to achieve a strong market position. The process involves acquiring individual insights to truly understanding customer needs in order to build a strong reputation and deliver specialised products and services. This strategy and specialised knowledge enables firms operating in a niche setting to avoid fierce competition and create opportunities for growth (Wilson and Gilligan, 2003). When operating in niche markets, there are also associated risks, such as exposure to the niche saturation or the possibility that growth in the sector might attract larger competitors.

Many small firms operate in such niche markets, providing high quality bespoke products and services to their customers. In this type of setting, marketing activities are tailored as opposed to the standardised approach used in the mass market. They are likely to involve:

- Close and on-going communications with customers
- Flexibility in the product or service offering to suit individual needs
- One-to-one after sales support
- A relational approach to all marketing activities.

This attention to detail and close relationship with customers is also evident in the luxury market, e.g. the car industry, where Lamborghini will manufacture to order and each car will be unique to customer specifications. Customers will even be invited to watch their car rolling off the production line.

Exercise 2

Think of as many businesses as you can which have built their success on a specific niche. For example, Innocent Smoothies leveraged the niche of pre-mixed, over the counter smoothies. Once they had established their success, they branched-out into multiple other sectors and eventually were bought by the Coca Cola Company.

■ Strong customer relationships

Key to small business success is the ability to offer a bespoke service to customers. This approach ensures that customers develop loyalty to the firm, often getting to know the owner manager personally. In the early days of a business, the founder or founding team and their subsequent expertise often represent the value the business is offering – this is particularly relevant in the service industry, especially if this is an unknown or infrequently used service, such as legal advice. Customers with limited knowledge of the service they are receiving rely heavily on the expert providing advice in the area, resulting in strong personal bonds being formed with customers.

Given this closeness to customers, small firms will adopt a relational (as opposed to a transactional) approach to their marketing activities and customer interactions, with the emphasis on long term valuable relationships.

■ Highly responsive to market

Given that small firms are often close to their customers, they have accurate and up to date information on both customer needs and feedback. This enables them to identify changes in customer requirements easily and adapt their product or service offering accordingly. In turn, this responsiveness creates customer loyalty to both the product and the people in the firm.

When small firms go through a period of rapid expansion however, this closeness to the customer and ability to respond quickly to their needs, must be protected since it represents a clear competitive advantage. It is at this stage that small firms need to ensure that their marketing information systems are developed to capture this important data, so becoming less reliant on the management's ability to manage the customer base.

Marketing activities in the SME context

Inherent in the study of small firms is the idea of growth and development from the original state of a new start-up firm to that of a mature enterprise capable of creating and sustaining wealth and employment. Marketing is now an accepted and central tool in the development of small firms into mature enterprises. However, scholars have noted that for many small firms, marketing is perceived as being at best peripheral to the management function.

Carson (1993) identified two common factors which led to an underutilisation of marketing in small firms:

- They use marketing in a general, wasteful and inappropriate way, resulting in it having limited impact on performance
- They often grow without formal and planned marketing effort and as a result owner managers feel it unnecessary to invest time and effort in formal marketing planning.

In these circumstances a 'credibility gap' occurs between the satisfactory growth performance experienced by a firm and the theoretical and hypothetical performance which might occur with the use of planned marketing.

In addition, Carson (1993: 192) points out that there are major functional differences between the management decision making approaches of entrepreneurs and marketing professionals:

"Entrepreneurial decisions are inherently informal whereas marketing decisions are inherently formal; entrepreneurial decisions are haphazard, creative, opportunistic and reactive, whereas marketing decisions are sequential, systems oriented, disciplined and structured; and entrepreneurs' decision time span is short term whereas marketing time spans are both short term, medium term and long term."

If, as Carson suggests, marketing is not perceived as being a central concern of small firms, then questions must be posed in considering what types of markets they participate in and how well they perform. One of the largest studies of small firms' performance analysed over 2000 UK companies (Cambridge Small Business Centre, 1992). The size of firms included in the study ranged from fewer than 5 employees (micro enterprises) to up to 500 people (so-called 'large SMEs'). This research showed that small firms were heterogeneous, sold into a wide variety of markets and were heavily reliant on a small number of customers. This dependence is particularly apparent among the micro and very small enterprises, where nearly half of these firms relied on one customer to provide 25% or more of their sales.

This issue of a high dependency on a limited customer base is not something which has altered much in the intervening years, with the recent GEM Report also identifying this on-going issue in the sector (Kelley et al., 2016). This over reliance coupled with limited power in the supply chain demonstrates small firms' vulnerability in terms of competitive position.

The marketing /entrepreneurship interface

The marketing/entrepreneurship interface has developed a substantial body of literature over the last two decades (Collinson & Shaw, 2002; Day, 1998; Ennew & Binks, 1998; Hills & LaForge, 1992; Hultman, 1999; Stokes & Wilson, 2006). Scholars from both the world of marketing and of entrepreneurship have long identified similar concerns. This has seen the emergence of increased study in the area of overlap between the two disciplines. Academics working in this field are undertaking research in a number of key areas, namely entrepreneurial management, networking and the resource and skills implications of adopting an entrepreneurial approach to marketing activities.

Marketing has much to offer the study of entrepreneurship (Murray, 1981; Hills, 1987) and likewise entrepreneurship can look to marketing as the key function within the firm, which can encompass innovation and creativity. Omura et al. (1993) perceive the interface between the two disciplines as having distinct areas of difference and overlap. Traditional marketing operates in a consistent environment where market conditions are continuous and the firm is satisfying clearly perceived customer needs, whereas pure entrepreneurship operates in an uncertain environment, where market conditions are discontinuous and the needs of the market are as yet unclear. The diagrams in Figure 8.3 show these differences:

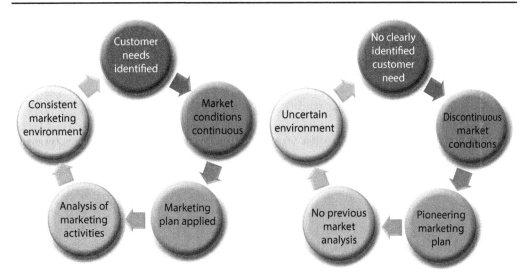

Figure 8.3: The traditional marketing (left) and pure entrepreneurial (right) approaches

The overlap between these two distinct disciplines exists in two areas:

- one where market conditions are continuous and entrepreneurship aids the process of identifying as-yet-unperceived needs

- and secondly, in a discontinuous market, where entrepreneurship guides marketing strategy to develop existing needs in a new environment.

In essence the research perceives the interface as focusing on identifying opportunities in a changing environment (Collinson & Shaw, 2000).

Marketing and entrepreneurship have three key areas of interface: they are both change-focused, opportunistic in nature and innovative in their approach to management. Carson et al. (1995) perceive the central focus of the interface as being change.

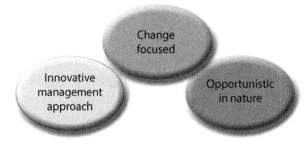

Figure 8.4: Three key areas of interface

Shane and Venkataraman's (2000: 218) description of contemporary entre-preneurship below highlights that many of the actions undertaken by the entrepreneur are key concepts in marketing theory:

8

"The study of sources of opportunities; the processes of discovery, evaluation, and exploitation of opportunities; and the set of individuals who discover, evaluate, and exploit them."

The above quote suggests that successful marketing is undertaken by firms who identify new opportunities, apply innovative techniques to bring the product / service to the marketplace and successfully meet the needs of their chosen target market. Again, the central element of managing many activities in a fluid, changing environment is stressed.

If we accept three key areas of the marketing/entrepreneurship interface as being change-focused, opportunistic in nature and innovative in management approach, this has implications for education. Specifically, this suggests that curricula are adequately developed to encourage students to learn how to deal with change, identify viable opportunities and develop their innovative skills. Equally, small firm owners require to develop their marketing knowledge and skills, in order to increase their competitiveness.

This issue of the skills or competencies required to successfully apply marketing in an entrepreneurial small firm is one of the key strands of research at the marketing/entrepreneurship interface. Carson et al. (1995) identify four key competencies associated with entrepreneurial marketing management:

Four key competencies:

- Experience of both the industry and the job

- Knowledge of the product and market

- Communication skills in being able to direct the organisation and articulate previously unclear or unknown opportunities

- Sound judgement in being able to identify good market opportunities.

These competencies should be supported by high levels of perception and intuition. Judgement is also crucial in appointing key personnel and in identifying the correct type of training/support required for the firm. These types of competencies are intangible and not easily acquired over a short period of time. The challenge facing firms attempting to adopt an entrepreneurial approach to their marketplace is how to harness and develop these competencies and ensure they are managed in a supportive environment. Traditionally, training for managers has focused on the tangible and more readily measureable competencies of knowledge, with skills such as judgement and intuition being perceived as secondary.

In the entrepreneurial small firm, a wider range of skills and competencies must be developed. This also has implications, not only in managerial training in industry, but also within higher education, where again the focus has traditionally been on acquiring the knowledge base, while what have been loosely termed 'transferable skills', have been given less importance in curriculum development. This scenario is gradually changing but awareness of the importance of this wide range of competencies is still low (Collinson and Shaw, 2000). Work experience between academia and industry, which encourage both knowledge and skills acquisition, is an important vehicle to enable change. Adopting the partnership approach suggested by Henriksen (1999) enables a greater understanding between academia and industry of each other's needs and objectives.

Entrepreneurial focus of marketing

■ Entrepreneurial culture

In discussing the area of marketing in traditionally entrepreneurial contexts, it must be recognised that it is not something which applies only in the small firm scenario. As can be appreciated from the description of an entrepreneur given earlier by Shane and Venkataraman (2000), entrepreneurship is an area which is relevant to both large and small firms. The reasons why it is so often associated with SMEs are: first, entrepreneurial activity is often more visible in the smaller firm; and second, when firms experience growth, it can be difficult to sustain an entrepreneurial focus in a multi-layered more corporate structure.

Researchers at the interface have attempted to ascertain changes in entrepreneurial activity over a firm's life cycle by measuring the entrepreneurial effort in marketing activities coupled with the entrepreneurial scenario faced by the firm.

The term *entrepreneurial effort* encompasses a number of characteristics exhibited by the entrepreneur or management team, namely:

- Zeal
- Commitment
- Determination
- Persistence
- Opportunity
- Focus

The term *entrepreneurial scenario* is characterised by:

■ The perceived level of risk facing the firm

■ The available resources

■ The individual's need for skills, knowledge, experience and personal independence.

In combining these two sets of factors the return on entrepreneurial effort can be ascertained. This reflects the degree to which the venture develops and grows over time as a consequence of the entrepreneur's efforts and changing circumstances (Carson et al., 1995). One of the key problems facing small firms is that as they grow it can be increasingly difficult to maintain the same level of entrepreneurial effort as was expended in the initial stage of the firm's life. In addition to this barrier, it is the natural tendency to veer towards activities that reduce levels of risk and consolidate the firm's position.

■ Networking: An entrepreneurial marketing tool for small firms

The networks within which entrepreneurs and their organisations are embedded play an important role in marketing, providing access to accurate information and advice used in marketing decisions. One reason why these networks contribute to the marketing effectiveness of entrepreneurial organisations is that when lacking market information and knowledge, they make use of their personal contact networks to provide them with the required support (Shaw, 1998). A second reason relates to the restricted time and resources which small firms have available to them. For many entrepreneurs, the conversations they have with people on a regular basis while running their business constitute the market scanning that they use to stay informed of changes in the marketplace.

Related to this is that the information provided to entrepreneurs from their networks is trustworthy, reliable and acted upon. An important reason for this is that the individuals providing this information and advice have been found to share more than an instrumental relationship with the entrepreneur and their business. More commonly, they also share friendship and trust, which enables entrepreneurs to make quick market decisions, without the need to validate the information received.

Whilst many small firms do not conform to the marketing strategies of their larger counterparts, research has found networks contribute to the product, pricing and promotional decisions taken by entrepreneurs. Once demand for a product or service is established, research has shown that by fostering relationships with customers, products can be continually reviewed and modified to ensure that they consistently meet the market needs (Collinson & Shaw, 2002).

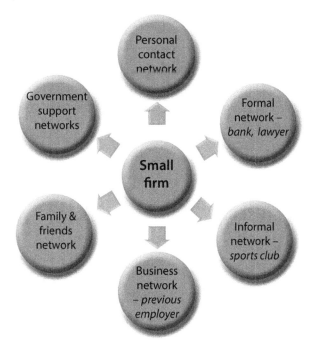

Figure 8.5: Small firm networks

Conclusion

Understanding the small firm sector is crucial for governments across the globe. These types of businesses count for high levels of both employment and wealth generation, support innovation and are the backbone of both developed and developing economies.

Small firms undertake marketing activities in a different context to larger organisations, often resulting in a more fluid approach to management – this does not however mean that it is less effective. Many small firms are often entrepreneurial in their outlook and opportunity focused, resulting in their marketing planning process seeming less rigorous and less sequential than traditional marketing plans. When a firm is large and has established a sustainable and consolidated market position it becomes easier to quantify and forecast the return on investing in structured, planned and strategically orientated marketing, making that investment justifiable and predictable.

In the context of SMEs, businesses have not necessarily reached a point of market consolidation and sustainability and therefore may not yet have the means of justifying significant spend on formal and structured marketing operations. This makes marketing activities in SMEs more budget-sensitive and often less clearly identifiable as marketing rather than something else, such as individual networking, personal relationship building, opportunity seeking or experimentation. This chapter will have helped you identify some of the characteristics of small business marketing and how this is intermeshed with many of the other pressures and forces at play when businesses are on a journey of growth and change.

Review questions

1 Why is it important to understand the small firm sector?

2 Why is networking important for small firms?

3 What is Entrepreneurial Marketing?

4 What are the main characteristics of small firms?

5 How does the small firm context impact the ways in which marketing is conducted?

6 What are the key competencies required to successfully run an entrepreneurial firm?

Case study: Arran Aromatics – A growth focused business

Arran Aromatics is a small business based on the island of Arran off Scotland's west coast. It started life in 1989 as a cottage based firm, operating from the kitchen of the founders Janet and Iain Russell. The business remains a family concern over 25 years later, with Andrew Russell, son of the founders, as Director of Branding. The initial product range consisted of soaps and body creams, infused with original fragrances inspired by the landscape and natural produce of the island.

The business grew quickly in the early years, expanding into the perfume and luxury candle sectors. Retail outlets opened and ranges expanded extensively over the next 20 years. The company branched out into the boutique hotel sector, supplying the Hotel du Vin and Malmaison chains. They also introduced a baby range in 2003. In 2016 the company had retail outlets across Scotland, an online store, a visitor centre, three manufacturing sites and a growing presence in Asia.

This small firm of 120 people has had a challenging development, receiving substantial support from Highlands & Islands Enterprise in the form of financial rescue packages, government subsidised training, manufacturing assistance and executive training. There are many restrictions that being an island based business creates; as a small community there is a lack of technical expertise and staying true to the company's heritage and community values means logistical compromises need to be made since Arran is linked to the mainland only by sea.

In 2015 they undertook a radical rebranding strategy to rationalise their range of products, refocusing a brand which had lost its core identity. In addition to this they closed a number of key stores, placing more focus on the on-line market and their presence in Asia. New CEO, Jacqui Gale, brought extensive experience in the retail sector to the business and has enhanced their networks while introducing a more strategic focus to their planning approach.

From a managerial perspective, a key challenge has been in people management and in introducing more rigorous control mechanisms into a small family run business. Given the recent changes and a focus on high growth over the next five years, a key focus is ensuring the clear communication of development plans across the business.

Since starting in 2015, the new CEO has restructured the board and the reporting systems within the business, undertaken a rebranding project, introduced training to enable a more retail focused culture and rationalised working conditions to improve efficiencies.

This small firm experienced high growth in its early years and was on the brink of bankruptcy due to poor financial management. Thanks to government support, it has survived and is now in the process of embedding structured management systems to support future growth. Nevertheless, this is a key example of how, even with a popular product range and a loyal customer base, success cannot be guaranteed.

References

Bolton, J. (1971) *Report on the Committee of Enquiry on Small Firms*, London: HMSO

Cambridge Small Business Centre (1992) *The State of British Enterprise*, Department of Applied Economics, University of Cambridge

Carson, D. (1993) A philosophy for marketing education in small firms, *Journal of Marketing Management*, **9**, 189-204

Carson, D., Cromie, S., McGowan, P. and Hill, J. (1995) *Marketing and Entrepreneurship in SMEs, An Innovative Approach,* Prentice Hall.

Carson, D. & Cromie, S. (1989) Marketing planning in small enterprises: A model and some empirical evidence, *Journal of Marketing Management,* **5**(1), 33-49.

Carter, S. & Collinson, E. (2002) Small business marketing, in the *International Encyclopedia of Business and Management,* International Thomson Business Press.

Collinson, E. and Shaw, E. (2000) Entrepreneurial marketing, in the *International Encyclopedia of Business and Management,* International Thomson Business Press.

Collinson, E. & Shaw, E. (2001) Entrepreneurial marketing – a historical perspective on development and practice, *Management Decision,* **39** (9), 761-766

Curran, J. & Blackburn, (1991) *Paths of Enterprise: The Future of the Small Business,* London: Routledge

Day, J. (1998) Defining the interface: A useful framework, in *Proceedings of the Academy of Marketing Symposia on the Marketing and Entrepreneurship Interface: 1996 – 1998,* Hulbert, Day and Shaw (Eds.), Northampton, Nene University College.

Ennew, C.T. and Binks, M.R. (1998) Marketing and entrepreneurship: Some contextual issues, in *Proceedings of the Academy of marketing Symposia on the Marketing and Entrepreneurship Interface: 1996 – 1998,* Hulbert, Day and Shaw (Eds.), Northampton, Nene University College.

Henriksen, L. (1999) Small firms and economic development : Research, Policy and Practice, *Journal of Small Business and Enterprise Development,* **6** (3), 215 – 219.

Hills, G.E. (1987), Marketing and entrepreneurship research issues : Scholarly justification, in *Research at the Marketing/Entrepreneurship Interface,* Gerald E. Hills (Ed.), University of Illinois at Chicago, pp. 3-15.

Hills, G.E. and LaForge, R.W. (1992) Research at the marketing interface to advance entrepreneurship theory, *Entrepreneurship, Theory and Practice,* **16** (3), 33 – 59.

Hultman, C.M. (1999) Nordic perspectives on marketing and research in the marketing/entrepreneurship interface, *Journal of Research in Marketing and Entrepreneurship,* **1** (1), 54-71.

Kelley, D., Singer, S. & Herrington, M. (2016) Global Entrepreneurship Monitor 2015/2016, 5th February, http://www.gemconsortium.org/report/49480

Liu, H. (1995) Market orientation and firm size: An empirical examination in UK firms, *European Journal of Marketing,* **9**(1), 57-71.

Murray, J. (1981) Marketing is home for the entrepreneurial process, *Industrial Marketing Management,* **10**, 93-9

Omura, G. S., Calantone, R.J. & Schmidt, J.B. (1993) Entrepreneurism as a market satisfying mechanism in a free market system, in G.E. Hills et al. *Research at the Marketing Entrepreneurship Interface,* Chicago, University of Illinois, pp.161-171.

Schumacher, (1973) *Small is Beautiful*, London: Abacus.

Shane, S., & Venkataraman, S. (2000) The promise of entrepreneurship as a field of research. *Academy of Management Review*, **25** (1), 217-226.

Shaw, E. (1998) Social networks: their impact on the innovative behaviour of small service firms, *International Journal of innovation Management*, Special Issue, 201-222

Small Business Administration (2015) *Small Business Profile*, SBA, Office of Advocacy

Stokes, D. (1995) *Small Business Management: An Active Learning Approach*, 2nd ed. London: DP Publications.

Stokes, D. & Wilson N. (2006) *Small Business Management and Entrepreneurship* 5th ed., Thomson Learning.

Ward, M. & Rhodes, C. (2014) *Small Businesses and the UK Economy*, House of Commons standard Note: SN/EP/6078, Section - Economics Policy & Statistics, 9th December.

Wilson, D. & Gilligan, R. (2003) *Strategic Planning*, Butterworth Heinemann.

8

9 Networks

Lindsay Stringfellow

"Networking is marketing. Marketing yourself, marketing your uniqueness, marketing what you stand for"

Christine Comaford-Lynch

We are all familiar with the adage "it's not what you know but who you know", and the principle that many people get ahead and find opportunities through their network of contacts. A typical way in which we successfully secure our first job, and perform well in our career will often depend on networking. Successful networking is not about the superficial exchange of business cards and the ability to blow your own trumpet, but is about how we relate to other people and build trust. In business-to-business deals, this type of marketing as networking is critical but is often hidden from view. We will uncover the role that network principles and networking play in business contexts in this chapter.

When your clients are not consumers

Most marketing concepts and examples that we see discussed in the chapters in textbooks tend to be consumer-focused. As we are all consumers, we readily identify with the strategies and tactics of marketers which relate to the influences that we experience in our day-to-day lives. However, for every business to consumer (B2C) cycle of 'market, sell and serve' there are multiple cycles of 'produce, distribute, retail and serve' in business to business (B2B) (McDonald, 2014). The total value of transactions involved in B2B activities of manufacturing, logistics, purchasing and distribution dwarfs B2C. B2B marketing refers to the marketing of all goods and services that are not for personal consumption, including channels of distribution. In the following section we briefly review some of the traditional characteristics associated with business markets and buying processes before outlining more recent discussion about the broader contribution of the network perspective of value creation in B2B scholarship.

■ Characteristics of the business vs the consumer market

There are many similarities between the business and consumer market in terms of marketing activities and the challenges that are faced. Market research, environmental scanning, segmentation, targeting and positioning, gauging your value proposition and communicating your offering are all activities which have to happen in both B2B and B2C transactions. However, there are particular characteristics that are commonly seen as differentiating business or organisational markets from consumer markets, which are summarised in Table 9.1:

Buyers	Typically **large buyers** and multiple needs to satisfy **Geographic concentration** is often greater Number of consumers is typically **much smaller**
Demand	Often **derived demand** (from consumer demand) Total demand is often **inelastic** Greater **fluctuations** in demand
Selling	Often purchases are made **direct** rather than through intermediaries **Longer sales process** given the larger transactions

Table 9.1: Typical features of business markets

The typical features listed above should also be considered alongside different situations business buyers find themselves in. These can vary in complexity in the same way as consumer purchasing decisions can. In general they are characterised as falling into three different groups:

1 **Straight rebuy:** typically a simple decision involving items that have been purchased before and are purchased frequently, such as office supplies.

2 **Modified rebuy:** this occurs when buyers might want something different, or see an opportunity to review their suppliers and find someone offering better terms in delivery/price/quality etc.

3 **New task:** this refers to purchases that are a one-off or being made for the first time. This type of purchase will involve the most uncertainty and risk, and will therefore take the most time and effort.

■ Buying process and procurement

The main difference in B2B is that professional buyers often carry out this activity in business markets. Just as it is important that we take into account the consumer's 'black box' and understand their internal influences and decision-making processes, we also need to understand what motivates key individuals such as a purchasing manager. There may also be multiple people participating in the decision process, in what is referred to as a buying centre, consisting of various people from across the organisation, each of whom have expertise or a vested interest in the purchase. It is most likely that a buying centre will be involved in new task buying situations as opposed to straight or modified rebuys.

The primary roles of the buying centre are featured in Table 9.2:

Role	Responsibility
Initiator	First recognises the need to buy a particular product or service to solve a problem.
User	Consumes or uses the end product or service.
Influencer	Their views and expertise influences the decision that is made.
Decider	Ultimately makes the final purchasing decision
Gatekeeper	Controls information flows and access to Influencers and Deciders
Buyer	Has the formal authority to execute the purchase decision and agree conditions

Table 9.2: Roles in the buying centre

9

The buying centre will typically consist of several people with differing interests, motivations, persuasiveness and position in the organisational hierarchy. Within this, individuals may assume one or multiple roles. For example, when buying new tables and chairs for a restaurant, a range of people might have a vested interest in the solution that is reached; some may favour style and design, others the affordability and longevity of the product, and for others, how many of a given design can feasibly fit into the restaurant and increase revenue. Ultimately, key individuals will make a choice based on their personal needs and preferences, meaning that B2B decisions often involve both rational and emotional elements in finding the right solution. B2B marketers need to think about targeting various individuals in the buying centre, researching what decision-making criteria they use, determining who is likely to be most influential and finding out how to overcome potential barriers. Ultimately, marketers need to try to understand the social dynamics, personal ties and interpersonal factors that will influence the decision. They need to get information and access to the network, win the business, and then carefully foster a relationship of mutual trust. These are some of the basic principles of networking we explore further on in the chapter.

■ B2B and beyond

Vargo and Lusch (2011) comment that the discipline of B2B or 'industrial' marketing really emerged as a consequence of the broader inadequacies of mainstream marketing, particularly in terms of the notion that one party produces value whilst another consumes it. This connects with their earlier influential work exploring the service-dominant (S-D) logic of marketing, which sees all parties engaged in exchange as service-providing, value-creating enterprises. In this sense, Vargo and Lusch (2011) propose that all exchange can be considered B2B.

These authors critique some of the characteristic differences from consumer marketing discussed above, and instead see B2B scholarship as making wider contributions towards our understanding of mainstream marketing. This emerges from the economic-actor-to-economic-actor focus (rather than producer to consumer), and the stronger focus B2B has on interactivity, relationships and networks. The extended network of actors such as suppliers, distributors, professional service firms and utility providers (as well as consumers) described at the beginning of this section form part of a resource network, which helps us to better understand value creation and context. In line with S-D logic, the theory of the market is thus "… one of value co-creation through mutual service provision, made possible by resource integration" (Vargo and Lusch, 2011: 186) within a service ecosystem. The foundational concepts on relationship marketing have been covered elsewhere in this textbook, and therefore in the next sections, we are going to focus specifically on the theory and understanding of networks and the 'social' as a resource.

Social capital and social network theory

In today's world, the term 'social network' is most often associated with online social networks facilitated through social media platforms such as Facebook. This contemporary form of connectivity represents one of the more visible means through which we can understand our lives, and the opportunities that might be available to us, through mapping out the various ties that we hold with our family, friends, colleagues, co-workers, school friends, and so on. In this section, we introduce some of the key theories, debates and associated concepts related to social capital, and outline the basics of social network analysis. To bring this into context, in the final section of the chapter we apply networking principles to help us understand how marketing works in professional service firms.

■ The development of social capital theory

Strange as it might seem, the idea that economic relations are embedded in social networks, rather than in an abstract idealised market, has only surfaced relatively recently. Work by social anthropologists and sociologists such as John Barnes (1954) and Mark Granovetter (1973) paved the way for researchers in a wide variety of disciplines to better understand the precise role that social relations play in understanding social behaviour. From our perspective, we can better understand how relational ties can provide marketing benefits, such as identifying new business opportunities, or entrepreneurial access to resources such as finance. In the section below, we briefly review some of the developments in social capital theory that have been particularly influential in business research.

Granovetter's (1973) research, in particular, has been highly influential, with his paper 'The Strength of Weak Ties' currently enjoying the status of the most cited work in the social sciences. Based on a large-scale survey of job seekers in the US, he found that the majority had found a job through a contact that they saw only occasionally or rarely, and are therefore classified as 'weak' ties. This finding contrasted with many people's perceptions that dense connections to strong ties, such as family and close friends, would be more likely to lead to success in finding work. Theories of network structure (explored in the next section) can help to explain the role of weak ties, in particular the concept of bridging ties, which refers to the role that some ties play in spanning and connecting otherwise disconnected groups within a network, thereby providing a source of unique information and resources. Strong ties by contrast tend to provide mostly redundant information. This also makes sense if we think about this in terms of social media and the transmission of information, as the more diverse and unconnected our network is, the more likely we are to find out a broader range of information related to, for example, what's happening at the weekend.

9

Exercise 1

Think about your own networks – e.g. personal, professional, social, academic. Within these networks, which ties would you classify as weak, and which ties would you classify as strong? Which do you think would be most useful for developing an opportunity for a summer internship? How would you use your networks to create such an opportunity?

Other researchers have, however, been sceptical of Granovetter's findings. James S. Coleman, another American sociologist, found that 'social capital' comes from smaller, denser networks of strong ties. He views social capital as resources that are bound up with family and community relations. It is these closer ties that bond actors together and lead to benefits such as trust, cooperation, group solidarity and the observance of norms (Coleman, 1988). There is also a related argument that can be made about the overall size of a network an individual can realistically maintain. The cost of maintaining linkages may increase as networks become larger and more complex, and therefore there may be upper limits of network size. Going back to the social media example, an individual might have a huge number of 'friends', but how many can be a real connection? If they are not a considered a real friend, perhaps they will miss out on key information as they only see a limited profile, or they are not invited to closed event.

Coleman (1988) also argued that individuals possess human and physical capital, in addition to social capital, and that certain obligations and expectations of reciprocity may be created which lead to the creation and exchange of these different forms. This notion of convertibility was also at the centre of French sociologist Pierre Bourdieu's (1986) description of overlapping forms of capital, which he proposes account for the structure and functioning of the social world. Bourdieu (1986) describes three primary forms of capital as:

1 Economic, the most material form of capital, including money and private property;

2 Cultural, which can exist in the form of knowledge, skills and disposition, in cultural goods, and in more formalised forms such as educational qualifications; and

3 Social, the aggregate of actual or potential resources which are linked to the network of relationships an individual holds.

To determine the rates of conversion and values of different forms of capital, Bourdieu (1986) introduces the concept of symbolic capital. Symbolic capital generates resources on the basis of honour, prestige or recognition:

a person is valued in a particular culture or situation, and the resources they possess are recognised as legitimate (Bourdieu, 1989). An influential vlogger who acquires more followers on the basis of the specific knowledge they possess (cultural capital converted to social capital), may then attract a company to sponsor them or send them complimentary products (social capital converted to economic capital). Their endorsement of that company or product will potentially legitimise it in the eyes of their followers, because of the symbolic capital or 'credit of renown' they possess.

Social network analysis and social capital

Whilst specific definitions of social capital vary, there is some general agreement that it is a "metaphor in which social structure is a kind of capital that can create for certain individuals or groups a competitive advantage in pursuing their ends. Better connected people enjoy higher returns" (Burt, 2000: 348). Ronald Burt, another key figure in the development of social capital and social network theory, argues that it is network mechanisms that define what it means to have more social capital, or to be 'better connected'. Here we turn to social network analysis, which refers to the mapping out and measuring of relationships and flows between actors, organisations, groups, etc.

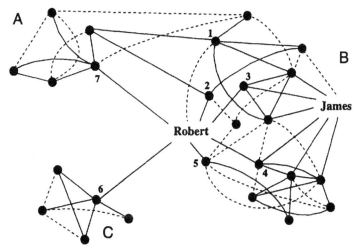

Density Table of Relations Within and Between Groups			
.65			Group A (5 people and 8 ties; 5 strong, 3 weak)
.05	.25		Group B (17 people and 41 ties; 27 strong, 14 weak)
.00	.01	.65	Group C (5 people and 8 ties; 5 strong, 3 weak)

Figure 9.1: Illustration of a social network (from Burt, 2000:349)

Figure 9.1 is an illustration of a network, where the dots are nodes in the network, indicating people. Relations between people are lines, with solid lines connecting pairs of people who have a strong relationship, and dashed lines indicating a weak tie.

Exercise 2

If we focus on the two individuals shown in Figure 9.1, Robert and James, as business owners operating in, say, the fashion retail industry, which of them do you think is in the best position according to their ties?

Robert and James have the same number of connections, six strong ties and one weak, but Burt (2000) argues that Robert has a better position than James for a number of reasons. He has the same ties within group B, but also has a strong relationship with contacts 6 and 7 which can provide information on groups B and C. If we imagine contact 6 was a friend working in the fashion industry, and contact 7 was a family relation working in China sourcing materials and producing garments for export. These relationships are network bridges that allow Robert access to groups A (a Chinese supply chain) and C (the fashion industry) which can benefit Robert by offering him privileged access to useful information on fashion trends, and the potential for faster or cheaper production of new clothing lines. If that relationship is broken, then there is no relationship between groups B and C, and more generally, this makes Robert a broker in the network.

Burt proposes that you should look for the weaker connections, which are holes in the social structure of the market, and "structural holes create a competitive advantage for an individual who spans the holes" (2000: 353). Some of the benefits that flow from Robert's bridge connections to other groups relate to information access, with a higher volume of, and less redundant bits of information. He can spread information and thus can potentially be seen as an opinion leader or innovator. His diverse contacts make him likely to be viewed as a more influential figure and therefore people are more likely to include him in new opportunities and ideas. Finally, Burt (2000) proposes that there are control advantages to his position; he can bring together otherwise disconnected individuals and groups, and decide on the terms of the relationships, brokering information and maintaining his own identity with different groups. It is these benefits that have led to a rapid growth in research attempting to understand the social networks of successful entrepreneurs, which is also discussed in Chapter 8. A subtle difference from the weak ties argument is that Burt proposes that strong ties (or network closure) can be important to realising the value offered by brokerage (Burt, 2001).

Table 9.3 illustrates some of the key properties and characteristics that are associated with social network analysis.

A. Transactional content and outcomes
- Expression of affect
- Influence, control and power
- Exchange of information
- Exchange of goods or services
- Solidarity

B. Relational nature of the links
- Intensity: The strength of the relation between individuals
- Reciprocity: The degree to which there is mutual benefit or symmetry in the relations
- Clarity of Expectations: The degree to which there are clearly defined expectations of behaviour
- Multiplexity: The degree to which individuals are linked by multiple relations
- Frequency: The frequency of interaction between ties
- Durability: The degree to which ties persist over time
- Content: The meanings which people attribute to their relationships e.g. kinship, friendship
- Ties' Strength: The total combination of factors such as intensity, frequency and reciprocity that characterise ties

C. Structural terms and characteristics
- Size: Total number of individuals participating in the network
- Density (Connectedness): Number of actual links as a ratio of the number of possible links
- Clustering: The number of dense regions in a network
- Stability: The degree to which a network pattern changes over time
- Reachability: The extent to which network members can contact each other (number of steps)
- Centrality: A measure of how many connections one node has to other nodes
- Bridge: A social tie that connects two groups
- Range: Number of connections combined with the social heterogeneity of ties
- Structural hole: A gap between individuals with access to complementary sources of information
- Broker: An individual who maintains ties with disconnected groups

Table 9.3: Key network concepts (adapted from Adler & Kwon, 2002; Burt, 2000; Tichy et al., 1979)

In general, we can conceptualise social networks and social capital in three broad areas. Section A refers to what is exchanged, such as information, goods and services, or the possible outcomes of social capital, which could be influence, power and solidarity with a cluster of connections. Determining what is exchanged or what resources can be accessed from a network will be related to that network's relational and structural characteristics. Section B refers to the relational nature of links in terms of elements such as frequency, intensity and reciprocity, which help researchers to understand the strength of the tie. Section C outlines key structural sources of social capital, from which researchers use measurements such as total network size, density, clustering and centrality as ways to quantitatively determine the potential opportunity within the formal network structure. There continues to be much debate between researchers over the relative benefits of structural opportunities, which may relate to features such as size and structural holes, and the benefits associated with embeddedness within closer, more trusting relationships.

Professional service firms and networking

The service sector in general has been at the heart of economic growth in the UK in recent years, and according to the Office for National Statistics, in 2016 it accounted for around 80 per cent of the economy. Following the financial crisis of 2008, the financial services sector has shrunk by around 10 per cent, but this has been off set by an increase of 25 per cent in IT and professional services, which include sectors such as accounting, architecture, law and management consultancy (Cadman, 2016). Reflecting back on our previous discussion of the convertability of different forms of capital, 'professionalisation' can be seen as the translation of one scarce resource (specialist knowledge and skills) into social, economic and symbolic rewards (MacDonald, 1995). From a marketing perspective, they are not typically seen as relying on mainstream marketing activities such as advertising and marketing research. Instead, marketing efforts are often connected with the network of relationships a professional or professional firm maintains, and aspects of how they interact with clients in professional engagements, which can help them to build trust and loyalty, and gain referrals for new business. In this final section, we explore some key elements that characterise professional services firms (PSFs), as well as the particular role that networking can play in how they market themselves and grow.

■ Key characteristics of PSFs

■ **Knowledge**: One of the defining features of PSFs is the important role played by knowledge and skills. Often professionals have advanced degrees and credentials, as well as tacit skills that enable professional service personnel to customise complex knowledge to meet client needs. Professional services transfer esoteric expertise which may be beyond the understanding of clients.

■ **Reputation**: Assessing a firm's competence relative to other suppliers is problematic and consumers are often obliged to use 'social proofs' of competence such as reputation or status. Reputation provides a number of key benefits, including the ability to attract the best staff and clients, increase loyalty, and enable a price premium to be charged. Although brands are often studied in the context of consumer goods, strong brands also serve as an important cue for quality for the clients of professional services.

■ **Social interaction**: For PSFs, satisfaction, loyalty and positive word of mouth are of key importance and they result from a combination of technical and functional (social) quality (Grönroos, 1982). Clients might not be able to judge the technical quality and will therefore often use functional quality based on, for example, courtesy, communication and understanding. Managing the functional or social quality of the service is particularly important for retention and loyalty. Loyalty has been shown to be particularly important for the performance of professional service firms given the high transaction costs associated with new clients.

■ **Trust**: Professionals are perceived to have a strong ability to create and maintain trust as a result of their primary commitment to the client (Laing and Lian, 2005). Trust has a pivotal role to play given the complexity, risk and uncertainty inherent in professional service delivery (Hart and Hogg, 1998). The clients of professional service firms need to feel sure the organisation or individual will perform services to the standards required, and it is also important for the profession to uphold standards and confidence in its activities to a wide community of stakeholders, such as the government.

■ Networking and marketing in PSFs

We can see from the discussion above that the maintenance of long term stable relationships is important for client and employee ties, as well as relationships with other organisations. Professional services encounters are likely to have more frequent and repeated one-on-one interactions between the client and provider, and exchange is more intimate. Networking and word of mouth are therefore viewed as important for building a positive reputation, generating referrals and enhancing performance in small professional service firms, particularly as they may lack the resources to undertake more formal marketing activities (Silversides, 2001).

Knowledge about the market, customers and competitors enables professionals to deliver value to their clients. Present and former clients are seen as important for enhancing (or degrading) the image of the professional service firm, as are former and current employees. However, the relationships between professionals and their clients have been changing in recent years. Many clients have become larger enterprises with managerial structures that treat professional services like any other commodity and will therefore switch providers more readily (Hart and Hogg, 1998). Clients have higher expectations: they are more educated and attuned to the concept of value; and clients often use information technology to compare providers, leading to a growth in price-based competition (Reid, 2008). While differentiation can be achieved through relationship quality, client retention is associated with escalating costs and diminishing returns.

Most professional service firms are built through referrals based on trust. There are a number of ways that professionals use networking to build trust, and also to market themselves and their businesses. Thought leadership refers to the publication and dissemination of ideas for commercial advantage. For example, many consulting firms make their forecasts and industry reports publicly available, and solicitors may publish white papers or blog on a particular client issue or technical area. The purpose of this is to demonstrate their expertise in a particular area. Giving out this kind of information also acts as collateral, which can be important for first time buyers – i.e. access to these extra materials reduces the perceived risk for clients. Social media platforms such as LinkedIn are another way in which network linkages can be fostered with clients and other professionals, as well as for information sharing, as discussed in the case study below:

Case study: LinkedIn and Law Firm Web Marketing

LinkedIn has emerged as one of the most successful social networking sites for business professionals. The facilitation of referrals and interaction with like-minded individuals has made LinkedIn a valuable tool, particularly for lawyers.

Recent studies have indicated that about 2/3 of legal corporate counsels use LinkedIn for marketing purposes. Additionally, executives of all industries and professions are using LinkedIn to explore new avenues and expand their business.

To help professionals establish a valuable LinkedIn presence and attain better cases, the following advice is given.

- Develop relationships with the referral sources.
- Network with potential clients.
- Build relations with members of the media.
- Showcase your practice more personally.
- Bolster relationships with existing clients.
- Broaden your network for expert witnesses.

Source:http://www.law-firm-web-marketing.com/tag/linkedin

Trust is integral to professional service firms and many authors who write about professional services marketing focus on what trust is, and how it can be nurtured. Maister et al. (1993) point to three skills of a trusted advisor, which are: (1) earning trust, through being reliable and sincere, listening and speaking truthfully; (2) giving effective advice that is customized, helpful and deals with the sensitivities, emotions and politics of the situation; and (3) building relationships through being understanding, thoughtful, considerate, sensitive to feelings and supportive. Trustworthiness depends on a combination of relational resources, including being reliable and credible, as well as having a degree of intimacy, meaning you are willing to expand the bounds of acceptable topics whilst maintaining mutual respect and boundaries. An aspect of trustworthiness which professionals must also think about is self-orientation. Instead of desiring to 'look intelligent' or 'to be seen to be right', professionals should listen carefully to clients to find out what's behind a problem. Building trust is important for retaining clients, fostering loyalty, cross-selling services and gaining referrals for new business.

Based on the knowledge that certain clients will give a stream of business to a supplier whereas others will not, most professional firms engage in client account management. This involves spending time identifying and defining the important clients/accounts for the business, which may be based on profit potential, targeting an industry sector or for prestige, a so-called a 'strategic account' that is pursued to signal reputation. The principles of CRM discussed in Chapter 5 are key to the process of account management and the idea that spending time to develop relationships with existing clients can help to foster success.

■   Academic research insight

We conducted research with small accounting practices in Scotland (Stringfellow et al., 2014, 2015) and uncovered further evidence regarding the role that networking plays in the business development and performance of professional service firms. Below we highlight some key findings with quotes from our respondents:

Structural factors

Homophily, meaning love of the same, highlights the network phenomenon that 'birds of a feather flock together'. Naturally people like to network with people that are similar to themselves along status and value dimensions:

> *There is probably a lot of generational thing there, in that people feel more comfortable with people of their own vintage. I think a lot of it is being able to have a conversation, whereas with a different generation it can be slightly different. You might be a bit more reserved and might not really understand what they're looking for.*
>
> Partner in Glasgow accounting firm

Homophily can also lead to problems, for instance, some respondents were caught out by the age of their client base and experienced succession issues. They could also find it hard to attract 'entrepreneurial new starts' because they "looked old and were not able to field thirty year old practicing accountants like PriceWaterhouseCoopers could". Value homophily was also important give the role of ethics in professional service firms. The importance of 'good quality clients' often came up and suggested characteristics of good quality clients would be: established businesses that know what they were doing; businesses that are responsive and appreciative of customer care rather than being price sensitive; and clients that are trustworthy and not simply trying to pay too little tax.

Reachability was also important. Clients who are smaller businesses, in particular, typically seek industry specialisations, value direct contact and accessibility to the firm's partners and will often value local reputation:

"... a lot of clients were attracted to the fact that they have direct contact with us.... quite a lot of our clients actually like the confidentiality and being able to pick up the phone and speak to us directly."

Partner in Edinburgh accounting firm

It is also the case that clients who are larger businesses tend to seek size and prestige. From a marketing perspective, Big Four firms such as KPMG and Ernst & Young (EY) can rely on a stronger brand, a larger and more specialised workforce, and greater reputation with financial institutions such as banks, which trust their size and financial clout.

Relational factors

In social network theory, generally as ties become stronger, more content is shared so that having begun as a business exchange, it may be reciprocated in further exchanges and eventually evolve to contain social or friendship aspects. In accounting firms, this can present problems:

"Your friends are not your clients. You have to remember that. Because you can be put in a very difficult situation, if that person's not declared income that you know about, you have to report it, and if you're friends with them, you might think twice. I don't go out w ith any of my clients. I don't see my clients socially, I think that's what I'm saying."

Partner in Edinburgh accounting firm

Professional ethics can therefore impact on the degree to which clients become friends and accountants were even more adverse to friends becoming clients. This reflects the importance of ethical standards for the reputation of the professional and the profession as a whole.

Trust was seen as fundamental to client relationships:

"A lot of what we do is about trust. I mean, people don't want to be going over the fine detail: they want to just say that he'll do this and it goes back to that. It's about comfort and peace of mind."

Partner in Glasgow accounting firm

Lack of knowledge and trust of new clients also presented a significant risk for professionals, given the potential risk that clients might mislead the professional to cover up their activity, e.g. to avoid paying tax.

Building trust was vital to client relationships, and to gaining access to referrals to new clients. However, in the wider business context, accountants often found it hard to get introductions and referrals from other businesses.

Unlike other business situations in which there is an element of quid pro quo, reciprocity and referrals were not always evident:

"Strangely enough with introductions and referrals it tends to be a one-way street. It used to be, if you knew bank managers, you could introduce new clients to the bank manager if they were looking for business and bank managers could similarly reciprocate… it tends to be more often than not a one-way street."

Partner in Perth accounting firm

Reciprocity was further hindered by the fact that it not generally seen as appropriate for professionals to reward clients or accept gifts from them due to their professional code of conduct.

What we can see from the above discussion is that networking is important to how professionals market themselves and their businesses. Accountants accept that networking is an increasingly important business activity:

"Historically things have changed as well. In the seventies if you got a client they would probably be a client for life but nowadays you get a client and you only expect them to stay with you for five or six years. You always have to keep trying to get new clients because the ones you've got will drop off, not because they fell out with you but that's just life now."

Partner in Glasgow accounting firm

"Being seen networking… If you're wanting new business you have to get out there. I think you do have to go along to things, you have to attend things and be seen to be proactive."

Partner in Edinburgh accounting firm

However, what we can also identify is that the structural and relational features of networking will vary from industry to industry and in different contexts. In larger firms, corporate events and hospitality may play a larger role in attracting clients, and in other professions where the ethical codes of conduct are less restrictive, we might find a larger role played by friendship and social interactions. Where innovation is key, we are likely to find a much larger role played by 'structural holes' due to the importance of cutting edge information (Maurer and Ebers, 2006).

Directed further reading

Stringfellow, L., Shaw, E., and Maclean, M. (2014) Apostasy versus legitimacy: Relational dynamics and routes to resource acquisition in entrepreneurial ventures, *International Small Business Journal*, **32**(5), 571-592.

Review questions

1 What key characteristics differentiate B2B from B2C marketing and can you offer any critique of these general features?

2 What types of considerations might impact on the B2B buying process?

3 What are the key debates in social capital theory?

4 What are the basic elements of social network theory in terms of relational and structural features, and possible outcomes?

5 What would constitute a favourable network position for someone starting a small business?

6 What are the key characteristics of professional service firms and how do these relate to the role that networking plays in their business?

7 What possible uses could social media offer for a professional?

References

Adler, P.S., and Kwon, S. (2002) Social capital: prospects for a new concept, *Academy of Management Review*, **27** (1), 17-40.

Barnes, J. A. (1954) Class and committees in a Norwegian island parish. *Human Relations*, **7** (1), 39-58.

Bourdieu, P. (1986) The forms of capital, in Richardson, J. (ed.) *Handbook of Theory and Research for the Sociology of Education*, New York: Greenwood Press, pp. 241-258.

Bourdieu, P. (1989) Social space and symbolic power, *Sociological Theory*, **7** (1), 14-25.

Burt, R. (2000) The network structure of social capital, *Research in Organisational Behaviour*, **22** (6), 345-423.

Burt R. (2001) Structural holes versus network closure as social capital, in Lin, N., Cook, K. and Burt, R.S. (eds). *Social Capital: Theory and Research*, Aldine de Gruyter: Chicago, IL, pp. 31–56.

Cadman, E. (2016) Services close to 80% of economy, www.ft.com/cms/s/0/2ce78f36-ed2e-11e5-888e-2eadd5fbc4a4.html#axzz4JOfPXUEv. Accessed 05/09/2016.

Coleman, J. (1988) Social capital in the creation of human capital, *American Journal of Sociology*, **94**, 95-121.

Granovetter, M. (1973) The strength of weak ties, *American Journal of Sociology*, **78** (6), 1360-1380.

Grönroos, C. (1982) An applied service marketing theory. *European Journal of Marketing*, **16** (7), 30-41.

9

Hart, S. and Hogg, G. (1998) Relationship marketing in corporate legal services, in Hogg, G. and Gabbott, M. (eds.) *Service Industries Marketing: New Approaches*, Frank Cass: London.

Laing, A. and Lian, P. (2005) Inter-organisational relationships in professional services: Towards a typology of service relationships, *Journal of Services Marketing*, **19** (2), 114–127.

MacDonald, K. (1995) *The Sociology of the Professions*, London: Sage.

Maister, D., Green, C. and Galford, R. (2002) *The Trusted Advisor*, Simon & Schuster: London

Maurer, I. and Ebers, M. (2006) Dynamics of social capital and their performance implications: lessons from biothechnology start-Ups, *Adminstrative Science Quarterly*, **51** (2), 262–292.

McDonald, M. (2014) There is a lot of B2B inside of every B2C transaction, AccentureStrategy, 6th October, https://www.accenture.com/us-en/blogs/blogs-B2B-inside-every-B2C-transaction. Accessed 01/09/2016.

Reid, M. (2008) Contemporary marketing in professional services, *Journal of Services Marketing*, **22** (5), 374-384

Silversides, G. (2001) Networking and identity: the role of networking in the public image of professional service firms, *Journal of Small Business and Enterprise Development*, **8** (2), 174-184.

Stringfellow, L., McMeeking K. and Maclean, M. (2015) From four to zero? the social mechanisms of symbolic domination in the UK accounting field, *Critical Perspectives on Accounting*, **27**, 86-100.

Stringfellow, L., Shaw, E. and Maclean, M. (2014) Apostasy versus legitimacy: Relational dynamics and routes to resource acquisition in entrepreneurial ventures, *International Small Business Journal*, **32** (5), 571-592.

Tichy, N.M., Tushman, M.L. and Fombrun, C. (1979) Social network analysis for organisations, *The Academy of Management Review*, **4** (4), 507-519.

Vargo, S. and Lusch, R. (2011) It's all B2B… and beyond: Toward a systems perspective of the market, *Industrial Marketing Management*, **40**, 181-187.

10 Not-For-Profit

Ross Curran

The term profit is widely understood as total money earned from the sale of a product or service, less the costs of production. Yet upon closer inspection we see profit represents a convenient signifier of success, allowing business leaders to evaluate their organisations' performance both in relation to competitors, and over time. In general, organisations with growing financial profit are viewed as successful, thus profit relates to the marketing functions of an organisation, as increases in profit may indicate the success or otherwise of particular campaigns and strategies. Within the non-profit sector then, success becomes more opaque, and the task of marketers more complicated. Although many of the strategies and techniques deployed by non-profit marketers share similarity and overlap with their for-profit counterparts, their success is measured through variables such as donor contributions, volunteer retention, and public trust in the organisation. This chapter offers an overview of some of the challenges and opportunities marketers face, from a distinctly non-profit perspective.

The non-profit sector

The contribution of the non-profit sector to all corners of society should not be understated. In the UK, some non-profit organisations (NPOs) contribute to sheltering the homeless, while some restore and preserve stately homes for future generations of heritage tourists. Some non-profits tackle international crises, while others run campaigns to change people's behaviour. Even political parties are classed as NPOs. Consequently, stereotypical views of the non-profit sector as a loose collection of sandal-wearing, tree-hugging do-gooders could not be more outdated. Of course, these exist, but they represent only a tiny minority, and notions of a sector characterised by amateurism are entirely mistaken. Figure 10.1 offers a simplified representation of the non-profit, private, and public sectors.

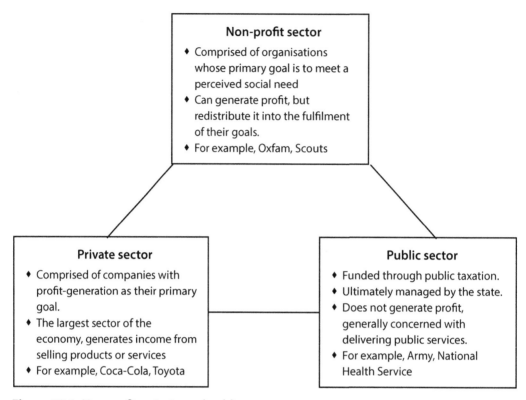

Figure 10.1: Non-profit, private, and public sectors

As Figure 10.1 shows, the non-profit sector is distinctive from its private and public sector counterparts, in that it can be characterised as comprising of organisations that are non-governmental, and undertake activities aimed at delivering a social good. Yet readers should note that in reality, the environment these sectors comprise is considerably more complex. For example, the UK Government accounts for almost one third of charity funding on a sector level, providing, in some cases, up to seventy per cent (Sargeant, 1999), therefore raising questions about the independence of some organisations from government influence.

The growing popularity of social enterprise generates further definitional challenge. In the absence of a legal definition, and different interpretations across national borders, social enterprise can best be considered "…an innovative and dynamic interface between social demands, humanity, and commerce" (Mulholland et al., 2013:40). Thus, social enterprises cut through sections of the private, public, and non-profit sectors working with organisations positioned in all categories, while holding at their core a desire to meet a social need, through commercial activity. In this sense, social enterprises contrast with public sector organisations, which may also seek to address a social need, but rely on public funding collected through taxation to do so. There are also distinctions between private sector organisations and social enterprise. For example, private companies can engage in corporate social responsibility programmes which address social issues, however, unlike social enterprises, addressing such issues is neither their core aim nor their main priority.

The term 'non-profit' is something of a misnomer, complicated by its interchangeability with terms such as third sector and voluntary sector, but also by the fact that such organisations are entirely entitled (and should even aspire) to generate a profit. However, status as a NPO does govern how such profit can be distributed, preventing any private individual benefitting, and encouraging its use in meeting the socially motivated goals of the organisation. Instead, perhaps partly as a consequence of this resource-constrained environment, the non-profit sector has become increasingly professionalised, with NPO marketers applying marketing practices previously viewed as exclusively 'private-sector' concepts.

The growth of the non-profit sector has accompanied its professionalisation, and it now employs an estimated 765,000 staff (comparable to the UK hospitality industry), and makes a contribution to the UK economy of over £23billion when volunteer hours are included (National Council for Voluntary Organisations, 2012). Indeed, the growing professionalisation of the sector has led to controversy over levels of non-profit executive pay (sometimes reaching six figures), raising questions from donors (often the public) and the intended beneficiaries of these NPOs about the appropriateness of such high salaries part-funded through donations from the public (Third Sector, 2015). In support of the sector's professionalisation, seminal management theorist Peter Drucker commented:

10

> "The non-profits are, of course, still dedicated to 'doing good'. But they also realise that good intentions are no substitute for organisation and leadership, for accountability, performance, and results. Those require management and that, in turn, begins with the organisation's mission" (Drucker, 1989:88-93).

Today, non-profit marketing is noted as being at the forefront of innovations to marketing practice, with the recent *Ice Bucket Challenge* (https://youtu.be/qgqsgXSJ7g8), and *END7: How to Shock a Celebrity* (https://youtu.be/sYimJKg-9QiE) campaigns highlighting the ability of non-profit marketers to reach large audiences, evoke strong emotional responses and encourage positive actions. All this is achieved with budgets and resources smaller than their private-sector counterparts. These challenges, and potential strategies for success are considered in the following sections.

Exercise 1

Consider a non-profit organisation of your choice. Does it engage in significant marketing activity? What recent campaigns has it run?

Non-profit marketing challenges

The previous section highlighted the distinctiveness of the sector and its organisations; successful marketing in the non-profit sector is therefore complicated by the unique challenges these organisations face. Indeed, non-profit marketers have to contend with an array of challenges which simply do not occur in the same way in private sector contexts. These are further exacerbated by generally tightly constrained resources. A selection of these distinctly NPO challenges are presented in Figure 10.2:

Figure 10.2: Non-profit marketing challenges, adapted from Andreasen and Kotler (2008)

Unlike their private sector counterparts, NPO marketers are often tasked with marketing a product, service, or social behavioural change, which is perhaps unfashionable, difficult to convey through traditional marketing mediums, carries little aesthetic appeal and may be inflexible or intangible. Furthermore, NPO marketers often have little scope to alter the core offering as they would in many private sector settings, where changing packaging, or the product design may be feasible. To understand these challenges, consider the task faced by marketers for a charity encouraging recycling behaviours. The organisation wants to encourage people to recycle more, and it cannot feasibly alter this goal as it aligns with its core mission. Recycling cannot easily be depicted in an attractive, appealing way using traditional non-digital mediums, as perhaps a new clothing brand, or fast-food menu item could in the private sector.

How many times have you viewed a charity aid appeal on television, been moved by its message, and angered at the tragedy it portrays? Now how many times have you actually responded to such appeals with donations? Particularly in large marketing campaigns, NPO marketers are challenged by the bystander effect, whereby members of the public assume they do not need to respond to campaigns, as they expect others will. The need for many NPO campaigns to hold broad appeal, and to communicate over mass-media channels (e.g. television, radio, newspapers) can render marketing messages impersonal. However, more interactive, targetable communication mediums, such as social media, offer opportunities to improve personalisation, and mitigate the bystander effect, as demonstrated by UNICEF's *Likes Don't Save Lives* campaign in Sweden. This tackled the bystander effect head on, by explicitly stating that viewers needed to respond by making donations rather than giving online support alone. You can familiarise yourself with the campaign here: https://youtu.be/2_M0SDk3ZaM.

Unlike in the private sector, where marketers can tailor particular products to the needs of niche market segments, NPO marketers are often tasked with inducing supporting action (e.g. financial donation, volunteer contribution) amongst multiple audiences. For example, during the Ebola outbreak in West Africa beginning in 2013, NPO marketers undertook marketing campaigns to raise funds for the international response, launching campaigns to attract volunteers, while at the same time communicating with affected populations to convey steps that could be taken to reduce the spread of Ebola. The challenge of multiple audiences can therefore lead to marketers simplifying their message, rendering it appropriate to more than one audience, or running several distinct campaigns simultaneously, piling further pressure on already limited resources and risking the creation of confusion amongst numerous audiences.

NPO marketing is further complicated by particular cultural sensitivities and ingrained opinions. While private sector marketers have been famously caught out on more than one occasion (a quick Google will provide some amusing blunders!) the nature of many NPO missions requires them to raise

10

issues that could be considered taboo and potentially offensive in certain countries, and amongst some sections of society. For example, campaigns to combat the AIDS epidemic encouraging condom use may cause embarrassment or shock amongst some sections of certain populations, perhaps opposed to their use for religious reasons or simply not used to topics of a personal nature being publicly raised. NPO marketers have to develop an understanding of propriety within the societies for which their campaigns are being developed, and decide how this might contribute to or detract from reaching their marketing goals, without detracting from the organisation's overall reputation.

In some instances, where NPO marketers are seeking to create behavioural change within a target group, they can find their message tasked with challenging long-established behaviours and opinions, reinforced daily by the family, friends and respected opinion leaders in a target audience's community. For example, sexual health and children's rights campaigners face a difficult task challenging ingrained opinions within community leaders in Malawi (Butler, 2016). Thus, marketers may consider strategic campaigns aimed at converting the views of key opinion leaders where possible, and circumventing their influence where it is not.

Ethical dilemmas represent another challenge for NPO marketers who must consider the appropriateness of their marketing strategies in relation to achieving the organisation's goals. For example, should an NPO form a marketing partnership with a large private sector organisation that generates income from the sale of weapons? Campaign and fundraising methods also raise ethical questions. Some large charitable organisations sell the right to fundraise using their brand to companies that then recruit donors through cold-calling, and face-to-face interventions on main shopping streets. Despite brandishing branded clothing and documentation, many of these fundraisers are in the employ of private companies, who have contractual arrangements with the NPO entitling them to a percentage of money raised (The Telegraph 2012). Marketers themselves may find their conscience tested if managing marketing campaigns for NPO organisations on controversial, or polarising issues that challenge assumptions or behaviours contrary to their own culturally or religiously informed beliefs. As another example, when a Greek division of Amnesty International developed a computer game to extend discussion on using the death penalty, an ethical debate was stimulated. Although the game succeeded in its aim of raising awareness, many questioned the appropriateness of such methods to an organisation such as Amnesty, which campaigns on issues of genuine life or death (Kylander and Stone, 2012). In this case, the ends were deemed to justify the means. The game is available here: www. amnestythegame.com.

Finally, NPO marketing is complicated by the difficulty in identifying success. For example, where private sector marketers for a cosmetics brand can assess the number of units sold before and after a marketing campaign, NPO marketers rarely have the luxury of such clear-cut metrics. NPO impact measurement is rendered particularly difficult, partly due to the intangible nature of their offerings, but also the slow pace of impact (and time required to change ingrained behaviours). Even as part of fund-raising campaigns, where money raised represents an accessible indicator of success, the eventual impact of those funds will not be fully understood in many cases for several years, and in some, not at all.

Exercise 2

Evaluate how the marketing of a new soft drink might prove easier than a non-profit organisation's marketing campaign to change attitudes to racism.

Non-profit brand orientation

Brands began essentially as a method of demarcating a craftsperson's output, but as a result of technological advances and the growing sophistication of brand audiences they have evolved to become:

> *"a complex multidimensional construct whereby managers augment products and services with values and this facilitates the process by which consumers confidently recognise and appreciate these values"*
>
> (de Chernatony and Dall'Olmo Riley, 1998: 427).

Today, brands consist of carefully managed identities, conveying a formulated personality and set of values to audiences with a view to differentiate an organisation from competitors, and gain support from their target audiences. Responding to the additional challenges faced by NPO marketers, the marketing literature shows that NPOs possess some of the most powerful brands in the world (Kylander and Stone, 2012). Consider Amnesty International, or the World Wildlife Fund. The barbed-wire-clad candle of Amnesty International and the World Wildlife Fund's Panda constitute iconic, globally recognisable brands which can afford NPOs the opportunity to attract significant funding, increase awareness of their work, and recruit and retain committed volunteers (Curran et al., 2016).

10

Globally recognisable NPO brands attest to growing brand orientation within NPOs. Brand orientation broadly, is the extent to which an organisation is characterised by its brand, and is reflected by the investment of time and resources, and the perceived importance of branding theory to the NPO. Although some NPO managers no doubt still perceive brands negatively through their traditionally private sector associations, when conducive to social benefit there is a growing willingness invest in and benefit from brands. Research by Hankinson (2001) suggests NPO brand orientation should be viewed from the perspective of a continuum to reflect varying intensities of orientation, and notes how as a theoretical construct brand orientation comprises:

- Organisational knowledge of the brand

- Realising strategic aims through the brand

- Proactive ongoing brand management

- The extent the brand is communicated (internally and externally)

Thus, NPO brand orientation could be enhanced through developing knowledge of the brand. This may relate to the recruitment of brand specialists into an organisation, or the undertaking of a brand audit to establish the strengths and weaknesses of a particular brand in relation to an audience. Brand orientation is also related to the extent to which branding is used to deliver on the core aims of an organisation. In relation to NPOs, this could relate to enhancing awareness of the organisation and building enduring trust between it and its beneficiaries. Research also suggests a strong brand orientation in NPOs is evidenced by management taking a hands-on approach to brand management, where consideration of the organisation's brand is incorporated into all decisions relating to an organisation. This is particularly important in developing strong brands over the long-term, as through this approach managers can ensure the organisation behaves in a manner commensurate with the values inherent in its brand, fostering the formation of trust with its audiences.

Finally, a strong brand orientation is contingent on effective communication with internal and external stakeholders conveying the message of an organisation externally to donors, and beneficiaries, but also internally to volunteers and paid staff. Figure 10.3 illustrates potential internal and external audiences for non-profit brands.

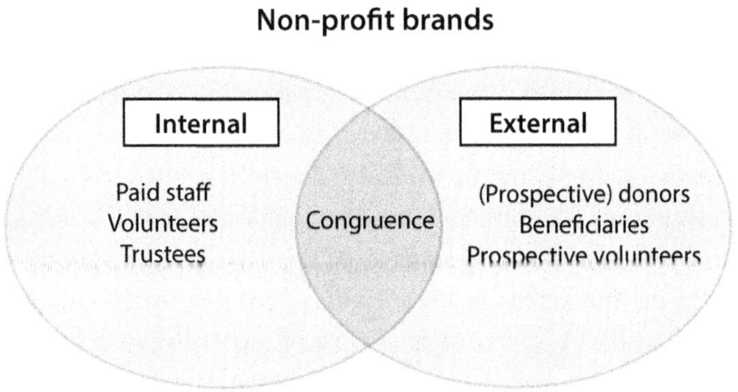

Non-profit brands

Figure 10.3: Non-profit brands. Adapted from Kylander and Stone (2012)

Figure 10.3 emphasises how non-profit brands communicate internally, to paid-staff and their volunteers, as well as to the trustees of an organisation, who are responsible for board-room level decisions in the organisation. Internally, commitment levels, and the likelihood of paid staff continuing volunteering have been shown to be influenced by positive perceptions of the NPO's brand (Hankinson, 2004). Similarly, branding has been associated with maintaining and enhancing commitment of volunteers and trustees in NPOs (Laidler-Kylander, 2012).

Externally, literature supports the idea that prospective donors are positively influenced to donate through NPO branding. For example, brands that convey high levels of trust can reassure donors that their contribution will be used to benefit a genuinely good cause (Rose et al., 2016). Beneficiaries themselves may also be encouraged to seek the support of a particular NPO as a result of messages conveyed through its brand, for example telephone support service Childline emphasises its mission to support children suffering abuse. Furthermore, the organisation's logo conveys the way in which Childline operates (by incorporating telephone related images). Prospective volunteers can also be influenced positively or negatively by NPO brands. For example, as CV development is a common motivator for volunteer action (Musick & Wilson, 2008), many prospective volunteers are keen to associate themselves with NPOs publicly perceived in a positive light, thus strong, successfully branded NPOs are likely to attract volunteers more easily than those with weaker brands.

Kylander and Stone (2012) suggest that NPO brands work best when the NPO's internal, and external brand offerings are complimentary of each other, as both internal and external stakeholders rally around a uniting brand identity. Figure 10.3 emphasises the importance of congruence between these elements in order to develop high levels of trust. Developing trust between brand audiences and an NPO brand is of particular importance if long-term support for the brand is to be maintained, and is arguably more important to NPOs than in the for-profit context, where organisations can receive feedback (or measure success) far more easily. Trust therefore establishes relationships which represent an important feedback channel for NPOs (Laidler-Kylander & Stenzel, 2014). The importance of trust is again highlighted by scandals that have hit the sector in recent years. For example, Kids Company was a large UK-based charity offering support to children from deprived inner-city areas in the UK. However, allegations of financial mismanagement and a subsequently dropped police investigation into alleged instances of misconduct caused major funders to withdraw support and led to the NPO's swift collapse. As NPOs become more brand orientated, their application of traditionally private sector branding techniques has become more complex. One aspect of branding that could be particularly useful for NPOs through its ability to develop and enhance trust (which is particularly important for NPOs) is brand heritage, which is introduced below.

Exercise 3

Consider a health related non-profit organisation such as the British Heart Foundation. Use Figure 10.3 to map the audiences for its brand by conducting your own online research. Now do the same for a public and private sector organisation. Do you notice any differences?

Non-profit brand heritage

Brand heritage is gaining increasing attention from marketers who note the power of heritage in influencing the appeal of brands to external audiences (Schultz, 2001), and it can contribute positively to the brand orientation of a NPO. The idea of brands possessing heritage components is supported by evidence from the automotive industry, which demonstrates that brand heritage can contribute to consumer satisfaction and purchase intention (Wiedmann et al., 2011). Given the large number of heritage-rich NPO brands (e.g. the Samaritans, the Royal National Lifeboat Institution) brand heritage represents a potentially fruitful and useful area for researchers and marketing managers alike. This is also an area where NPOs have led the way in pioneering marketing activities.

To understand what brand heritage is, we first need to revisit the notion of heritage. Heritage is typically associated with the built environment around us, for example, Edinburgh Castle, and the ancient city of Palmyra in Syria could both be considered sites rich in heritage. Such places help us understand and make sense of our past, connect us with each other, and allow us to position ourselves as part of a large community of people. Thus, heritage is a personal concept, associated with notions of reassurance, certainty, and shared community (Balmer, 2013). Brand heritage therefore involves harnessing the heritage perceptions generally held towards traditional heritage-rich sites, but within an organisation's brand. This idea has led brand heritage to be described as the 'linking glue' (Ardelet et al., 2015: 2) connecting the benefits of heritage, with organisational branding.

Brand heritage is suggested by Urde et al. (2007: 4) to be "a dimension of a brand's identity found in its track record, longevity, core values, use of symbols and particularly the organisational belief that its history is important." This highlights the five brand heritage elements of track record, longevity, core values, history and symbols (Wiedmann et al., 2011; Urde et al., 2007).

Within brand heritage, **track record** is in effect evidence of an organisation's ability to deliver its promises over time. Consider the Samaritans in the UK, (a charity offering free confidential counselling) which began in 1953. Its long track record of integrity and success contributes to reassuring donors, volunteers, and beneficiaries that it can deliver on its goals and maintain its promise of confidentiality.

Positive perceptions are strengthened by **longevity**, which emphasises the length of time an organisation has been active. NPOs with longevity can sometimes be perceived as more trustworthy and dependable. Consider your feelings toward a brand associated with a travel company you wish to book with. One has been selling travel for 100 years, while the other has only opened 6 months ago. The longevity of the former business is likely to reassure and inspire confidence in you that the booking will be honoured and will proceed smoothly. A similar effect can occur in relation to NPOs for whom longevity can represent a positive attribute.

10

Exercise 4

Think about a site you consider rich in heritage. Write down the feelings and emotions this site elicits. Now consider whether these emotions would be useful to a NPO?

Core values are also central to a brand's identity as they contribute to establishing brand heritage over a prolonged period of time, and represent a promise to brand audiences conveying what the organisation believes in. Consider how you would feel about an NPO that was previously opposed to windfarm construction, but subsequently altered its position to be in favour. Regardless of your personal stance on the issue, you might consider the organisation's overall position unclear.

The **history** aspect of brand heritage emphasises the brand's relationship with the past, and helps subsequent brand audiences relate it to their futures. The personal nature of history and the ability for it to be shared between large numbers of people allow brand audiences to arrive at firm opinions regarding who and what the organisation represents, supported by overlap between the histories of an organisation and its brand audience. NPOs can help promote their history by curating exhibitions and visitor centres, inviting the public to learn more about it. This tactic is used widely by private sector organisations, for example the Heineken Experience in Amsterdam, which invites visitors to learn about how the lager brewing company was founded, and grew into the success it is today.

Finally, these elements of brand heritage are manifested through various tangible and intangible symbols, for example the brand logo, but also the office buildings of an NPO such as Gilwell Park House, which is situated on a grand country estate near London and houses the headquarters for the UK Scouts. Alternative symbolic representations of brand heritage in the Scouts include the uniforms worn by the children and volunteers, as well as the terminology used, which conveys the heritage and historical roots of the Scouts.

Our understanding of NPO brand heritage remains at an early stage, yet an initial piece of empirical research has shown brand heritage can enhance the engagement levels of volunteers, and subsequently improve their satisfaction with how they are managed, as illustrated by Figure 10.4.

Brand heritage has the ability to enhance dedication, absorption, and vigour of volunteers, and therefore increase their levels of overall engagement and satisfaction towards their managers (Curran, 2016). Marketers can consider their management of brand heritage to help retain volunteers for longer, reducing re-training costs and improving the standard of service deliverable. Importantly, the benefits of brand heritage are not exclusively restricted to older, long-established organisations. Instead, brand heritage can be attained through affiliating an organisation with other heritage-rich brands or sites. Nevertheless, brand heritage remains an emerging concept, and our understanding of it is evolving rapidly.

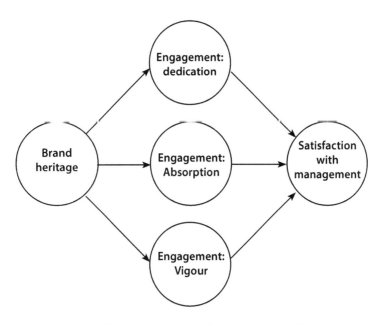

Figure 10.4: Brand heritage influence on non-profit organisations. Source Curran et al. 2016

Exercise 5

Assess the heritage of a NPO of your choice by considering it in relation to the components of brand heritage.

Conclusion

This chapter has outlined the relevance of marketing to organisations operating in the non-profit sector, and highlighted the growing professionalisation and importation of marketing strategies previously considered characteristic of the private sector. The chapter also notes the particular challenges NPO marketers face in comparison to their private-sector colleagues. The adoption of branding by NPO marketers was then considered, highlighting the inherent brand strength that can be leveraged by many NPOs, and the potential reach of such brands while cautioning against them departing from the organisation's genuine values. Brand heritage was also introduced as an evolving area of research that has demonstrated an ability to improve volunteer engagement and satisfaction, toward aiding volunteer retention.

10

Case study: Brand heritage and the Scouts

The Scouts are a non-profit youth organisation founded by Robert Baden-Powell as a result of his experiences during the Boer War (1899-1902).The first Scout camp took place in 1907, and so began its mission to inspire developmental qualities of self-discipline, improvement, aspiration, and generosity amongst young boys across the country.

In the 1980s and 1990s however, the Scouts found attendances waning, and their supply of volunteers became increasingly limited. The organisation's leadership realised they had gained an unfashionable image, were perceived as outdated, and out of touch, and began taking remedial action. Consequently, since the early 2000s the organisation has reported continued growth in both its membership, but also the number of volunteers it recruits. But how did the Scouts create such a remarkable turnaround? Part of the answer lies with the marketing strategy the Scouts adopted to reinvigorate their brand, and make it more appealing to a 21st century audience.

Celebrity outdoor adventurer Bear Grylls was appointed Chief Scout in 2009, a move widely praised within the Scouting community, "appointing Bear as Chief Scout was an inspired choice", said one Scout volunteer interviewed during a recent research project. Indeed, the position of Chief Scout, although broadly ceremonial, can allow the Scouts to gain headlines, and harness the positive reputation of the appointee, with the potential to broaden the audience of the Scout message. Bear Grylls acts as the public face of Scouting, and has advocated Scouting through many of his television appearances, books, and online outlets to his non-Scouting followers. Appointed at age 34, Bear was the youngest ever Chief Scout, allowing the Scouts an opportunity to modernise its image, but also to alter it. With a background in elite military operations for the British Armed Forces, Bear contributes an edgy dynamism to the Scouts' brand, allowing it to move on completely from outdated notions of boys in long socks, brown shirts, and big hats.

Social media has contributed enormously to the Scouts' re-invigoration. A quick Google search reveals the Scouts are highly visible across Twitter, Facebook, YouTube, and Instagram platforms. These allow the organisation to demystify what it offers, and highlight the range of activities, and capacity for fun it can deliver. Using these media also allows the Scouts to communicate more effectively with its target audiences (young people) who are more likely to be reached through these as opposed to newspapers, magazines, or local recruitment events.

The external marketing efforts have also been accompanied by modernisation to align them with the internal offering available from the Scouts. For example, the principal offerings have been overhauled, with Scouts now able to experience a wider range, and broader variety of activities than ever before. This has accompanied updates to the Scouts' award system which previously included gender-specific badges. The available awards are now more diverse and inclusive. Additionally, the Scouts have sought to become more youth-led, meaning the organisation is encouraging its young members to contribute to shaping what the organisation offers both now, and in the future. The youth-led initiative has contributed substantially to making the Scouts more appealing to those it seeks to serve, through giving them a powerful, and genuinely influential voice which contributes to making it the relevant, dynamic organisation conveyed in its external marketing today.

Source: Adapted from Quinn 2009, The Scout Association 2016, and Moss 2015

What the Graduate says: Sam Abrahams, First Aid Africa

Sam Abrahams is a graduate of Heriot-Watt University, and the current CEO of First Aid Africa, which he started during his studies. He shares his views and experiences on non-profit marketing below.

> "In 2008, the Heriot Watt First Aid Africa society was started, thanks to support from the Heriot Watt University Student Association. These days it is an international charity, with offices in five countries, supporting emergency healthcare training to communities across East and Southern Africa. With funding from the Scottish government, as well as the British Medical Society and the general public, the charity has thrived since its inception to become an innovative voice in the international development community.
>
> This growth would not have been possible without a multi-faceted approach to marketing. In the early days of the organisation, the yearly budget for Marketing was £50. We spent this on t-shirts and iron-on prints. We accidentally burnt the t-shirts and so our budget was effectively zero.
>
> Despite advances in targeted advertising, social media, and the Internet, positive word-of-mouth marketing remains a priority for all international development charities. And so we learned a lesson in 2008, which would serve us well throughout the coming years, "individual opinion is everything". The First Aid Africa brand represents not just the hard work of many local staff and volunteers, but also the efforts and actions of 1000 international volunteers and staff who have worn our logo over the years.

10

A basic logo, created on Microsoft P aint, by taking an outline of the mainland continent of Africa and superimposing a First Aid style 'white cross' on the centre, came to represent the ambitions of hundreds of thousands of individuals lobbying for better access to emergency care.

The Red Cross (also recognized as the Red Crescent or Red Crystal) is an important symbol, internationally protected, representing neutrality in peacetime and in times of conflict. It is a brand almost as recognizable as Coca-Cola or McDonalds' 'golden arches' and it stands as a testament to the positive influence that charitable brands can have in the toughest of circumstances.

In our journey as an international charity, we have seen the impact of targeted advertising, utilizing social media to provide access to first aid information to over 10,000 people in East & Southern Africa. Equally however, we have recognized the impact that individual supporters can have, not just in terms of recruiting volunteers, but also in regards to our ongoing efforts to spread the word about access to emergency healthcare.

We have utilized local television and radio articles, national print media and poster campaigns, and shared our ideas through public forums and University platforms. More than ever before, it is clear that there is no single path into non-profit marketing, at the same time as those in our sector are recruiting more and more specialists within the fields of marketing and donor engagement.

None of this is to ignore the fact that it is easier than ever for charitable brands to target a specific audience. Given the same £50 we had just a decade ago, we would surely now spend it on targeted advertising. On a recent "sponsored campaign" on social media we reached over 20,000 people within our target demographic for only £15. Significantly more than we could have reached with five burnt t-shirts less than a decade ago. The new reality in non-profit marketing, from ice-bucket challenges to push-ups for PTSD, is that, while we know social media is not the silver bullet many people once believed it might be, those individuals who are able to capture the public's attention, will remain the most employable.

As always with the field of international development, graduates are being asked to show their experience before they are given a job. This paradox has long caused anxiety amongst those aiming to get involved with the sector, but the truth is, that with social media being more accessible than ever, students who are able to demonstrate an aptitude for online marketing in their time at university, will become more and more attractive to those of us looking to employ people from 2018 and beyond."

Sam Abrahms (CEO First Aid Africa)

You can find out more about exciting First Aid Africa volunteering opportunities and its current projects by visiting their website http://www.firstaidafrica.org.

Exemplar paper

Liu, G., Chapleo, C., Ko, W.W. and Ngugi, I.K., (2015). The role of internal branding in nonprofit brand management: An empirical investigation. *Nonprofit and Voluntary Sector Quarterly*, **44**(2), 319-339.

> The authors contribute to our understanding of the internal role played by NPO brands, and highlight the potential of these brands to motivate commitment and support from paid-staff, thus allowing it to make real its externally projected brand promises. Drawing on self-determination and leadership theory, the paper presents evidence from a survey of UK NPO sector staff highlighting specifically how their emotional attachment to a brand and service involvement contribute to their subsequent performance. Consequently, they offer appropriate suggestions for NPO managers to fully utilise their NPO brands.

Further reading

Although NPO marketing literature remains underdeveloped when compared to its private-sector counterpart, it is growing in sophistication and breadth. To deepen your understanding of the value of NPO marketing first consult management guru Peter Drucker's seminal 1989 paper, entitled "What businesses can learn from nonprofits". Here, Drucker emphasises how NPO marketing represents a hotbed of innovation and best-practice, from which he suggests private-sector marketers should learn from. Of additional value, is the work of Stanford University based Nathalie Laidler-Kylander, who offers a range of texts and research papers unpacking non-profit marketing, and exploring the role branding plays in such organisations. Principally, Laidler-Kylander develops the concept of the brand IDEA, which is presented in her 2012 work with colleague Christopher Stone, entitled, 'The role of brand in the nonprofit sector'.

10

Multiple choice questions

1 What answer below best describes what constitutes a brand?
   a. Name, signs, symbols, employees, URLs etc
   b. The balance sheet of an organisation.
   c. The brand is what consumers perceive an organisation to be like.
   d. The brand is the strategy the managers decide to adopt.

2 The greatest innovations in marketing emerge in the private sector.
   a. True
   b. False

3 Internal non-profit brand audiences comprise of:
   a. Customers, volunteers, and shareholders.
   b. Shareholders and the government.
   c. Volunteers, employees and trustees.
   d. Donors, government regulators, and the public.

4 Brand heritage can be a strong advantage to an organisation, it is difficult for competition to imitate and can elicit strong feelings of trust.
   a. True
   b. False

5 External non-profit brand audiences include:
   a. Managers, employees, and shareholders.
   b. Its volunteers.
   c. Its leadership.
   d. Prospective volunteers, beneficiaries (current and prospective), prospective donors, and the public.

6 A non-profit organisation should be completely different internally, compared with how it is perceived externally?
   a. True.
   b. False.

7 What challenges do non-profit marketers face?
   a. Intangibility and inflexibility of offering.
   b. Multiple audiences.
   c. Breaking through a bystander mentality among the public.
   d. All of the above.

8 What statement best describes some benefits of brands?
   a. They act as a barrier to competition, create higher profits, and increase trust.
   b. They ensure the consumer is aware of increased value of a brand.

    c. They make it easy for consumers to return a product if it is faulty.

    d. They ensure consumers do not remember negative aspects of a brand.

9 An example of a well-known public-sector organisation would be:

    a. The National Health Service

    b. Oxfam

    c. Apple

    d. Royal National Lifeboat Institution

10 Brand heritage is composed of:

    a. All of the above.

    b. Track record, longevity, core values, history and a brand.

    c. Brand heritage elements of track record, longevity, core values, history and marketing.

    d. Track record, longevity, core values, history and symbols.

References

Andreasen, R. A. and Kotler, P. (2008) *Strategic Marketing for Nonprofit Organisations.* 7th edn. New Jersey: Person Education.

Ardelet, C., Slavich, B. and de Kerviler, G. (2015) Self-referencing narratives to predict consumers' preferences in the luxury industry: A longitudinal study, *Journal of Business Research*, **68**(9), 2037-2044.

Balmer, J. M. (2013) Corporate heritage, corporate heritage marketing, and total corporate heritage communications: What are they? What of them?, *Corporate Communications: An International Journal*, **18**(3), 290-326.

Butler, E. (2016) The man hired to have sex with children, http://www.bbc.co.uk/news/magazine-36843769. Accessed 16/08/2016.

Curran, R., Taheri, B., MacIntosh, R. and O'Gorman, K. (2016) Nonprofit brand heritage: Its ability to influence volunteer retention, engagement, and satisfaction, *Nonprofit and Voluntary Sector Quarterly*, **45**(6), 1234-1257.

de Chernatony, L. and Dall'Olmo Riley, F. (1998) Defining a 'brand': beyond the literature with experts' interpretations, *Journal of Marketing Management*, **14**, 417-443.

Drucker, P. F. (1989) What business can learn from nonprofits, *Harvard Business Review*, **67**(4), 88-93.

Hankinson, P. (2001) Brand orientation in the charity sector: A Framework for discussion and research, *International Journal of Nonprofit and Voluntary Sector Marketing*, **6** (3), 231-242.

Hankinson, P. (2004) The internal brand in leading UK charities, *Journal of Product & Brand Management*, **13**(2), 84-93.

10

Kylander, N. and Stone, C. (2012) The role of brand in the nonprofit sector, *Stanford Social Innovation Review*, **10**(2), 35-41.

Laidler-Kylander, N. (2012) Nonprofit brand and brand management, in Burke, R. and Cooper, C., eds., *Human Resource Management in the Nonprofit Sector: Passion, and Purpose,* Cheltenham: Edward Elgar Publishing, 160-177.

Laidler-Kylander, N. and Stenzel, J. S. (2014) *The Brand IDEA: Managing nonprofit brands with integrity, democracy, and affinity*, San Francisco: Jossey-Bass.

Moss, R. (2015) How the Scout Association is shaping men of the future by making mental health and diversity a priority, 25th November, http://www.huffingtonpost.co.uk/2015/11/26/scouts-helping-future-generation-of-men-mental-health_n_8637610.html. Accessed 16/08/2016.

Mulholland, G., MacEachen, C. and Kapareliotis, I. (2013) Rise, fall, and re-emergence of social enterprise in Wankel, C. and Pate, L., eds., *Social Entrepreneurship as a Catalyst for Social Change*, Charlotte: Information Age Publishing, 36-66.

Musick, M. A. and Wilson, J. (2008) *Volunteers: A social profile*, Indiana University Press.

National Council for Voluntary Organisations (2012) UK Civil Society Almanac, https://data.ncvo.org.uk/a/almanac12/how-big-is-the-voluntary-sector-compared-to-the-rest-of-the-economy/. Accessed 17/08/2016.

Quinn, B. (2009) Survivalist Bear Grylls names as new chief scout, *The Guardian*, 17th May, www.theguardian.com/global/2009/may/17/bear-grylls-chief-scout. Accessed 16/08/2016.

Rose, G. M., Merchant, A., Orth, U. R. and Horstmann, F. (2016) Emphasizing brand heritage: Does it work? And how?, *Journal of Business Research,* **69**(2), 936-943.

Sargeant, A. (1999b) *Marketing Management for Nonprofit Organisations*, Oxford: Oxford University Press.

Schultz, D. E. (2001) Zapping brand heritage, *Marketing Management*, **10**(4), 8-9.

The Scout Association (2016) Youth Shaped Scouting, http://members.scouts.org.uk/supportresources/search/?cat=708. Accessed 18/08/2016.

The Telegraph (2012) 'Chugging': A high street fundraiser's diary, 24th June, www.telegraph.co.uk/news/uknews/9351651/Chugging-a-high-street-fundraisers-diary.html. Accessed 16/08/2016.

Third Sector (2015, March) Who are the highest earners?, *Third Sector,* 34-39.

Urde, M., Greyser, S. A. and Balmer, J. M. (2007) Corporate brands with a heritage, *Journal of Brand Management*, **15**(1), 4-19.

Wiedmann, K.-P., Hennigs, N., Schmidt, S. and Wuestefeld, T. (2011) Drivers and outcomes of brand heritage: consumers' perception of heritage brands in the automotive industry, *The Journal of Marketing Theory and Practice*, **19**(2), 205-220.

11 Celebrities

*Tom Farrington, Andrew MacLaren and
Kevin O'Gorman*

"Sic transit gloria mundi"

This is commonly translated as 'thus passes the glory of the world' and often interpreted to mean 'worldly things are fleeting.' The phrase came into popular use due to its inclusion in the coronation ceremony of the popes from 1409 to 1963, to highlight the transitory nature of life and earthly celebrity, and serves our purpose well here.[1]

We are living in a celebrity age

This chapter is about how the idea of 'celebrity' is used to influence, promote, represent and add value to the marketing process. In contemporary society, celebrities are important – this is something that is hard to argue against. Redmond and Holmes (2007) tell us how we embrace the celebrity myth, exploring the ways in which these magical figures give us strong imagery of identities and social meaning that we aspire to reflect within ourselves. Despite the fact that we are often aware of celebrities as mythical inventions created by the media, they can still represent forms of identity we seek to reflect in our personal identities, beyond other identities we feel we are ascribed by society. In the 1970s the celebrated American Football player O.J. Simpson appeared as the central figure in Hertz rent-a-car's advertising campaign – this was a break-through celebrity moment as black Americans were given a positive public reference for their identity that was not related to stigmatised stereotypes of black crime or violence[2] (Williams, 2001). O.J. Simpson went on to cultivate his fame in a way that transcended his popularity and success as

---

1 If you are interested in coronation rites and rituals, Woolly, R.M. (1915) *Coronation Rites.* Cambridge, Cambridge University Press is the text for you; the event above is described on p. 163.

2 When Hertz's campaign was launched in America, the country was going through a prolonged period of civil unrest in relation to racial equality issues.

a professional athlete and saw him occupy a position as 'a celebrity' in a contemporary way: he was famous because he was famous. This is an example of how ideas of celebrity have evolved over time. We instinctively understand what a celebrity is when we hear the word, but knowing the mechanics of 'celebrity' as a concept and recognising its different manifestations will help develop your ability to use and leverage notions of celebrity in practice.

Celebrity has become a media process, according to Turner (2013: 24), which has turned the idea of being famous into a commodity that can be packaged and sold to audiences who have an appetite to consume it. He presents two categories of fame:

> *The first is composed of people who possess "political, economic or religious power", whose decisions "have an influence on the present and future fortunes of society which they direct". The second group is what we now think of as celebrities and they are people "whose institutional power is very limited or nonexistent, but whose doings and way of life arouse a considerable and sometimes even a maximum degree of interest"* (Alberoni, 2007: 72)

Something that has shifted in recent times is the sense of agency any member of the public has in theory to elevate their own fame through means such as social media, thus changing our relationship with the idea of fame as not just something to be consumed passively as a 'fan', but something we can aspire towards ourselves. Therefore, we are developing an even greater appetite for celebrities as our relationship with them is more internalised and visceral than ever before. And the result of this from a marketing perspective is that celebrities have more power and influence when it comes to marketing activities (Redmond & Holmes, 2007).

Our appetite for celebrity as a consuming public is now so fierce that we have entered a new realm of what forms a celebrity. Beyond the two concepts presented by Turner (2013) above, Rojek (2001) discusses the idea of 'celetoids', being celebrities who have neither earned their fame, nor had fame ascribed by the public. Celetoids are entirely constructed by media producers or marketers in order to resonate with a particular audience to achieve a particular end, these are what Pierre Bourdieu (1998) describes as 'puppets of necessity'.

Puppets of necessity are a product of what is known as the celebritisation process (Stern et al., 2001). This is seen as the cultural process whereby the idea of celebrity is fostered in response to the audience's appetite for it, and it takes place at a macro level. Celebrification is something that happens to an individual; it is a process of becoming through media ritual that unifies "the spectacular with the everyday, the special with the ordinary" (Dyer, 1979: 35). In general we can consider ourselves to live in a celebritised age, where the process of celebritisation is all around us and is reproduced through mainstream media channels (such as talent shows like the X-Factor), and in informal and organic ways on social media through viral content.

Celebrity marketing

The pursuit of celebrity status exists in some of the oldest literature; the hero of the epic Gilgamesh, a Sumerian king (c. 2700-2500 BC) sought immortal fame. However, the epic was written to highlight the stupidity of fame as a goal and emphasise that fame for fame's sake is ultimately self-destructive. Unsurprisingly, in the Ancient World the means for promoting oneself to celebrity were extremely limited. There are well-known historical political figures: Emperor Qin Shi Huang (Emperor of China, c. 220 BC); Boudica (Queen of the British Celtic Iceni, c. 60AD); or religious figures Gautama Buddha (c. 500BC); St Paul (Saul of Tarsus c. 60AD) – but not what would be normally be considered celebrities. However, the cult of celebrity as distinct from being well-known is nothing new, for example, Socrates (Greece 470/469 – 399 BC) was a visible character, spoke well in public, hung out in the right places and, according to contemporaries, had a striking physical appearance. However, celebrities were not a class of their own. Dictators and emperors might fall in love or socialize with actors and actresses but that would never change their status.

Celebrity has its roots in the concept of fame: to spread abroad the fame of, render famous by talk. This comes from the Latin *famare*, meaning 'to tell or spread abroad.' The word celebrity originally came into English around 1610 from the Latin *celebritas*, meaning 'famous', or 'thronged'.

Until 1849, the OED attributed two meanings: "Due observance of rites and ceremonies; pomp, solemnity"; and "A solemn rite or ceremony, a celebration". Both of these definitions link to the Latin roots as they reference ideas of fame and importance. Nowadays our understanding of celebrity includes the assumption that a celebrity is widely known and generates interest among the public by virtue of their personality, i.e. there is intrinsic interest from others in the individual. According to the current Oxford English Dictionary, celebrity as we use it today in English means "a celebrated person, a public character."

11

Cultural elitism vs popularity

Traditional ideas of fame, which are couched within themes of power, influence, skill and endeavour are closely linked to concepts of taste (Bourdieu, 1984), which reinforce class divides and hierarchies within society. Bourdieu considered different areas of endeavour or activity to be distinctive 'fields' that had their own sets of rules, characteristics and values. He considered these fields to be understood in terms of different forms of capital (economic capital, cultural capital, social capital and symbolic capital):

> *"A capital is any resource effective in a given social arena that enables one to appropriate the specific profits arising out of participation and contest in it."*
> (Bourdieu, 1984: 26)

Each field values different forms of capital in its own way, but the concept of taste derives from an individual's level of cultural capital, which is their accumulation of knowledge, skills and behaviours associated with and valued by that field. Cultural capital emerges from education and experience within a certain field and even the material choices we make that relate to this, such as the books we decide to buy or the type of furniture we choose to have in our home. Bourdieu's concept of cultural capital is important for our understanding of celebrities because the intuitive concept of celebrity is tightly wedded to high levels of cultural capital and to Alberoni's (2007) initial ideas, presented above, of political, economic or religious power. Those who rise to the top of their particular field tend to possess high levels of cultural capital, thus they have elite levels of education and experience within their field. Often this also translates to high levels of economic capital (they are wealthy) and social capital (they have access to networks of power and influence within their field) too. With these high levels of valued capital forms comes recognition and typically fame too. However, there is a paradox with traditional celebrity forms, which sits at odds with the contemporary ideas of celebritisation.

Those individuals who occupy elite positions within a particular field are often not interested in fame and by the very nature of their elite and scarce level of expertise, they do not value the opinions of their fans because their fans do not necessarily have the level of cultural capital required to fully appreciate the person's abilities. Therefore, the cultural elite often practice what Bourdieu (1975) terms disinterested restricted production. This is where these elite members of the field continue with their pursuits with a disregard for the opinions or recognition of the masses and instead value only the opinions and recognition of their contemporaries among the elite echelons of the field. It is in this situation that we hear terms such as 'they are a chef's chef' or a 'comedian's comedian' or a 'writer's writer', meaning they only value recognition from those within their own world. Despite this, their purposeful disinterestedness often creates mystery and intrigue and makes them even more compelling for the masses. British comedian Stewart Lee is well known for deliberately patronising his audience for not being fluent enough in the comedy genre to appreciate the complexity and skill contained within his shows. Lee is notorious for relentlessly performing and touring, something that has led to him boasting a highly refined and hard-earned level of cultural capital in his field and being referred to as the 'comedian's comedian.' Lee is therefore someone who pursues disinterested restricted production whereby he does not seek to sell-out arenas

The consequence of the dichotomy between traditional celebrity figures (who have predominantly earned their recognition through achievement) and contemporary celebrity figures (who take advantage of the media process of celebritisation) is that when the elite members of a field are 'disinterested', space then opens up for other figures to occupy positions of recognition among the consuming public. As a consuming society we have entrenched the trend of celetoids versus traditional 'stars' by willingly consuming the celebrity of hollow figures who claim to be 'chefs' or 'comedians' or 'musicians', because our appetite for that consumption far outstrips the supply available from the disinterested traditional celebrities.

Case study: The celebrification of contemporary chefs

In the mid-nineteenth century the cookery book moved into the realm of popular publishing, exemplified by *Mrs Beeton's Book of Household Management*, which "both represented and sought to create the material and discursive practices around food that distinguished English middle-class homes" (Beetham, 2008: 394). To Mrs Beeton, dining was the privilege of civilization: the transformation of the natural into the social. Mrs Beeton opined that the "the rank which a people occupy in the grand scale may be measured by their way of taking their meals" (Beeton, 1861: 905). It had become less socially acceptable to declare high status based exclusively on wealth, social position or racial superiority, instead status was increasingly related to individual tastes and lifestyles that are constructed as sophisticated, savvy, and cosmopolitan.

11

The advent of television produced its own particular style of celebrity chef, an early example being the American cook, Julia Child, the wife of a US State Department officer who was posted in Paris after the Second World War. Child made French food accessible to the masses, which to some observers signalled the end of the exclusivity, mystique and high status of French haute cuisine. In 1970s France there was a change in the relationship between gastronomy and the economic field, as corporations purchased Michelin starred restaurants and the symbolic capital of the chefs. These individuals shifted from 'chef de cuisine' to 'chef d'enterprise' with their increasing endorsements, promotion and sponsorships of events and products.

Another key turning point has been the repositioning of cooking and dining in a celebrified taste project based on culinary heritage and lifestyle construction. Jamie Oliver's television show, *The Naked Chef*, was one of the first to position food at the centre of a lifestyle narrative that could be effectively transferred to goods and services. By adopting a 'leisure identity', Oliver repositioned cooking as a leisure pursuit rather than domestic work. While previous cookery programmes often involved some aspect of lifestyle, the rise of today's celebrity has accompanied a television format that increasingly centres upon lifestyle, symbols of travel and exotic places. Celebrity chefs draw on an assemblage of culinary and destination heritage to enhance their status. Viewers can choose which celebrity they want to 'consume' via their identifications and aspirations rather than cooking style or menu preference. Consumers' tastes are structured around attaining glimpses of elite comforts and symbols of authenticity and foreign travel in these programmes.

Celebrities also have an identity comprised of class, gender, fame and power heralding new forms of class distinction and classification. The consumption of celebrity relies on a feeling of identification and perceived similarities that forges bonds across members of a social group. There is a distinct class element to the choices that consumers make. Presenters tend to exaggerate or play down their accent and backgrounds to align with their audiences: Jamie Oliver plays down his middle-class roots, putting on a working class London accent; Nigella Lawson and The Two Fat Ladies display their cultural capital through their speech and behaviour, emanating the distinction they have acquired from their social circle and upbringing.

There are, however, risks for those who are 'classically trained' who move into the lifestyle television format. Often these programs tend to underplay their skills and creativity, the very elements that underpin their culinary legitimacy and standing within the field of the professional 'elite' (Hollows and Jones, 2010). The most important quality required of cultural producers is a rejection of economic interest, which works as an effective signal to prove one's claim to authenticity (Bourdieu, 1993). Haute cuisine becomes consecrated through the acts of professionals, and cultural inter-mediaries and the language and philosophy associated with gastronomy give the field a degree of autonomy, governed by aesthetic rather than economic concerns (Fantasia, 2010). It also changes the object of consumption; as Hyman (2008) points out, people are increasingly anthropophagous, consuming the person's name, fame and power rather than the cultural capital they possess. Consuming the food they make then becomes a vehicle for the consumption of the celebrities themselves. The physical act of eating therefore exemplifies the privileging of consuming celebrity status over the cultural position of the chef.

An important consequence of the celebrification of the culinary field is that it now overlaps with the fields of politics, fashion, popular entertainment, marketing and tourism, to name but a few. The most valued capital in the field has changed as a consequence, moving away from culinary traditions to lifestyle attributes: we are as likely to see an ex-model or sports star become a celebrity chef as someone with Michelin stars (the rating given to the world's best restaurants). The culinary elite are also becoming more openly commercial: Marco-Pierre White's endorsement of Knorr stock cubes; Darren Simpson's recommendation of KFC; and numerous product range endorsements on housewares, including Ramsay, Lawson, and Oliver. Whilst celebrity status may offer greater financial reward, the symbolic capital they risk losing within the culinary world can be significant as they try to make short term gains.

Contemporary mass manufacturing of celebrities

So where does contemporary, instant and entirely transient celebrity come from? Well, we don't really need to look much further than 'reality' TV. This medium has manufactured celebrities whose fame is neither ascribed nor earned, but rather results from marketing efforts, planned production and intense media attention. The process of celebritisation is a feature of contemporary marketing activity that draws upon consumers' desire for television. On the whole this is caused by 'structured' reality television, a format that often employs everyday people in preference to branded celebrities and blends authentic experiences within highly structured pseudo-environments. *Keeping Up With The Kardashians*, *The Only Way is Essex* (hereafter *TOWIE*), and *Made in Chelsea* (hereafter *MIC*) have come to represent a booming television genre that sees specific groups of people, united by a socio-economic context or geography, apparently followed in their day-to-day lives by a documentary-style film crew. These celebrities are make-believe and real all at the same time.

11

Contemporary consumer culture is replete with manufactured celebrity products, serving as packaged resources for consumers to draw their identity from. Reality television shows such as *Big Brother* were an important precursor to structured reality, as audiences are already aware of constructed reality. In structured reality television, cultural and social stereotypes are often drawn upon and subsequently reinforced. For example, *TOWIE* uses the stereotypes of Essex man and woman: He is flash, arrogant and sexually prolific. She is obsessed with beauty treatments and snaring the aforementioned Jack-the-lad. This mirrors US-based programmes such as *The Real Housewives of...* in being aspirational, escapist and focused almost exclusively on the romantic attachments of the cast.

This process can be more easily understood when viewed through three different, but intersecting theoretical lenses: Tournaments of Value, Spectacle and Transformative Performances. Each one of these offers an explanation as to how celebrity is bestowed upon some individuals who would have the more traditional skills or attributes, which would normally be identified with fame and nascent celebrity.

■ Tournaments of value

Tournaments of value are temporally demarcated events, participation in which confers levels of status and prestige amongst all participating members, the highest levels of prestige and status for the winner. Reality shows in general are rife with tournament rituals including *The X-Factor*, *The Apprentice* and *Masterchef*, and there is also a popular genre of celebrity-focused contests such as *Celebrity Big Brother*, *Celebrity Masterchef* and *I'm a Celebrity...Get Me Out of Here!*, within which structured reality celebrities are eligible to compete, either by public vote (*Celebrity Big Brother*) or expert evaluation (*Celebrity Masterchef*).

For example, in *I'm a Celebrity...*, contestants are sent to live in jungle conditions in New South Wales, Australia, and must complete 'Bush Tucker Trials' and other challenges in order to win rewards, such as food for the group. A Bush Tucker eating trial may involve the celebrity being required to eat snakes, spiders, rats, and a nauseating selection of animal body parts, which may be served to them dead or alive. Viewers are given accessible, interactive voting options to select a celebrity for a trial, and eventually to vote for the celebrity they would like to win the show, who is declared the King or Queen of the Jungle. The trials operate as a rite of passage (Taheri et al., 2016), where celebrities have an opportunity to demonstrate their worth, and subsequently change their social status within the group, as well as externally with the media and consumers. When viewed alongside the everyday social interactions and struggles that take place between cast members, and the progressive evictions, it can be seen that the journey of celebrities through the tournament is one of sensemaking (Weick, 1993), in which norms, values and hierarchies are reproduced or reconfigured.

Such programmes offer reputational resources that can be leveraged by celebrities in order to increase their economic capital and enter new fields. Mark Wright (of *TOWIE*) came second in the 2009 series of *I'm a Celebrity...* and has subsequently acquired presenting roles in four other television programmes, made numerous television guest appearances, and has become the face of menswear for a large online retailer. Within these tournaments of value, viewers are able to see the structured reality stars through a different lens, where the individual has greater scope for interaction and initiative, and can join the social network of a wider group of celebrities. It is often the relationships that form between celebrities in the programme that become a source of fascination for the viewers, and Wright gained headlines from his flirtatious encounters with an Australian model, as well as his 'bromance' with the eventual winner, boy band member Dougie Poynter. In a subsequent interview with MTV, Wright (2011) revealed his desire for the show's transformative potential, as he was upset with being portrayed as a womaniser in *TOWIE*, and claimed he "… wanted to show people the real me. The real me is what I showed in the jungle" (in reference to Wright's subsequent appearance in *I'm a Celebrity...*). Tournaments of value offer the celebrity a promise of agency; a new format of public scrutiny through which they can layer additional socially constructed meanings into the interactive negotiation of reality and the authenticity of their celebrity self.

Spectacle

The spectacle is a form of representation of everyday things, which hypernormalises and oversimplifies complex ideas (Debord, 1994; 1998). Spectacle draws out simplified signs and symbols of these ideas and organizes them around the production and consumption of images, commodities, and staged events (Kellner, 2003). Donald Trump was considered to have used spectacle effectively in his Presidential campaign in the USA by hypernormalising common ideas of immigrants, terrorists and prosperity in order to create clear messages for his followers. This process propagates stylised forms of celebrity that are often idolised and emulated within mainstream society (Kellner, 2003), echoed in the way Donald Trump himself is characterised as a semi-fictional character. The rise and demise of celebrities in this regard is an intrinsic part of the phenomenon; as newcomers emerge others go out of fashion and are eventually discarded, as individual celebrities follow (or resist) the celebrity life-cycle. In the context of structured reality and celebritisation, we see tropes associated with love, friendship, sex, debauchery, and infidelity, all leveraged in the creation of celebrity forms. These universal archetypes are key drivers in the legitimation of structured reality in the celebritisation process. What makes structured reality unique in this process is the speed and proliferation with which it creates celebrities through forms of spectacle; accelerating the life-cycle alluded to above through an ever-quickening production process which constantly demands new 'fodder' in the form of new reality programme ideas, and new actors to satiate the demands of the public.

Structured reality is emblematic of a new stage of spectacle which encourages the creation of new cultural spaces and forms, and new subjects. Television in general has developed from a one-way communication tool, in which audiences are 'compliant and pliant', to a medium from which consumers draw resources in order to enact social relations, through engaging other consumers, as well as celebrities, production agents, and other involved parties.

Drawing on a report Twitter published about the ways in which consumers use the social network to engage with TV shows, Moth (2012) points towards the increasing connectivity of television with other forms of media, with 60% of all Twitter users accessing the social network while watching TV, and more than 90% of online conversations about TV occurring on this particular platform. *MIC* is highlighted as having a particularly high ratio of viewers to people tweeting, with one in four viewers also actively engaged on Twitter during most episodes. One episode included in the report showed that 215,220 tweets were generated from 110,162 users, which could reach a potential audience of 124.2m (Moth, 2012). Consumers can be seen as closer to the celebrities in structured reality, in both time and space. Because of the short shooting schedules and relatively fast editing and production of structured reality, events are televised within weeks of being filmed, meaning that there can be near real-time dialogue between the celebrity and their audiences, across a seemingly limitless digital network space. The interactivity of the spectacle thus differentiates structured reality from other reality formats in which production and consumption are largely separated, e.g. *The Apprentice*, or formats in which the celebrity is cut off from 'reality' for the duration of the programme and prohibited from interacting with the consuming public and media, such as *Big Brother*. Cast members' personal use of platforms such as Twitter is another way for them to generate intense and hyper-real media depictions of themselves.

■ Transformative performances

Through transformative performances celebrities come to embody the structural forms created by media producers and marketers. These structural forms can be represented through social constructions of masculinity or femininity, place, ethnicity, or through leveraging standard industry conventions of the body. This effectively transforms celebrities into cultural vessels that perpetuate the intended meanings created in the celebritisation process. According to the nature of structured reality programming this can be viewed as a type of metaphorical 'rebirth', through which celebrities assume new personae through their participation in and transformation through the programme. For example, the cast and production team of TOWIE have been particularly skilful at drawing on relevant signifiers to create formulaic and fashionable celebritised personas. One of the best-known male cast members, Joey Essex, has become a poster boy for the contemporary 'primped' metrosexual, ever more willing to adopt aesthetic sensibilities. The appearance of cast members in structured reality is often commoditised and uniformed; in TOWIE, the men are without exception clean-cut, tanned, physically fit and dressed in similar attire, typically jeans, t-shirt and suit jacket. Reference to specific brands such as Range Rover and Rolex are made both physically and in conversation and are deployed in structured reality as artifacts that objectify, for instance, class and gender relations, and which are able to produce meaning for cast members. This process is the means by which celebrities are often described as being caricatures of themselves.

Celebrity endorsements

11

As described by McCracken (1989), the endorsement process sees a pre-existing (and powerful) set of meanings associated with a particular celebrity being transferred through endorsement to a brand, and then on to the consumer, who consumes these meanings as part of the brand. It is thus crucial that the celebrity be matched to the brand through the emphasis of pre-existing similarities between the two (Hackley & Hackley, 2015). In his book-length study of celebrity and endorsement, Pringle (2004: 195) picks out ten of the "most obvious and important genres of celebrity usage" in advertising:

- **Celebrity as presenter**: the celebrity takes the place of a non-celebrity in explaining the advantage of using this particular product or service. Public knowledge of that celebrity may add layers of trust, reliability, and practicality to the presentation, but it is also likely that the celebrity is here chosen for their physical attractiveness or the sound of their voice.

- **Celebrities playing themselves**: the 'real-life' persona of the celebrity (or at least their publicised persona) is used to instil a sense of integrity and authenticity to the endorsement. This relies upon, contributes to, and may even satirise the establishment of celebrity identity myths (Cocker et al., 2015), being the (allegedly) biographical collection of incidents and associations that allow the viewer quick and easy access to the particular meanings associated with that public figure.

- **Celebrity as brand character**: a celebrity is typecast as a scripted character whose actions showcase the utility of the brand, usually in self-contained comedy sketches. Slapstick, catchphrases, and jingles bring a sense of comfortable familiarity to the consumer, not unlike the bells, whistles, and repetitive action of children's television. This can also lead to brand characters played by non-celebrities becoming celebrities in their own right.

- **Celebrity expertise**: where the particular skills or knowledge for which the celebrity is famous are incorporated into the promotion. This lends credence to the consumer who makes the same informed choice as the expert, even when the home consumer lacks the skills or know-how to make full use of the product.

- **Celebrity as role model**: the consumer is encouraged to put themselves in the celebrity's shoes, thus weaving the product or service into individual fantasies of fame, fortune, and self-fulfilment. Mimicry is a vital aspect of learning in both humans and animals. It is well-established in the sociological literature that individuals modify their behaviour based on their observations of others (Bandura, 1977), and the same is largely true when consumers identify with celebrities as role models (Ruvio et al., 2013). The increasing uniformity of poses deemed most flattering on social media is a physical manifestation of this phenomenon.

- **Celebrity cast against type**: public perceptions of the celebrity's character are unsettled or entirely subverted, e.g. a very wealthy or conceited celebrity 'secretly' enjoying very cheap goods. The purpose of this inconsistency is to lend the appearance of fallibility to the celebrity, rendering them more relatable as a human being. This is one way in which a celebrity can broaden their appeal: by incorporating seemingly oppositional characteristics into a richer identity myth that is more intriguing and accessible to the consumer. We might imagine a popstar singing songs critical of fame and excess while wearing designer clothes and spending millions on their latest video, thus soliciting simultaneous admiration from both the materialist and the pseudo-Marxist. It is also important to remember that celebrities can (and often do) embody such contradictory meanings *prior* to being cast against type.

- **Celebrity acting a part**: a celebrity plays an everyday, stock character role, which could conceivably be played by a non-celebrity (e.g. supermarket shopper or homemaker), often as part of a series of adverts in which plot and characters develop as part of a long-running campaign. By utilising techniques of editing and scripting learned from mainstream film and television, this technique may even instil a sense of anticipation in the consumer for the next instalment of the campaign. Again, familiarity and recognition are two of the meanings made instantly transferable from celebrity to brand, and from brand to consumer, through this technique.

- **Celebrity revelation**: a celebrity reveals something intimate or unexpected about themselves that is connected to the brand, often by answering a simple 'dinner-party' style question. These purported insights into the inner psyche allow the consumer to feel a fresh sense of connection with the celebrity, and in responding internally to that same question, enter into an imagined dialogue with the public figure. It is important to consider the stage management that goes into soliciting these revelations.

- **Celebrities interacting**: celebrities that we usually wouldn't see in the same place at the same time are shown united in their use of the brand. This multiplies the power of the endorsement and assists the viewer in fantasising that consuming that same brand somehow elevates their social status, allowing them to virtually commune their idols.

- **Celebrity representations**: here a visual representation of a celebrity (often several celebrities) such as a cartoon, is employed to endorse the brand. This allows marketers to explore and exaggerate brand associations beyond the physical restrictions of the celebrity and setting. This technique could also involve bringing a fictional character to life, or even integrating footage of a deceased celebrity into new contexts.

11

> ## Exercise
>
> The world of celebrity has undergone significant change since 2004, when Hamish Pringle developed these ten genres. Write down at least one recent example of each of the above, think about why that particular celebrity was chosen, and assess the success of the campaign.
>
> Select an appropriate approach from the above list, attach a celebrity of your choice, and outline how you would use their fame to market a particular product or service.

Conclusion

This chapter has looked at the historical rise of celebrities, explored the ways in which they become or are made noticed, and traced relationships between celebrities and brands. Who or what is a celebrity, and how quickly their fame passes, can depend largely on the channels through which the alleged abilities and/or personalities are conveyed. As these channels are in a constant state of renewal and replacement, understanding the formulation and usage of celebrity is just the beginning for marketers. Putting this knowledge into practice will require careful and critical adaptation to the channels and famous faces in use.

Review questions

1   What are the four forms of capital described by Bourdieu?

2   In your own words, describe Alberoni's two categories of fame.

3   What are the three intersecting theoretical lenses mentioned above through which the manufacture of celebrities can be understood?

4   What are two of the risks facing professional chefs who wish to move into the lifestyle television format?

5   In your own words, explain three of Pringle's genres of celebrity usage.

Directed further reading

Hackley, C. & Hackley, R. A. (2015). Marketing and the cultural production of celebrity in the era of media convergence. *Journal of Marketing Management*, **31**(5-6), 461-477.

Hewer, P. & Hamilton, K. (2012). Exhibitions and the role of fashion in the sustenance of the Kylie Brand mythology. Unpacking the spatial logic of celebrity culture. *Marketing Theory*, **12**(4), 411-425.

Thomson, M. (2006). Human brands: Investigating antecedents to consumers' strong attachments to celebrities. *Journal of Marketing*, **70**(3), 104-119.

Stringfellow, L., MacLaren, A., Maclean, M. & O'Gorman, K. (2013). Conceptualizing taste: Food, culture and celebrities. *Tourism Management*, **37**, 77-85.

References

Alberoni, F. (2007). The powerless 'elite': theory and sociological research on the phenomenon of the stars. In, Redmond, S. & Holmes, S. (eds.) *Stardom and Celebrity: A reader*, Sage, pp. 65-77.

Bandura, A. (1977). *Social Learning Theory*: Prentice Hall.

Beetham, M. (2008). Good taste and sweet ordering: Dining with Mrs Beeton. *Victorian Literature and Culture*, **36**(2), 391–406.

Bourdieu, P. (1975). *The Invention of the Artist's Life*, JSTOR.

Bourdieu, P. (1984). *Distinction: A social critique of the judgement of taste*, Harvard University Press.

Bourdieu, P. (1993). *The Field of Cultural Production: Essays on art and literature.* New York: Columbia University Press.

Bourdieu, P. (1998). *On Television*, London: New Press.

Cocker, H. L., Banister, E. N. & Piacentini, M. G. (2015). Producing and consuming celebrity identity myths: Unpacking the classed identities of Cheryl Cole and Katie Price. *Journal of Marketing Management*, **31**(5-6), 502-524.

Debord, G. (1994). *The Society of the Spectacle*. New York: Zone Books.

Debord, G. (1998). *Comments on the Society of the Spectacle*. London: Verso.

Dyer, R. (1979). *Stars*, London: British Film Institute.

Hackley, C. & Hackley, R. A. (2015). Marketing and the cultural production of celebrity in the era of media convergence. *Journal of Marketing Management*, **31**(5-6), 461-477.

11

Hollows, J., & Jones, S. (2010). Please don't try this at home. *Food, Culture and Society,* **13**(4), 521-537.

Kellner, D. (2003). *Media Spectacle.* New York: Routledge.

McCracken, G. (1989). Who is the celebrity endorser? Cultural foundations of the endorsement process. *Journal of Consumer Research,* **16**(3), 310-321.

Moth, D. (2012). 'Stats: Twitter's relationship with TV revealed.' Econsultancy. https://econsultancy.com/blog/61871-stats-twitter-s-relationship-with-tv-revealed. Accessed 02/02/2017.

Pringle, H. (2004). *Celebrity Sells*: John Wiley & Sons.

Redmond, S. & Holmes, S. (2007). *Stardom and Celebrity: A reader*, Sage.

Rojek, C. (2001). *Celebrity*, Wiley Online Library.

Ruvio, A., Gavish, Y. & Shoham, A. (2013). Consumer's doppelganger: A role model perspective on intentional consumer mimicry. *Journal of Consumer Behaviour,* **12**(1), 60-69.

Stern, B., Zinkhan, G. M. & Jaju, A. (2001). Marketing images: construct definition, measurement issues, and theory development. *Marketing Theory,* **1**(2), 201-224.

Taheri, B., Gori, K., O'Gorman, K., Hogg, G. & Farrington, T. (2016). Experiential liminoid consumption: the case of nightclubbing. *Journal of Marketing Management,* **32**(1-2), 19-43.

Turner, G. (2013). *Understanding Celebrity.* Sage.

Weick, K. E. (1993). The collapse of sensemaking in organisations: The Mann Gulch disaster. *Administrative Science Quarterly,* **38**, 628-652.

Williams, L. (2001). *Playing the race card: Melodramas of Black and White from Uncle Tom to OJ Simpson* (Vol. 134). Princeton University Press Princeton, NJ.

Wright, M. (2011). Cited in an interview included in MTV. http://www.mtv.co.uk/im-a-celebrity/news/im-a-celebrity-mark-wright-upset-over-towie-portrayal. Accessed 02/02/2017

12 Revision

Tom Farrington and Andrew MacLaren

"What great things would you attempt if you knew you could not fail?"

Robert H. Schuller

This chapter gives a broad recapitulation of the topics covered in *Marketing Perspectives*. Some closing thoughts are given on keeping marketing as a subject in perspective, alongside notes on where we are in the lifetime of marketing, before each chapter in turn is offered in revision form, with the key learnings from each chapter being refreshed.

Perspectives on marketing

This book has attempted to give you a tour through some specific perspectives on marketing. Marketing is a broad subject area and whole books could be (and have been) written on the subject matter covered in every chapter here. So do not be tricked into thinking this book covered everything one needs to know on the subjects discussed. However, it did give you a basis on which you can develop your knowledge of each subject area.

One of the lovely things about marketing is its range of characteristics, from scientific and mathematical precision, all the way to pure creativity and artistic verve. Regardless of your interests and persuasions, you can find a home within the field of marketing that suits you.

Something that a book called 'Marketing Perspectives' would be wise to do as it concludes is to remind its readers of the necessity of keeping things in perspective. Marketing is a young professional field and so is management as an academic field. That means there is a lot of change and development still to take place. As technological innovation rapidly siezes control of society, the nature of work continues to evolve. The nature of marketing and the business world in ten years' time is likely to include things that we currently cannot even conceive of. The jobs that many people reading this chapter will be doing in their careers do not yet exist because they belong to an industry that has yet to be invented. So do your best to see the underpinning ideas that emerge from each chapter and remember there is no alternative to real experience. The best way you can prepare yourself for a successful career in business is to combine your theoretical knowledge with real practical experience. You wouldn't trust a doctor to treat you if they'd never engaged with a patient before, nor should you expect to be an expert marketer just by reading some books and journal articles – practical and theoretical knowledge need to be grown together.

Even the simplest innovations can represent significant opportunities for people in a certain context. Something as simple as standardised time had a revolutionary impact on the ability for businesses to operate more effectively and efficiently. Time is such a recently formalised concept that we should always keep in mind that it is both a construct we invented and one that we made significant progress without. For marketers, this reminds us not to take the status quo for granted, no matter how normal it seems or how difficult it is to imagine how we lived without it before (think about how normal Facebook and social media seem to us now).

Arguably the introduction of formal time-keeping across large geographical expanses came in North America when the railroads required to run on a standard timetable for safety reasons (avoiding collisions in particular). It was a Scottish engineer (Sir Sanford Fleming, who was involved in the development of railroads in Canada) who introduced the idea of global time zones. All railroads in Canada and the United States adopted these standard time zones in 1883. However, formalised time zones were not passed into law until the United States Standard Time Act of March 19th, 1918. This means that upon the publication of this book, internationally standardised time is less than 100 years old (please forgive the irony of stating how old time is). Another more recent example is of 'sun time' in the Middle East in the 1960s. Arab locals would make arrangements according to the sun, e.g. '2 in the evening' would be 2 hours after sunset. This caused issues with Western business people arriving in the Middle East following the oil deals made in the 1950s, who preferred to make the arrangements in relation to GMT. Can you imagine how that simple difference would have influenced the way everybody had to think when conducting matters of business? The lesson here is that being able to retain a solid perspective on what the world is like right now and what it was like before, best prepares you for being able to shape the future.

The following sections briefly return to the concepts in each chapter, and highlight what has been covered in this book.

Recapitulation

■ History

Historical research is a growing field within the academic discipline of marketing. This chapter looked at debates over the purpose of studying the history of marketing, as well as discussions of what that history might include. The benefits of historical understandings are summarised by Stearns (1998) as:

- Helping us to understand people and societies.

- Helping us to understand change and how things came to be.

- Contributing to our personal and social identities.

- Providing moral understanding and groundings for good citizenship

Similarly, a healthy understanding of the histories of marketing provides the discipline with identity, assists in moral understanding and helps to ensure that marketing can act for progress for business, consumers, and wider society. Historical research in marketing has developed in two broad areas:

- Marketing history (analysis of companies, industries or economies in order to explore the histories of advertising, retailing, product design, distribution, and other elements of the marketing mix)

- The history of marketing thought (scrutinising the philosophical development of marketing ideas, concepts and theory).

The pivotal historical points introduced were:

- The pre-modern expansion of trade between groups

- The development of ancient civilisations in Greece and Rome

- The regression of marketing in the warring Middle Ages

- Marketing's re-emergence amidst the growth of the later Middle Ages and early modern periods (including the impact of colonial expansion)

- The industrial revolution and its expansion of trade and consumption

- The mass consumption of the post-Second World War era.

The case study of Cadbury offered an example of a company with a rich marketing history spanning nearly 200 years, whose success relied upon

12

developments in three areas: production and management, standardisation and mass-selling, and branding and advertising. The case study illustrated the vast importance of marketing over time in the case of just one company or product type, and the importance of understanding how marketing drives change across industries, companies and across wider society. The chapter concluded by noting the lack of research in areas such as gender, race and cultural heritage, and the role of class in the history and development of marketing.

■ Money

One of the primary concerns of organisations is the financial implications of the resources required to conduct marketing activities, and so marketing managers and scholars must be familiar with this area. This chapter discussed engagement with the marketing budget, financial and non-financial measurements of marketing activities, and reporting on their performance to the organisation.

The following table described some of the most common roles of a budget within an organisation:

Role	Description
Planning	Preparing a budget encourages management to bring together all aspects of the organisation through the process of formal financial planning. Budgets are prepared in coordination with each business function and in line with overall objectives of the organisation.
Performance evaluation	Comparing the actual financial performance of activities at the end of a period with the budgeted financial performance allows the organisation to assess performance. Management attention is required for areas where actual results differ from expected results.
Communication	The budget can be used as a tool by management for bringing together the different business function of the organisation. The budget is a means of communicating the objectives to be achieved in financial terms.
Motivation	Targeted levels of performance set by management can have a motivating impact but care must be taken. If a performance level is seen to be too difficult to achieve, the target may be viewed as unrealistic and employees could cease trying to achieve it. If a target is too easily achievable the organisation may be underperforming. A careful balance must therefore be struck.

Some of the most commonly used approaches to budgeting are listed in the table below:

Approach	Description
Periodic budgeting	With this approach to budgeting the plan for each financial period is set up-front and rarely altered. If the budget period is one year then expenditure will be spread out evenly over that period, with the amount of expected income and expected expenditure of the year split into one-twelfth of the total and allocated to each month of the year.
Incremental budgeting	Occurs when the organisation prepares the budget for the next period by showing incremental effects based on past budgeted or actual results. In brief, this often means that the budget for the current period for a line item will be a set percentage higher or lower than the corresponding figure in the previous period.
Zero-based budgeting	Each area of the organisation starts with no allocated budget. Each of these business areas then creates their own budget from scratch for the appropriate period based on their anticipated activities. This can be time consuming and costly, and is often a difficult task.
Continuous budgeting	A continuous budget is one that is continually updated at the end of a specific period, typically one month with respect to an annual budget. The actual results are compared with the budgeted results and if there are any differences that are considered to be permanent, the remaining eleven months of the budget are updated to reflect this.
Flexible budgeting	This is where the budgeted cost is adjusted in line with the level of activity achieved during the period of the budget. This is helpful when the budgeted level of activity is not the same as the actual level of activity. Differences in performance can arise not through efficiency savings or gains but through differences in volume.

In setting the marketing budget, the chapter recognised a number of approaches:

- **Percentage of sales**: marketing expenditure is determined by calculating a set percentage of expected sales.

- **Affordable method**: allocating the marketing expenditure based on what the organisation can afford to spend.

- **Competitor comparison**: Amounts are allocated to the marketing expenditure based on what competitors in the market are spending.

- **Objective and task**: Budgets are prepared on the basis of determining the resources that will be required to meet the objectives set out in the marketing plan. This is the recommended method for preparing a marketing budget.

12

A number of metrics for measuring the performance of the marketing function were introduced:

- Short-term financial metrics: marketing spend, net profit and cash flow, return on investment (ROI), return on customer (ROC).

- Long-term financial metrics: customer lifetime value (CLV), customer equity, brand equity.

- Non-financial metrics: market share, brand awareness, customer satisfaction, customer loyalty, marketing audits.

Reporting information on the financial costs and performance of marketing to interested parties was highlighted as a vital activity in marketing accountability. Reporting takes place across two main fronts: internal reporting (concerning the giving of accounts within the organisation) and external reporting (referring to the reporting of information to stakeholders outside of the organisation). The case study of Apex Hotels emphasised the importance to marketing managers of understanding their finances, in order to plan for and justify costs, and manage financial performance through the year.

■ The Internet

This chapter asserted the need for marketers to understand how and why people use the Internet, in order to create effective digital campaigns. A short biography of the Internet revealed its conception as a military communications network with no central node, being therefore significantly less vulnerable to nuclear attack. Paul Baran (one of the scholars at the heart of this conception) immediately recognised the significance of such a network for marketing, and predicted:

- Below-the-line (BTL) advertising

- Streaming entertainment

- Online education

- Online retail and its associated hierarchical structure

Key stages that followed include the development and commercialisation of associated technologies, the formalisation of standards of a digital language (HTML) and its communication (HTTP, WWW), and the shift in content creation from a few key players to almost anyone with Internet access.

For just under half of the world's population, access to the Internet is now widespread. For the relatively rich (that's probably you!), this access is mobile and part of everyday life. This presents many opportunities and challenges for marketing practitioners, which can be classified into four main themes:

- Explosion of data
- Social media
- Shifting consumer demographics/the digital customer
- Proliferation of channels.

Two themes are key to understanding some of the changes in consumption that impact marketing to Internet users:

- Consumer empowerment (which has levelled the playing field for interaction between consumers and brands)
- The hyper-connected consumer (multiple-screen media consumption).
- Digital channels are classified into three major categories:
- Owned media (over which the company has full control, e.g. their website)
- Earned media (online mentions of the company not paid for by the company, e.g. unpaid blog review)
- Paid media (advertising generated by the company in other websites, e.g. social media ads)
  - ☐ For example, Google AdWords is a form of the Pay-Per-Click (PPC) advertising model, calculated by dividing the cost of advertising by the number of clicks an advert generates.

The chapter concludes with a discussion of social marketing (which seeks to effect positive social change in people), noting that commercial marketing could learn a lot by examining genuine human or social need, rather than attempting to manufacture consumer wants.

■ Customers

The latter decades of the 20th century saw problems emerging with the traditional marketing mix model which had so successfully underpinned the boom years of the post WWII era. Increased competition (both national and international) and growing customer interest and involvement meant firms had to do more than simply apply the '4Ps' to any given situation.

12

The idea of balancing attraction and maintenance (more commonly known as retention) has become a dominant narrative in relationship marketing. This is perhaps best represented by the notion of marketing relationships being like a leaky bucket (see Figure 12.1) (Ehrenberg, 1988).

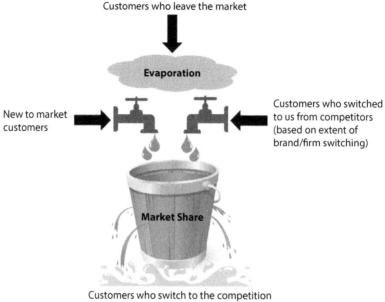

Figure 12.1: The leaky bucket (Ehrenberg, 1988)

In the 1990s, sophistication of technology and its application within the management world enabled firms to begin to gather information on customers and store this within databases. Increasingly sophisticated algorithms combined with customer purchase data at an individual customer level meant that firms could learn about customer choices, purchase patterns and trends and use this data to select products, choose displays, and, more importantly, target specific customers with specific offers. This strategy came to be known as customer relationship management (CRM).

The list below suggests that CRM activity is heterogeneous albeit connected directly to a firm's ability to gather information from customers and store it in an electronic database.

Types of CRM activity[1]

- Direct mail/email
- Loyalty card scheme
- Database
- Help desks and call centres
- Populating a data warehouse and data mining
- E-commerce
- Internet personalization

1 These types of CRM were suggested by marketing practitioners and reported by Payne and Frow (2005)

Many CRM practices manifest behaviour or outcomes which may damage or even permanently destroy relationships. Research by Frow et al. (2011) suggests that 35-75% of CRM initiatives fail in some way suggesting, perhaps, that firms are getting it wrong. Fang et al. (2011) note that the 'dark side' of relationships emerges when imbalanced tensions appear in relationships and other authors see favouritism and differential treatment of customers as the root cause where some customers are advantaged and others disadvantaged by the initiative (Nguyen & Simkin, 2013).

In most cases, CRM initiatives fail because companies lose sight of the human element of the relationship over the position a customer holds on a database. Additionally, firms can be somewhat one-dimensional in their relationships with customers despite the heterogeneous nature of relationships (Fournier & Avery, 2011).

Customers often seek additional benefits associated with purchasing from an organisation, such as:

- **Confidence benefits -** purchasing this product/service is a safe option with less risk;
- **Social benefits -** being known and recognised by a provider and;
- **Special treatment -** where customers with a repeat purchase pattern get additional benefits such as special deals or enhanced service levels.

Achieving high levels of loyalty can be seen as both a defensive (protecting an existing customer base) and offensive strategy (aiming for increased sales, margins and profitability). Additionally, the use of loyalty programmes relates strongly to firms' use of CRM techniques, whereby customers signed up to the programme provide important purchase data (e.g. supermarket loyalty cards).

Jacoby and Keyner (1973: 2) defined loyalty as a "non-random purchase over time of one brand from a set of brands by a customer using a deliberate evaluation process". This important definition suggested an attitudinal element to loyalty which had at that point not been considered and suggested that loyalty could be a state of mind as well as a behavioural trait.

12

Critically, Oliver supplements the focus on attitudinal forms of loyalty with an additional behavioural element suggesting a strength of character around loyalty where the customer resists alternatives due to a deeply held commitment to rebuy. The definition forms the basis of a four stage model of loyalty (see Figure 12.2). The model envisages the customer moving through loyalty stages as their level of commitment increases.

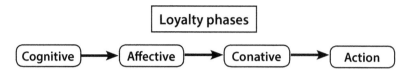

Figure 12.2: The four stage model of customer loyalty (Oliver, 1997)

Benefits of customer loyalty schemes might be financial (such as cash back, points or air miles), non-financial (such as priority in queuing or upgrades), but customers may also seek (or firms offer) higher level bonds (see below) which deepen the relationship the customer has with the firm (Lovelock & Wirtz, 2011):

■ **Social bonds** – giving the customer personalised levels of service (e.g. use of name)

■ **Customisation bonds** – meeting customers' individual needs (e.g. type of pillow in a hotel)

■ **Structural bonds** – aligns customer needs with those of the firm more closely (e.g. an SMS about flight status or a customised account)

The growth of research on customer loyalty made organisations and academics alike start to wonder about the extent to which having loyal customers would actually create any return on investment (ROI). In fact so critical was this notion that the term return on relationships (ROR) is often used to indicate the financial benefits from relationship marketing activity.

Firms began to realise that both offensive (marketing activity) and defensive (loyalty/retention) measures were needed to combat defection (the term given to customers who leave the market). In 1990 a crucial research study showed dramatically the impact that reducing defection could have on the bottom line. Reicheld and Sasser (1990) indicate the range of reasons customers might have for defecting which include:

■ **Price:** Customers who defect when a cheaper price is available elsewhere.

■ **Product:** Customers who switch to a supplier with a superior product

■ **Service:** Customers who switch suppliers due to poor service.

■ **Market:** Customers who switch markets because of failure or business relocation

■ **Technological:** Defection due to a technological advance in the sector (could be a switch outside the industry)

■ **Organisational:** Sometimes customers within larger organisations are forced to switch supplier due to political decisions within an organisation.

■ Consumers

The Consumers chapter offered a broad history of consumers and consumerism, key reference points of which included:

- ■ 'Sumptuary' laws restricted consumers in pre-modern Europe
- ■ Jevons repositioning of the consumer as the creator of value in the late 1800s
- ■ The slave trade and modern slavery
- ■ The rise of consumerism proper in the 20th century

A definition of consumerism as a culture-ideology is then introduced, before discussion of academic debates over consumer culture and identity. The reversal of the traditionally passive consumer/active producer roles is unpacked, and the question of empowerment briefly explored, with the spread of the Internet making three particular opportunities for empowerment available to the consumer:

- ■ Control over the composition of the choice set
- ■ Progress cues
- ■ Information about other consumers

It is made clear that marketers are no longer able to simply put something in front of people and hope they like it; they must actively understand and appeal to the specific cultures and subcultures created by consumers. Contemporary marketing scholars now largely concur that we are living in a consumer culture, whereby the dominant values of society are organised through and defined in relation to our consumption practices, so what we consume is the ultimate reference point for how we see and understand the world. Consumer Culture Theory is introduced as offering ways of exploring these relationships.

Several manifestations of consumer power in contemporary marketing practice are then examined: crowdsourcing, blogs, and viral marketing. Crowdsourcing is differentiated by operational type:

- ■ **Integrative**: the company collecting various (and hopefully complementary) resources from the network
- ■ **Selective**: multiple responses to the open call, with the company selecting the best solution

Crowdsourcing can also be broken down into four types, corresponding to the aims of the activity:

- ■ **Crowdfunding**: where a large number of funders each contribute small amounts of money to a project

12

- **Crowd labour**: the recruitment of often unidentified individuals contributing work to very specific tasks through virtual labour markets

- **Crowd research**: a form of market research that gathers opinion from target demographics

- **Creative crowdsourcing**: the consumer contributes original ideas, products, or content relative to a particular challenge.

The pros and cons of platform capitalism and the sharing economy are then discussed, before the chapter moves on to a look at blogs. Blogs are short 'posts' of text, typically displayed in reverse chronological order, which can be personal or topical, and cover a range of different subjects. Blogs are shown to be highly influential, and are said to empower consumers in four ways:

- **Consumer control over the marketing relationship**: bloggers and blog consumers are able to block material that they do not wish to say using browser plug-ins and email filters, or download and disseminate material that they enjoy.

- **Availability of information**: the blogging community is able to interpret individual marketing campaigns in relation to vast swathes of information online, and in relation to the views of other consumers. This leads to:

- **Aggregation**: whereby like-minded consumers unite online to talk about particular marketing campaigns, where even inconclusive discussions can lead to perceptibly positive or negative overall impressions. Such discussions may lead to the formulation of groups specifically opposed to a brand, working to investigate their business practices.

- **Participation**: through this, consumers can actually create content, which may satirise the marketing campaign, or highlight its merits.

Viral marketing campaigns are discussed as a cost-effective, potentially widely influential way of communicating marketing messages. Emphasis is placed on:

- **Choosing the right initial recipients**: they should have access to a large social network, the ability to persuade others, and sufficiently represent your target market.

- **Carefully composing the message**: the message must clearly and simply communicate the value proposition with a consistent brand image, and be easy to pass on.

- **Control mechanisms**: you'll need to make sure that the right message is being spread, and keep tabs on who is spreading it. This is useful to measure impact, but also keeps you aware of any backlash.

The chapter concluded with a look into what makes consumers truly happy: spending their money on other people.

■ Services

In the Services chapter we looked at the scope and definition of services. We also presented the four underpinning characteristics of services. Service encounters were discussed, exploring the dynamic exchange that takes place between a service provider and a customer. These elements were considered in relation to the 4Ps model of the marketing mix and an extended marketing mix concept was presented (the 7Ps). Finally, the chapter explored how services are managed and measured.

Services are a very big part of global contemporary business. You are over three times more likely to be working for a services company when you leave university than a manufacturing company: the vast majority of jobs in the developed economy are in services.

In economic terms a service is the non-material equivalent of a good. That is an inverse definition, which is often not very helpful as a definition, it is like saying a cat is a non-dog equivalent of a four-legged mammal. In more useful definitions, service provision has been defined as an economic activity that does not result in ownership (e.g. psychotherapy) and this is what makes it different from providing physical goods (e.g. a pair of socks or a shirt).

Here are the four core characteristics of sevices:

Characteristic	What that means	Example
Intangibility	You can't touch it or take it home	You will come home from a theme park feeling exhilarated hopefully, but that feeling is intangible.
Heterogeneity	It's different every time	Getting on a 6am flight because you're going on holiday will feel different to getting on a 6am flight to fly somewhere for a business meeting. Both customers and providers' roles make it difficult to make services experiences consistent.
Inseparability	The production and consumption happen at the same time	You have to be present to get a haircut, and so does the hairdresser.
Perishability	Services have a very specific shelf-life	You can't stay in a hotel 7 days ago, the empty bedrooms the hotel had 7 days ago have perished and can no longer be sold.

12

Following our understanding of the characteristics of services and service encounters, there are three additional elements to the marketing mix that are used to supplement the 4Ps of the marketing mix.

- **People**: People are the product in a service setting so they must be taken care of and be considered carefully.

- **Physical evidence**: Tangible cues reduce consumer decision-making risk.

- **Processes**: These are the operating processes that take the customer through from ordering to the delivery of the service.

Parasuraman et al. (1988) map out the service process in order to allow the points of friction, error or failure to be identified and addressed. The model they developed to measure service quality is called the SERVQUAL model. The SERVQUAL model leads to the identification of points of friction or 'gaps', as presented below:

Gap	Definition
Gap 1 - Service providers' misconception of the customer.	The gap between what the customer expects/perceives and what the management thinks the customer expects/perceives
Gap 2 - Inadequate resources	The gap between what is provided and what is required to match consumer expectations
Gap 3 -Inadequate or inconsistent service delivery	The gap between the service design and service delivered.
Gap 4 - Exaggerated promises	The gap between the service delivered and the service advertised
Gap 5 – Jumping to conclusions	The gap between what service staff think is the right course of action in delivering the service and what the customer would actually like to happen.

As service delivery and management has become more sophisticated and we as consumers of services have become more discerning in what we seek to gain from consuming them, the experience economy has developed to become an established part of the services landscape. Pine and Gilmore's (1998) assertion is that services can be built upon in order to use them as a stage for creating an experience.

■ Small businesses

The small businesses chapter discussed marketing in the context of the small firm. It looked at what constitutes a small to medium sized enterprise, identifying their key characteristics and how this context affects the marketing function. The area of entrepreneurship was also discussed, towards an explanation of entrepreneurial marketing.

Small to medium sized enterprises (SMEs), make up the highest proportion of firms operating in most countries across the globe. In the US there
are currently over 28 million small firms, employing nearly 56 million people
(Small Business Administration 2015). In 2013 over 99% of the 4.9 million
businesses in the UK were SMEs, employing 14,424,000 people. The European
Commission's SME Performance Review estimates the Gross Value Added
of SMEs as €473 billion or 49.8% of the UK economy (Ward & Rhodes, 2014).

In many small firms, resistance to change and fear of losing control (both
financially and in decision making) result in them remaining small in size,
with limited growth aspirations.

SME characteristics

- Owner manager's style
- Limited skills resources
- Limited financial flexibility
- Supply chain power
- Quality & niche offering
- Strong relationships with customers
- Quick response to marketplace

Carson (1993) identified two common factors which led to an underutilisation of marketing in small firms:

- They use marketing in a general, wasteful and inappropriate way,
  resulting in it having limited impact on performance
- They often grow without formal and planned marketing effort and as
  a result owner managers feel it unnecessary to invest time and effort in
  formal marketing planning.

In these circumstances a 'credibility gap' occurs between the satisfactory
growth performance experienced by a firm and the theoretical and hypothetical performance which might occur with the use of planned marketing.

Marketing has much to offer the study of entrepreneurship (Murray, 1981,
Hills, 1987) and likewise entrepreneurship can look to marketing as the key
function within the firm, which can encompass innovation and creativity.
Omura et al. (1993) perceive the interface between the two disciplines as
having distinct areas of difference and overlap. The overlap between these
two distinct disciplines exists in two areas;

- One where market conditions are continuous and entrepreneurship aids
  the process of identifying as-yet-unperceived needs

12

- In a discontinuous market, where entrepreneurship guides marketing strategy to develop existing needs in a new environment.

Marketing and entrepreneurship have three key areas of interface: they are both change-focused, opportunistic in nature and innovative in their approach to management. Carson et al. (1995) perceive the central focus of the interface as being change.

Carson et al. (1995) identify four key competencies associated with entrepreneurial marketing management:

Four key competencies

- Experience of both the industry and the job
- Knowledge of the product and market
- Communication skills in being able to direct the organisation and articulate previously unclear or unknown opportunities
- Sound judgement in being able to identify good market opportunities

The issue of the skills or competencies required to successfully apply marketing in an entrepreneurial small firm is one of the key strands of research at the Marketing/Entrepreneurship Interface.

■ Networks

For every business to consumer (B2C) cycle of 'market, sell and serve' there are multiple cycles of 'produce, distribute, retail and serve' in business to business (B2B) (McDonald, 2014). The total value of transactions involved in B2B activities of manufacturing, logistics, purchasing and distribution dwarfs B2C.

Buyers	Typically **large buyers** and multiple needs to satisfy **Geographic concentration** is often greater Number of consumers is typically **much smaller**
Demand	Often **derived demand** (from consumer demand) Total demand is often **inelastic** Greater **fluctuations** in demand
Selling	Often purchases are made **direct** rather than through intermediaries **Longer sales process** given the larger transactions

The typical features listed above should also be considered alongside different situations business buyers find themselves in. These can vary in complexity in the same way as consumer purchasing decisions can. In general they are characterised as falling into three different groups:

1   **Straight rebuy**: Typically a simple decision involving items that have been purchased before and are purchased frequently, such as office supplies.

2   **Modified rebuy**: This occurs when buyers might want something different, or see an opportunity to review their suppliers and find someone offering better terms in delivery/price/quality etc.

3   **New task**. This refers to purchases that are a one-off or being made for the first time. This type of purchase will involve the most uncertainty and risk, and will therefore take the most time and effort.

The main difference in B2B is that professional buyers often carry out this activity in business markets.

Vargo and Lusch (2011) comment that the discipline of B2B or 'industrial' marketing really emerged as a consequence of the broader inadequacies of mainstream marketing, particularly in terms of the notion that one party produces value whilst another consumes it.

Granovetter's (1973) research found that the majority job seekers in the US had found a job through a contact that they saw only occasionally or rarely, and are therefore classified as 'weak' ties. This finding contrasted with many people's perceptions that dense connections to strong ties, such as family and close friends, would be more likely to lead to success in finding work.

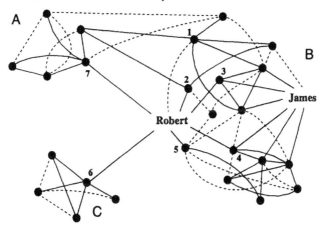

Density Table of Relations Within and Between Groups			
.65			Group A (5 people and 8 ties; 5 strong, 3 weak)
.05	.25		Group B (17 people and 41 ties; 27 strong, 14 weak)
.00	.01	.65	Group C (5 people and 8 ties; 5 strong, 3 weak)

Figure 12.3: Illustration of a social network (from Burt, 2000: 349)

Ronald Burt, another key figure in the sociological development of social capital and social network theory, argues that it is network mechanisms that define what it means to have more social capital, or to be 'better connected'. Here we turn to social network analysis, which refers to the mapping out and measuring of relationships and flows between actors, organisations, groups, etc. Figure 12.3 is an illustration of a network, where the dots are nodes in the network, indicating people. Relations between people are lines, with solid lines connecting pairs of people who have a strong relationship, and dashed lines indicating a weak tie.

Burt (2000) proposes that you should look for the weaker connections, which are holes in the social structure of the market, and "structural holes create a competitive advantage for an individual who spans the holes" (p. 353).

The table below illustrates some of the key properties and characteristics that are associated with social network analysis.

A. Transactional content and outcomes

Expression of affect

Influence, control and power

Exchange of information

Exchange of goods or services

Solidarity

B. Relational nature of the links

Intensity: The strength of the relation between individuals

Reciprocity: The degree to which there is mutual benefit or symmetry in the relations

Clarity of expectations: The degree to which there are clearly defined expectations of behaviour

Multiplexity: The degree to which individuals are linked by multiple relations

Frequency: The frequency of interaction between ties

Durability: The degree to which ties persist over time

Content: The meanings which people attribute to their relationships e.g. kinship, friendship

Ties' strength: The total combination of factors such as intensity, frequency and reciprocity that characterise ties

C. Structural terms and characteristics

Size: Total number of individuals participating in the network

Density (connectedness): Number of actual links as a ratio of the number of possible links

Clustering: The number of dense regions in a network

Stability: The degree to which a network pattern changes over time

Reachability: The extent to which network members can contact each other (number of steps)

Centrality: A measure of how many connections one node has to other nodes

Bridge: A social tie that connects two groups

Range: Number of connections combined with the social heterogeneity of ties

Structural hole: A gap between individuals with access to complementary sources of information

Broker: An individual who maintains ties with disconnected groups

■ Not-for-profit

Within the non-profit sector, success becomes more opaque, and the task of marketers more complicated. Although many of the strategies and techniques deployed by non-profit marketers share similarity and overlap with their for-profit counterparts, their success is measured through variables such as donor contributions, volunteer retention, and public trust in the organisation. This chapter offered an overview of some of the challenges and opportunities marketers face, from a distinctly non-profit perspective.

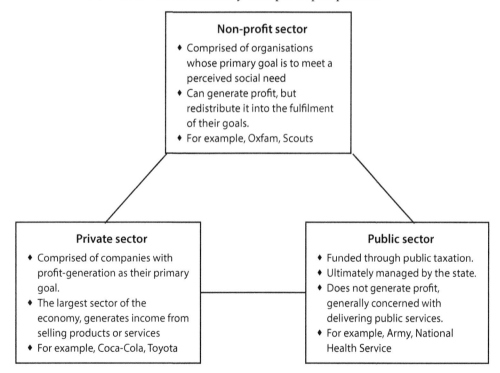

Figure 12.4: Non-profit, private, and public sectors

12

The non-profit sector is distinctive from its private and public sector counterparts, where the non-profit sector can be characterised as comprising of organisations that are non-governmental, and undertake activities aimed at delivering a social good. Social enterprises cut-through sections of the private, public, and non-profit sectors working with organisations positioned in all categories, while holding at their core a desire to meet a social need, through commercial activity.

"The non-profits are, of course, still dedicated to "doing good". But they also realise that good intentions are no substitute for organisation and leadership, for accountability, performance, and results. Those require management and that, in turn, begins with the organisation's mission" (Drucker, 1989: 88-93).

Non-profit marketers have to contend with an array of challenges which simply do not occur in the same way in private sector contexts. These are further exacerbated by generally tightly constrained resources. A selection of these distinctly NPO challenges are presented in Figure 12.5:

Figure 12.5: Non-profit marketing challenges, adapted from Andreasen and Kotler (2008)

Research by Hankinson (2001) suggests NPO brand orientation should be viewed from the perspective of a continuum to reflect varying intensities of orientation, and notes how as a theoretical construct brand orientation comprises:

- Organisational knowledge of the brand
- Realising strategic aims through the brand

- Proactive ongoing brand management
- The extent the brand is communicated (internally and externally)

Finally, a strong brand orientation is contingent on effective communication with internal and external stakeholders conveying the message of an organisation externally to donors, and beneficiaries, but also internally to volunteers and paid staff. Figure 12.5 illustrates potential internal and external audiences for non-profit brands.

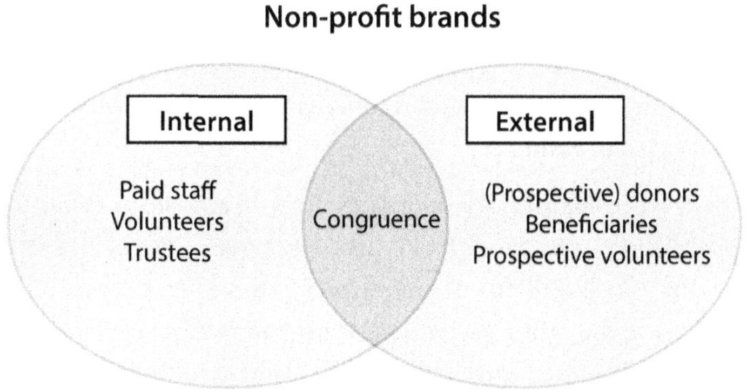

Non-profit brands

Figure 12.6: Non-profit brands. Adapted from Kylander and Stone (2012)

Brand heritage is gaining increasing attention from marketers who note the power of heritage in influencing the appeal of brands to external audiences (Schultz, 2001), and it can contribute positively to the brand orientation of a NPO.

Given the large number of heritage-rich NPO brands (e.g. the Samaritans, the Royal National Lifeboat Institution), brand heritage represents a potentially fruitful and useful area for researchers and marketing managers alike, this is also an area where NPOs have led the way in pioneering marketing activities.

Brand heritage is suggested by Urde et al. (2007: 4) to be "a dimension of a brand's identity found in its track record, longevity, core values, use of symbols and particularly the organisational belief that its history is important." This highlights the five brand heritage elements of track record, longevity, core values, history and symbols (Wiedmann et al., 2011; Urde et al., 2007). Brand heritage has the ability to enhance dedication, absorption, and vigour of volunteers, and therefore increase their levels of overall engagement and satisfaction towards their managers (Curran et al., 2016).

12

■ Celebrities

This chapter showed how the idea of 'celebrity' is used to influence, promote, represent and add value to the marketing process. In contemporary society, celebrities are important, that is something that is hard to argue against. Redmond and Holmes (2007) tell us how we embrace the celebrity myth and these magical figures give us strong imagery of identities and social meaning that we aspire to reflect within ourselves.

Celebrity has become a media process, according to Turner (2013: 24), which has turned the idea of being famous into a commodity that can be packaged and sold to audiences who have an appetite to consume it. He presents two categories of fame:

> *"The first is composed of people who possess 'political, economic or religious power', whose decisions 'have an influence on the present and future fortunes of society which they direct'. The second group is what we now think of as celebrities and they are people 'whose institutional power is very limited or non-existent, but whose doings and way of life arouse a considerable and sometimes even a maximum degree of interest'* (Alberoni, 2007: 72)

■ **Celetoids** - are entirely constructed by media producers or marketers in order to resonate with a particular audience to achieve a particular end, these are what Pierre Bourdieu (1998) describes as 'puppets of necessity'

■ **Celebritisation** - This is seen as the cultural process whereby the idea of celebrity is fostered in response for the audience's appetite for it and it takes place at a macro level.

■ **Celebrification** - is something that happens to an individual, it is a process of becoming through media ritual that unifies "the spectacular with the everyday, the special with the ordinary" (Dyer, 1979, p. 35).

Celebrity has its roots in the concept of fame: to spread abroad the fame of, render famous by talk. This comes from the Latin *famare*, meaning 'to tell or spread abroad.' The word celebrity originally came into English around 1610 from the Latin *celebritas*, meaning 'famous', or 'thronged'.

Contemporary consumer culture is replete with manufactured celebrity products, serving as packaged resources for consumers to draw their identity from. This process can be more easily understood when viewed through three different, but intersecting theoretical lenses: Tournaments of value, Spectacle and Transformative performances. These combine to tell us that (1) we have an interest in the competitive aspect of reality TV (Tournaments of ritual), (2) we like certain elements of that reality to be exaggerated or stylised (Spectacle), and (3) we rely on stereotyping and cultural hallmarks to help us understand the environment (Transformative Performances).

Traditional ideas of fame, which are couched within themes of power, influence, skill and endeavour are closely linked to concepts of taste (Bourdieu, 1984), which reinforce class divides and hierarchies within society. Bourdieu considered different areas of endeavour or activity to be distinctive 'fields' that had their own sets of rules, characteristics and values. He considered these fields to be understood in terms of different forms of capital (economic capital, cultural capital, social capital and symbolic capital).

"A capital is any resource effective in a given social arena that enables one to appropriate the specific profits arising out of participation and contest in it." (Bourdieu, 1984: 26)

Therefore, the cultural elite often practice what Bourdieu (1975) terms 'disinterested restricted production'. This is where these elite members of the field continue with their pursuits with a disregard for the opinions or recognition of the masses and instead value only the opinions and recognition of their contemporaries among the elite echelons of the field.

The consequence of the dichotomy between traditional celebrity figures (who have predominantly earned their recognition through achievement) and contemporary celebrity figures (who take advantage of the media process of celebritisation) is that when the elite members of a field are 'disinterested' then space opens up for other figures to occupy positions of recognition among the consuming public.

Conclusion

As we bring this book to a close, we wish to remind you that marketing is a doing subject. It is simple and complex all at the same time. It is vast and myopic all at the same time. It can be devious and manipulative as well as empowering and emancipatory. Being equipped with theoretical knowledge and a critical perspective on your subject will prepare you to practice marketing in a more creative, considered and ethical way. A successful technology entrepreneur once warned that there is no 'silver bullet' with marketing. You have to keep multiple plates spinning and be prepared to react and change when things don't go as you hoped they would. The business space you are entering into is increasingly noisy and crowded and it is also ever-expanding as new worlds such as Virtual Reality environments are being created.

12

References

Alberoni, F. (2007). The powerless 'elite': theory and sociological research on the phenomenon of the stars. *Stardom and Celebrity: A reader*, 65-77.

Bourdieu, P. (1975). *The Invention of the Artist's Life*, JSTOR.

Bourdieu, P. (1984). *Distinction: A social critique of the judgement of taste*, Harvard University Press.

Bourdieu, P. (1998). *On Television*, London: New Press..

Burt, R. (2000) The network structure of social capital, *Research in Organisational Behaviour*, **22** (6), 345-423.

Carson, D. (1993) A philosophy for marketing education in small firms, *Journal of Marketing Management*, **9**, 189-204

Carson, D., Cromie, S., McGowan, P. and Hill, J. (1995) *Marketing and Entrepreneurship in SMEs, An Innovative Approach*, Prentice Hall

Curran, R., Taheri, B., MacIntosh, R. and O'Gorman, K. (2016) Nonprofit brand heritage: Its ability to influence volunteer retention, engagement, and satisfaction, *Nonprofit and Voluntary Sector Quarterly*, Advance online publication. Doi:10.1177/0899764016633532.

Drucker, P. F. (1989) What business can learn from nonprofits, *Harvard Business Review*, **67**(4), 88-93.

Dyer, R. (1979). *Stars*. London: British Film Institute.

Ehrenberg, A. (1988). *Repeat-Buying: Facts, theory and applications*. London: Edward Arnold.

Fang, S. R., Chang, Y. S., & Peng, Y. C. (2011). Dark side of relationships: A tensions-based view. *Industrial Marketing Management*. **40**, 774-784.

Fournier, S., & Avery, J. (2011). Putting the Relationship Back Into CRM. *MIT Sloan Management Review*, **52**(3), 63-72.

Frow, P., Payne, A., Wilkinson, I. F. & Young, L. (2011). Customer management and CRM: addressing the dark side. *Journal of Services Marketing*, **25**(2), 79-89.

Granovetter, M. (1973) The strength of weak ties, *American Journal of Sociology*, **78** (6), 1360-1380.

Hankinson, P. (2001) Brand orientation in the charity sector: A framework for discussion and research, *International Journal of Nonprofit and Voluntary Sector Marketing*, **6** (3), 231-242.

Hills, G.E. (1987), Marketing and Entrepreneurship Research Issues : Scholarly Justification, in *Research at the Marketing/Entrepreneurship Interfac*e, Gerald E. Hills (Ed.), University of Illinois at Chicago, pp. 3-15

Jacoby, J., & Kyner, D. B. (1973). Brand loyalty vs. repeat purchasing behavior. *Journal of Marketing Research,* **10**(1), 1-9.

Kylander, N. and Stone, C. (2012) The role of brand in the nonprofit sector, *Stanford Social Innovation Review*, **10**(2), 35-41.

Lovelock, C., & Wirtz, J. (2011). *Services Marketing: People, Technology, Strategy* (Vol. 7th (International Edition)). Upper Saddle River, New Jersey: Pearson.

Murray, J. (1981) Marketing is home for the entrepreneurial process, *Industrial Marketing Management*, **10**, 93-9

Nguyen, B., & Simkin, L. (2013). The dark side of CRM: advantaged and disadvantaged customers. *Journal of Consumer Marketing,* **30**(1), 17-30.

Oliver, R. L. (1997). *Satisfaction: A behavioral perspective on the consumer.* McGraw-Hill.

Omura, G. S., Calantone, R.J. & Schmidt, J.B. (1993) Entrepreneurism as a market satisfying mechanism in a free market system, in G.E. Hills et al. *Research at the Marketing Entrepreneurship Interface*, Chicago, University of Illinois, pp.161-171

Parasuraman, A., Zeithaml, V. A., & Berry, L. L. (1988). Servqual: A multiple-item scale for measuring consumer perception. *Journal of Retailing,* **64**(1), 12.

Payne, A. and Frow, P. (2005). A strategic framework for customer relationship management. *Journal of Marketing,* **69**(4), 167-176.

Pine, B. J., & Gilmore, J. H. (1998). Welcome to the experience economy. *Harvard Business Review,* **76**, 97-105.

Redmond, S., & Holmes, S. (2007). *Stardom and Celebrity: A reader*: Sage.

Reichheld, F. F., & Sasser Jr, W. E. (1990). Zero defections: quality comes to services. *Harvard Business Review,* **68**(5), 105-111.

Schultz, D. E. (2001) Zapping brand heritage, *Marketing Management*, **10**(4), 8-9.

Small Business Administration (2015) *Small Business Profile*, SBA, Office of Advocacy

Stearns, P. N. (1998). 'Why Study History?', American Historical Association, https://www.historians.org/about-aha-and-membership/aha-history-and-archives/archives/why-study-history-(1998). Accessed 7th August 2016.

Turner, G. (2013). *Understanding Celebrity*: Sage.

Vargo, S. and Lusch, R. (2011) It's all B2B… and beyond: Toward a systems perspective of the market, *Industrial Marketing Management*, **40**, 181-187.

Urde, M., Greyser, S. A. and Balmer, J. M. (2007) Corporate brands with a heritage, *Journal of Brand Management*, **15**(1), 4-19.

Ward, M. & Rhodes, C. (2014) *Small Businesses and the UK Economy*, House of Commons standard Note: SN/EP/6078, Section- Economics Policy & Statistics.

Wiedmann, K.-P., Hennigs, N., Schmidt, S. and Wuestefeld, T. (2011) Drivers and outcomes of brand heritage: consumers' perception of heritage brands in the automotive industry, *The Journal of Marketing Theory and Practice*, **19**(2), 205-220.

12

Index

Printed in the United States
By Bookmasters